T0313728

HARVARD ECONOMIC STUDIES

Volume CXXVIII

The studies in this series are published by
the Department of Economics of Harvard University.
The Department does not assume responsibility for
the views expressed.

MARKET CONTROL
AND PLANNING
IN
COMMUNIST CHINA

DWIGHT H. PERKINS

Harvard University Press

CAMBRIDGE, MASSACHUSETTS

Library of Congress Catalog Card Number 66–10808
Printed in the United States of America

TO KNIGHT BIGGERSTAFF

Preface

Four years ago at Harvard I began work on a study of Communist China's price system. Since then the subject has evolved into an analysis of the role of market forces within the context of Chinese central planning. Research has taken me to various libraries around the United States and to the Far East, primarily Hong Kong, for slightly more than a year. My debts of gratitude to individuals along the way are correspondingly long and varied.

To Professors Abram Bergson and Simon Kuznets I owe a special debt. Professor Bergson patiently read through numerous outlines and two complete drafts of this monograph while it was being prepared as a doctoral thesis at Harvard. Professor Kuznets read the thesis and two subsequent drafts. It is customary to absolve all others from responsibility for the result, but without their generous advice and criticism this book would be of little interest to anyone but the author.

My interest in China began twelve years ago under the inspiration and guidance of Professor Knight Biggerstaff of Cornell University, to whom this book is gratefully dedicated. Professors John Fairbank and John Lindbeck of the East Asian Research Center at Harvard were particularly helpful in providing me with advice and introductions for my year in Hong Kong and elsewhere in the Far East. Many people in Japan, Taiwan, and Hong Kong were helpful to my research, but special mention should be made of Professor Ishikawa Shigeru of Tokyo and members of the staff of the Union Research Institute in Hong Kong.

My wife, Julie, has been a major help at all stages of research and writing, whether editing, typing, or introducing me to refugees whom she met in the course of her work in Hong Kong.

My first four years of graduate school were financed by a grant from the Ford Foundation Foreign Area Training Fellowship Program. The last two years of this grant, which included the year in Hong Kong, were spent on research for this monograph.

Finally, I wish to thank the *Quarterly Journal of Economics* and the *Journal of Political Economy* for permission to use my articles in those journals as the basis of Chapters III, IV, and VIII, and to the Iwanami Bookstore of Tokyo for permission to reproduce a chart from Ishikawa Shigeru, *Chugoku ni okeru shihon chikuseki kiko.*

D.H.P.

Cambridge, Massachusetts
May 1965

Contents

Chart

Tables

MARKET CONTROL AND PLANNING
IN COMMUNIST CHINA

Abbreviations and Equivalents

CB	*Current Background* (translations by the American Consulate General, Hong Kong)
CCPCC	Chinese Communist Party Central Committee
CCYC	*Ching-chi yen-chiu* (Economic research)
CHCC	*Chi-hua ching-chi* (Planned economy)
ECMM	*Extracts from China Mainland Magazines* (translations by the American Consulate General, Hong Kong)
FKHP	*Chung-hua jen-min kung-ho-kuo fa-kuei hui-pien* (Collection of laws of the People's Republic of China), 12 vols.
HHPYK	*Hsin-hua pan-yueh-k'an* (New China semimonthly)
HHYP	*Hsin-hua yueh-pao* (New China monthly)
JMJP	*Jen-min jih-pao* (People's daily)
JPRS	*Joint Publications Research Service* (translations)
NCNA	New China News Agency (the official Chinese Communist news agency)
SC	State Council
SCMP	*Survey of the China Mainland Press* (Translations by the American Consulate General, Hong Kong)
Shanghai Price Book	*Shanghai chieh-fang ch'ien-hou wu-chia tzu-liao hui-pien* (A collection of Shanghai pre- and postliberation price materials)
SSB	State Statistical Bureau
TCKT	*T'ung-chi kung-tso* (Statistical work)
TCKTTH	*T'ung-chi kung-tso t'ung-hsun* (Statistical work bulletin)
TCYC	*T'ung-chi yen-chiu* (Statistical research)
TKP	*Ta kung pao* (Impartial daily), Hong Kong, Peking, and Tientsin
URS	*Union Research Service* (Translations, Hong Kong)
WKKT	*Wo-kuo kang-t'ieh, tien-li, mei-tan, chi-chieh, fang-chih, tsao-chih kung-yeh-te chin-hsi* (Our country's iron and steel, electric power, coal, machinery, textile, and paper industries, past and present)

1 catty = 0.5 kg or 1.1 lb
2000 catties = 1 metric ton
6 mow = 1 acre
1 yuan = U.S. $0.4246

CHAPTER I

Introduction

All nations must devise means for directing the economic activities of individual firms and households. For the Chinese Communists control had to be exercised over more than 120 million farm households and 100 thousand industrial enterprises, and it had to be exercised in a way that would rapidly transform an economy that was both underdeveloped and devastated by twelve years of war and civil war. Of techniques available to the Peking regime, one of the most important was the market or price mechanism. In China, unlike most Western economies, the market was merely one technique among several. The centralized nature of the state, in particular, tended to prejudice the regime in favor of various nonmarket controls.

This analysis attempts, first of all, to determine what the role of the market and prices has been in the allocation of resources both within and between households, firms, and cooperatives. Special emphasis is placed on the reasons why the market in various circumstances was either accepted or rejected as a basic control device. There also is an attempt to discover the degree of efficiency with which the market was used in those areas where it continued to perform some function. No analysis is attempted of the effect of prices and the market on central planners, that is, on those whose job it was to direct rather than be directed. The discussion is also confined to the domestic market because foreign trade prices were determined on substantially different principles and had little effect on domestic prices. The period covered begins with Communist attainment of power in 1949 and carries through 1963, but special emphasis is placed on the post-1952 period, when recovery and full political control had been achieved and a state-run pattern of development had begun to emerge.

The market's role in any economy depends in large degree on the nature of a country's political and economic institutions and on the goals of those who determine these institutions. In a private-enterprise market economy, prices help determine four key relations: factor proportions used in production, the final product mix, the marketed portion of output, and distribution to consumers of that marketed portion. Given technology, the existing stock of capital, and other factors, it is mainly prices or the market that determine the rest. The advantages of this system are that it allows for a high degree of decentralized control over economic activity, and provides a sensitive device whereby consumer preferences determine what is produced.

Socialist ownership is not necessarily incompatible with a market-directed economy. Oscar Lange and Abba Lerner have demonstrated theoretically how a socialist system can simulate market controls without losing the theoretical efficiency of a perfectly competitive market, the advantages of decentralized controls, or consumer sovereignty.[1] They have gone even further to argue that a socialist economy can operate in a manner superior to that of the capitalist system because of freedom from distortions in the latter's price structure that arise from monopolistic practices.

The Chinese Communists, however, like their counterparts in the Soviet Union, accept neither consumer sovereignty nor decentralized controls as goals desirable in and of themselves. Instead, they start with a preference for output decisions settled primarily on the basis of centrally determined targets and rationed allocation of key commodities. This preference results from a variety of political, ideological, and economic factors, which are discussed at length in subsequent chapters. The technique by which these centralized decisions are reached is called "material-balances planning."

The key fact about material-balances planning, from the point

---

[1] Oscar Lange, "On the Economic Theory of Socialism," in Oscar Lange and Fred Taylor, *On the Economic Theory of Socialism* (Minneapolis, 1938); Abba P. Lerner, *The Economics of Control* (New York, 1944).

of view of this discussion, is that the technique does not ensure efficiency,[2] only balance. Attainment of a more efficient production technique or a more efficient product mix is possible, but there is no force in the system itself that puts pressure on planners or firms to use such a technique or product mix. Planners themselves must determine the most efficient method by means of complex calculations which, in a properly functioning market economy, are made automatically, or, more accurately, in a decentralized manner.

Difficulties involved in making such complex calculations have caused all economies of the Soviet type to supplement or modify material-balances planning with a variety of measures, not the least of which has been the market. In some sectors, for example, reliable data are not available in sufficient quantity or in time to make any of the necessary calculations. This is true with both agricultural production and much of consumers' goods distribution, for example. In other sectors, enough data are available and hence central planning is possible, but it is not efficient because it does not make sufficient use of local initiative.

The underdeveloped nature of China's economy makes the task of central planners both more and less complex. On the one hand, underdeveloped economies produce fewer commodities, and both production and distribution of these items are less interrelated than in developed economies. Even the consumers' diet, for example, is simple enough to allow the state to allocate a few key foods in a rationed manner without fear that the resulting distribution will be grossly inefficient. On the other hand, China lacks skilled personnel either for planning or collection of data. In addition, the dominant role of agriculture, a sector particularly subject to uncontrollable influences such as weather, makes planning difficult even for skilled personnel. Being back-

[2] The term "efficiency" is used throughout the discussion in the narrow economic sense of the word. One is not being efficient when, by rearranging inputs, it is possible to increase the output of one or several items without reducing the output of any other. It is, of course, possible to be inefficient in this economic sense while at the same time being efficient with respect to other goals, such as political and ideological goals. For a more precise and thorough discussion of the term as used in this context, see Abram Bergson, *The Economics of Soviet Planning* (New Haven, 1964), chap. i.

ward in relation to the developed nations does make it possible to adopt others' technology, but the fact that that technology was developed in capital-intensive countries of the West tends to make it less suitable for labor-intensive China; at least the Chinese Communists have felt so, and have tried to develop their own small-scale labor-intensive technology. Furthermore, China's size and hence the number of units that must be controlled is so large that this alone makes central planning for the nation as a whole difficult.

Most of the measures undertaken to reduce inefficiencies resulting from such conditions have included some degree of decentralization. Many forms of decentralization do not involve the market at all, but only various forms of administrative reorganization. These latter forms of decentralization are of concern in subsequent analysis only to the extent that they impinge on or enhance the role of the market.

Decentralization through the market creates many complex problems, particularly in an economy that is both socialist and still basically controlled by more direct means. First of all, for prices to have effect, decision makers in firms and cooperatives must try to maximize profits or have some other goal expressed in value terms. If their major concern instead is to surpass a physical production target, market forces will not have any influence on their actions. Alternatively, if decision makers are not ordered to maximize profits, but are strictly limited in obtaining finances, they still may respond to prices, since higher output and lower input prices would improve their financial position. This latter possibility has a corollary in the distribution of consumers' goods. If money incomes after taxes rise faster than the value of available consumers' goods, the result is rationed allocation of either a formal or *de facto* variety. An alternative is to allow prices to rise, but this has been undesirable in China on political grounds. As a result, efficiency in the consumers' goods market has depended on the state's ability to control general inflationary pressures.

Even if decision makers respond to the market, the result may be decreased rather than increased efficiency if prices are not determined on a rational basis. With consumers' sovereignty, prices must reflect consumer preferences, but the experience of Western countries with wartime price controls suggests that it is difficult to determine and maintain such a rational price structure when prices are set by other than a free market. If planners' sovereignty prevails, the problem is simplified, since only planners' preferences need to be ascertained. Planners' preferences, however, may be expressed in such terms as maximization of a country's rate of growth or maximization of consumer welfare. In either case, relative prices of individual commodities still may be meaningful only to the extent that they reflect consumer preferences and underlying cost conditions. Planners' preferences could be expressed in terms of preferences for individual commodities, but unless these commodities have intrinsic value for their own sake, rather than as means for increasing consumer welfare, military power, or economic growth and hence future welfare, then there is a question whether planners' preference for individual commodities means anything. It is possible that planners might have strong moral feelings about what a consumer ought to eat, wear, or use, but it is more likely that detailed commodity preferences, in China at least, simply reflect attempts by planners to guess what preferences should be according to some more general criterion. It is not unfair, therefore, to measure actual prices against what prices would have been on a free market and attribute the difference to inefficient price determination, except for military goods and the like, where the government is the only purchaser.

One qualification must be made to the above argument. A price structure that reflects true underlying preferences will increase production efficiency only if producers are trying to maximize profits under simulated perfectly competitive conditions. Since these conditions do not prevail in China, a "rational price structure" as described above may at times decrease efficiency. On the labor market, for example, excessive wage differentials (wages that do not reflect marginal productivity) may increase worker incentives while not interfering with efficient allocation, since allocation is hamstrung by a variety of direct controls.

There are several reasons why an analysis of the role of prices and the market in Communist China is a useful exercise. In the first place, it provides insights into the rationale and effectiveness of several key economic policies of the Chinese Communists. The problem of controlling China's economy has been something they have struggled with since the beginning of their attainment of power on the Chinese mainland. Many key programs, therefore, have been directed toward this end and can only be fully understood in this context.

Furthermore, this study has the advantage of covering a field for which substantial amounts of material, quantitative and otherwise, are available. This is not true of some other areas of the Chinese economy and Chinese economic policy, although many people have tended to exaggerate the difficulty of obtaining relevant data. More serious than the lack of data is the question of their validity. Since the issues involved are both complex and important, this question is dealt with at length in the appendixes. It is desirable here, however, to give some indication of the general approach to Chinese Communist statistics followed in the text. Deliberate falsification by central statistical authorities of underlying raw data is largely ruled out on grounds that it would serve little purpose and would be easily discovered by those whom the regime most wanted to fool, the Chinese people. Falsification of aggregate data would be somewhat easier but would also be of limited usefulness over the long run. In addition, except for 1958 and 1959, various types of aggregate data published by the regime usually possess a high degree of internal consistency. Consistency can, of course, be achieved through consistent falsification of all data, but it does not appear likely that this is the case in Communist China. A lack of deliberate falsification by central authorities, however, does not mean that data are necessarily reliable. There were many areas in which the ability of the regime to collect accurate data was severely limited. Chinese Communist statistics, therefore, must always be used with care. The data for 1958 and 1959, in particular, are generally of little use.

Finally this analysis is of relevance for other underdeveloped nations with similar problems, both within and without the Soviet bloc. There is a considerable theoretical literature on criteria upon which investment funds should be allocated in a planned economy, but very little on methods of controlling lower-level decision-making units so as to ensure that they will follow directives set down in the plan. Among various control devices, the market is particularly useful, since it makes possible a high degree of decentralized decision making and the resulting attainment of considerable economic efficiency, virtues a poor country can ill afford to ignore. The usefulness of Chinese experience in this regard is that the Chinese Communists have been willing to experiment and have had the necessary political power to do so. Centralized controls, therefore, have not been rejected for lack of ability to put them into force. Instead, centralized and market controls have been accepted or rejected on a variety of economic, political, and ideological grounds. The political and ideological grounds have often, though not always, been peculiar to the needs of a Communist totalitarian state. The degree of political power required by a totalitarian state, for example, is greater than what is necessary in a less tightly controlled society. Marxist-Leninist ideology also limits the choices open to a Communist regime in ways that have less than general applicability, even within totalitarian states.[3] The economic grounds, however, have had much more general applicability.[4]

Because the period during which the Communists have controlled the Chinese mainland has been short and changes in Communist economic policies have been both radical and frequent, it is necessary to treat the role and effectiveness of market controls historically as well as theoretically. A theoretical analysis in this case is best facilitated by a separate study of each sector of the economy. Nearly complete compartmentalization of various sectors has made it possible for the Chinese to treat each one individually, and policies and conditions in one area often have no effect on another. Rationing, for example, was a neces-

---

[3] Throughout the text, the term "political goals" or "political grounds" refers to issues related to achieving and maintaining political power, or control, over a society and the individuals within it. "Ideology" refers specifically to Marxist-Leninist or Marxist-Leninist-Maoist ideology, particularly the belief in socialism as a form of organization superior to capitalism.

[4] "Economic grounds" as used here refers to the desire to increase output or marketings of goods and services irrespective of how output or marketings are to be used.

sity in rural areas long before it had to be introduced in cities, and inflationary pressure on the urban consumers' goods market has had almost no effect on industrial producers, although the reverse is not true. But the regime has made several across the board changes in its economic policies. Socialization of the economy in 1955–56 and communization and the "great leap forward" in 1958–59 are two important cases in point. Furthermore, compartmentalization of the economy was itself a process which took place over a period of several years and was not completed until 1956. To keep these changes over time from confusing rather than enhancing the analysis, a brief historical summary is given in Chapter II. In addition, the discussion of each individual sector of the economy is organized either wholly or partially on a historical as well as an analytical basis because so many aspects of Chinese Communist market controls can only be understood in this context.

CHAPTER II

Historical Prologue

Chinese economic policies and institutions have undergone a number of radical changes since the establishment of the Communist regime in 1949. China's economic history from 1949 through 1963 can, as a result, be broken up into five quite distinct periods of development. Certain major characteristics of each period had important influences either directly or indirectly on the Chinese economy and Communist economic policy, including price policy and efficient operation of the market mechanism.

The first two periods are ones in which the Communist regime consolidated its control over the economy. In the first period, which ended in 1952, this consolidation involved recovery from war devastation, stopping of inflation, and breaking the political and economic power of those groups viewed by the regime as most opposed to its long-term interests. The second period was the one in which socialization of the economy and establishment of the mechanisms of planning were largely completed. The third period, which started with the Eighth Party Congress in 1956, was marked by considerable experimentation with relaxation of control both in the economy and in politics. Finally, there are the fourth and fifth periods, the fourth starting in mid-1958 with the crash development program of the "great leap forward" and communization of the countryside, and the fifth, whose precise starting date is difficult to pinpoint owing to a lack of adequate information, a period of agricultural crisis ending with a partial recovery. Although many policies and institutions of each period have carried over into later years, and thus the line of demarcation between them cannot be too sharply drawn, the character of each is distinct enough to justify this division.

As the Red Army moved south through China, the areas it occupied were economically prostrate and prices were spiraling upward. In Shanghai, for example, wholesale prices during the latter half of 1949, when the city was under Communist control, rose on the average by 51 per cent per month.[1] According to Communist statistics, industrial production throughout the country had fallen to nearly half the prewar peak level. Agricultural production also suffered, both from war destruction and from floods, and was certainly well below prewar levels.[2] Even where production was still substantial, a disorganized commercial and transportation network made it difficult to get goods to places where they could be used. The first task of cadres following closely behind or with the army was to put production back on its feet and restore order in the market.

Initially, therefore, the Chinese Communists encouraged free enterprise in all spheres of the economy. It was not long, however, before they began methodically to increase their control over the economy. Whether this process was as systematic at the time as it appears in retrospect is difficult to say. Certainly the unanticipated entry of China into the Korean War in November 1950 accelerated the pace of a number of policies, but it is not easy to tell by how much.

In retrospect, at least, the regime appears to have proceeded along two fronts in expanding its control over the economy. On the one hand, the Communists moved to establish a dominant position in major commodity markets and over prices and the financial system. On the other, they made a concerted attack on the economic, political, and social power of those groups in Chinese society whom they considered most inimical to the long-term interests of Chinese Communism. The history of these latter policies is relatively well known. It involved neutralization or elimination of politically defined classes of "rich peasants" and "landlords" in rural areas during the process of land reform (1949–1952), an attack on private business through the "five anti" movement, beginning in November 1951, and tightening of control over the bureaucracy by means of the "three anti" move-

[1] Shanghai Price Book, p. 355.
[2] See Table 5.

ment, beginning in August 1951.[3] There were many market- and price-related aspects to the pressure put on private businessmen, such as a profit squeeze. In effect, the state forced private businessmen to sell many products to it at low prices, to increase wages, and to pay large and apparently often arbitrary fines and heavy taxes.[4] These measures, however, are primarily of historical interest, since it is unlikely that the circumstances that recommended them to the Communists will ever be repeated. They are, therefore, dealt with only briefly in subsequent chapters.

Of more interest are the means by which the Communists established control over prices and financial affairs, since many policies pursued at that time have been continued with varying degrees of modification up to the present. The principal feature of this initial period's financial policy was the largely successful attempt to channel circulation of money into a relatively few tightly controlled paths. Gold, silver, and foreign exchange were barred from circulation almost immediately after arrival of the Red Army. Later on, handling of all foreign trade was placed in the hands of state-operated companies (March 1950) and trade was conducted in foreign currencies only, thus effectively cutting off the domestic economy from direct access to the international market and turning the *jen min pi,* as the Chinese Communist monetary unit is called, into an isolated currency. At the same time control over domestic circulation of the *jen min pi* was tightened. Authority to issue the *jen min pi* was turned over to the sole control of the People's Bank of China, and private banks were systematically consolidated and socialized between 1949 and 1951, or, what amounts to nearly the same thing from the stand-

[3] For a more detailed discussion of the "three" and "five anti" movements and how they were designed to "reform" and increase control over the bureaucracy and private industry and commerce, refer, among other sources, to W. W. Rostow, *The Prospects for Communist China* (Cambridge, Mass., and New York, 1954); and T. J. Hughes and D. E. T. Luard, *The Economic Development of Communist China, 1949–1958* (London, 1959). Discussions of the process of land reform are in K. C. Chao, *Agrarian Policy of the Chinese Communist Party* (New Delhi, 1960); Wu Yuan-li, *An Economic Survey of Communist China* (New York, 1956); and C. K. Yang, *A Chinese Village in Early Communist Transition* (Cambridge, Mass., 1959).

[4] See, for example, Hsiao Chi-jung, *Revenue and Disbursement of Communist China* (Hong Kong, 1955), chaps. iv and v.

point of central government control, turned into enterprises under joint public-private control. Only cash itself was left outside of direct central government control. Even here, attempts were made to keep its amount to a minimum by creation of a Soviet-like system of cash control whereby all currency of any significant amount, first of the army and the administrative bureaucracy (March 1950) and later of state enterprises (December 1950), had to be deposited in the People's Bank. In addition, savings deposits by individuals were encouraged by attaching their value to a commodity unit that would not depreciate as prices rose.

Accompanying these attempts was an equally vigorous campaign to balance the government budget through tight control over expenditures and increases in revenue. The "three" and "five anti" campaigns played their part in this movement, the former probably helping to reduce government expenditure and the latter contributing temporarily badly needed funds to the state treasury. Most important, however, was the organization and systemization of the new forms of tax revenue. The principal directive, "Regarding Settlement of the Unification of the Nation's Financial and Economic Work," was passed on March 3, 1950, by the Government Affairs Council.[5] It laid down, among other things, the basic tax structure which, although often revised, still exists today. This system provided the Communist government with an ever-increasing amount of revenue which, with the aid of the extra revenue from the "five anti" campaign, made it possible to balance the budget by 1952 and keep it approximately balanced in every year since except 1956.[6]

Even in this period, however, the Communist regime did not rely only on monetary and fiscal controls to stabilize prices. Their most important efforts were directed toward the recovery of production. They also gradually moved toward a position of dominance over the market for certain key commodities and eventu-

---

[5] For the text of the directive, see *HHYP*, April 15, 1950, pp. 1393–1395.

[6] The Chinese Communists claim that the budget was balanced in 1951, but evidence presented in Appendix C indicates that there was still a substantial deficit in that year. If one excludes certain items such as revenue from credits and insurance, which the Chinese Communists include in their revenue data, then the budget was also in deficit in 1953, 1954, and 1955.

ally over the greater part of the entire wholesale market. During this period they established the principle of government-determined prices even though they did not immediately attempt to stabilize these prices by government fiat. The culmination of this effort, however, came after 1952. Through 1952, the principal aim of Chinese Communist financial policy had been to gain fundamental control over the nation's finances so as to stabilize prices and to form a base from which to establish more complete control over all areas of the economy. Having thus created financial order, and with the Korean War rapidly approaching a permanent truce, the regime was able to launch a program of planned industrial development in 1953, although planning was still rudimentary and relied heavily on financial controls for its effectiveness.[7] The formal fiscal and monetary structure, however, had reached very nearly its present form by the end of 1952. Subsequent formal changes in the system left the basic structure intact and were designed merely to adapt the structure to changing demands upon it. There were also many informal changes of considerable importance, but these commonly did not involve the formal structure itself so much as the way in which that structure was used.

By the Eighth Party Congress in September 1956, the picture of Communist central-government economic control had changed radically from that at the end of 1952. By 1956 private enterprise in China had ceased to exist except for a few small traders and 3.7 per cent of the farm families.[8] A certain amount of socialization, to be sure, had been occurring for some time. The take-over of the banking system has already been mentioned. Most of the transportation network and nearly half of industry were state-run right from the beginning of the regime. But socialization of industry was not completed until the end of 1955. Similarly agriculture, handicrafts, and commerce were not fully socialized or run by cooperatives until 1956. Putting agriculture and handicrafts, in particular, under cooperative control was pushed through quite rapidly at the end of this period. This transforma-

---

[7] The real first five-year plan was not ready until July 1955, when it was presented to the National People's Congress.

[8] SSB, *Ten Great Years* (Peking, 1960), p. 35.

tion of the form of ownership had a profound effect on the function and mode of operation of the Chinese financial system. In particular, basic criteria of success of those making most decisions on what to produce and to whom the produce was to be distributed were fundamentally changed. To some extent this transformation in criteria of success actually took place before the drive for socialization. The government had set down strict rules on how profit of private enterprises was to be distributed and had largely taken control over allocation of resources out of the hands of entrepreneurs through monopolization of raw materials and markets. As a result, private firms had to buy from and sell to the state.[9] In agriculture, changes in criteria of success came about more because of the nature of cooperative leadership than from changes in the form of ownership itself. In this sense, the institution of agricultural cooperatives in China was more a transfer of land to state control than it was a matter of setting up cooperatives for their own sake.

In addition to changing criteria of success of China's economic decision makers, socialization marked a temporary high tide in Communist control over the economy. State ownership not only put members of the state or party bureaucracy in charge of almost all economic decision-making units; it also substantially reduced the degree of interdependence between various units, thus giving central policy makers greater freedom of action. The entire rural economy was cut off from direct contact with the urban industrial economy and to some extent from other individual units within the rural sector. This was accomplished by directives requiring most produce to be sold to state or cooperative stores and ensuring that all industrial products would be distributed by these same stores. Until the reopening of the free market in 1956, peasants could not take their produce to the cities, and in most cases were not even allowed to trade with peasants from other cooperatives. Also, the state, by means of strictly enforced agri-

[9] Commodities in this category (excluding handicrafts) made up 62 per cent of the total production of private industry in 1953, 79 per cent in 1954, and 82 per cent in 1955; see Yang Chien-pai, *Chieh-fang i-lai wo-kuo kuo-min ching-chi-chung chi-chung chu-yau pi-li kuan-hsi-te pien-hua.* (Changes in several important ratios in our national economy since the liberation; Shanghai, 1957), p. 14.

cultural taxes and purchase quotas for major crops, took away the freedom of the cooperatives to decide whether to keep or sell a large part of their production. The state, in addition, had nearly complete control of prices, and turnover and profits taxes meant that retail prices could be changed without influencing agricultural purchase prices. The purchasing power of rural money and the amount of industrial goods to be supplied to agriculture, as a result, could be determined relatively independently of the state's need of farm produce for the cities and for export. The word "relatively" is important here, since the question of the effect of rural incentives on production placed a limit on the state's arbitrariness.

The rural sector, however, was not alone in being isolated. State-controlled commerce and turnover and profits taxes also kept urban and rural consumer preferences from having much influence on the industrial product mix. These same taxes, plus tight bank control over other enterprise funds, effectively removed investment decisions from individual enterprises and transferred them to central planning authorities. State distribution of a large number of industrial raw materials and of a few consumers' goods allowed the state to operate somewhat independently of market conditions for these materials. It is this isolation of various sectors which, as stated in the previous chapter, makes it possible to deal with these sectors individually. Lack of interdependence cannot be pushed too far, however. Although influences may not always have been direct, consumer preferences still had some effect on the product mix, many of the devices used to separate sectors at times broke down, and factories were not able to operate without food for their workers or agricultural raw materials for their machines, just to name a few examples. Thus, lack of interdependence was only relative even in the middle of 1956, when state control of the economy was most complete.

The history of the first seven years of the Chinese Communist economy was, therefore, a history of gradually tightening central-government control over economic decisions, making it possible for the state to operate somewhat independently of the desires of its individual members and even to some extent of the interdependence that one finds among various sectors of most economies.

It was also a period in which the example of the Soviet Union was most clearly in evidence. Many basic economic forms chosen in this period were patterned after their Soviet counterparts, although the timing of their adoption was often quite different. It would not be too great an oversimplification to say that the Soviet Union supplied many of the organizational goals, while China supplied the technique for bringing the various organizations into existence. Even at this early date, however, much of the organization aimed at was being modified to fit conditions in China. This was particularly true in agriculture, where the main policy the Chinese took from the Russians was only the basic decision to collectivize. In industry, lack of experience and of sufficient numbers of skilled personnel dictated a heavier reliance on Soviet methods and Soviet technicians to carry them out than was the case in agriculture.

The Eighth Party Congress of September 1956 marked the beginning of nearly two years of economic liberalization on a limited scale. For a brief period this economic relaxation was accompanied by a political liberalization, the famous "hundred flowers" period, when freedom of speech was briefly encouraged, and which ended so abruptly in July 1957. Some proposals for liberalization brought forward at the congress were put into effect almost immediately, while others were not completed until early 1958, when the economy was already beginning to shift into the "great leap forward." It now seems clear that both the economic and political loosening of central control were meant to have limits. It is probable that one reason for the "hundred flowers" campaign was to use limited public criticism to prevent abuses and to stimulate the ingenuity of lower-level cadres. It was hoped that this would keep them from relying on the powers of their position to force compliance where other methods were more desirable. Objectives of economic liberalization were similarly limited; there was never any intention to return to a market economy. When the reopened free market began to spread beyond intended bounds, a directive was issued clearly stating what was and was not to enter this market. Similarly, directives giving greater power to local government organs and to individual enterprises, most of which were not issued until 1958, were accompanied by an increase in party control within these same units. Thus it appears that the objective of these measures, at least in the economic sphere, was to stimulate and give scope to individual initiative of lower-level cadres while ensuring that this initiative would be directed toward the interests of the state and the party.

Liberalization and decentralization involved a substantial increase in the importance of the role of prices and the market in the Chinese economy. Opening of the free market meant that supply and demand operating through the price mechanism again influenced production of a significant number of commodities. Transfer of authority to lower levels was accompanied by an increase in the relative importance of profits to state industrial and commercial enterprises. Centralized distribution of important commodities was relaxed, and commercial organizations and factories were given greater freedom to select commodities they needed rather than being forced to take whatever was allocated to them. These and many other changes all tended to give market and price controls a more vital role in the economy.

Many economic reforms promulgated during these two years are still in force. In many areas of industrial policy there was no dramatic turnabout comparable to that which took place in the political sphere at the end of the "hundred flowers" period. This was certainly not true in agriculture, however. At the end of 1957 the regime moved to decrease the size of cooperatives and to expand the size of private plots. By the end of September 1958, however, the cooperatives had become organizations over twenty times as large (communes), and private plots and the free market had been abolished.

These organizational changes in agriculture had a profound effect on the economy, but perhaps even more important was the complete change in attitude of the regime toward economic organizations and principles in general. Restraints on lower-level units in the form of planning targets or limited funds were for all practical purposes removed. Heads of factories and communes were given free rein and were told that spectacular achievements were expected. The result was that planning goals were continuously revised upward, and allocation of resources became a matter of who could get hold of the most, regardless of real need. When a firm found itself short of the necessary financing to carry out an enlarged scheme, it merely had to channel funds meant for working capital or other purposes into investment.

Once before, in late 1955 and early 1956, there had been the beginnings of a somewhat similar movement, but at that time strains had manifested themselves fairly quickly — principally in the form of rapidly deteriorating stores of commodities and strong inflationary pressures in those sectors where such pressures could still manifest themselves. Those who had advocated a planned approach to economic development had regained the upper hand, and there had followed a period of retrenchment during which commodity stores were rebuilt and inflationary pressures subsided. This was not the case in 1958 for several reasons. In the first place, there appears to be little reason to doubt that the best agricultural harvest under the Communist regime was that of 1958. In the industrial sector, many projects started during the previous five years were scheduled to be completed in 1958. Thus, even if economic development in that year had been carefully planned, there would still have been rational grounds for stepping up the pace.

Second, many areas where pressures had shown themselves in the past had ceased to exist. With the advent of communes, for example, the free market, the only market on which inflationary pressures could show themselves in the form of price increases, was gone. In addition, the State Statistical Bureau had become little more than an organization for cheering on the "great leap forward" with statistics of limited if any reliability. It is likely that there was a period of several months at least when the central authorities themselves had only the vaguest picture of what was really happening. Finally and most important, those in power had become deeply committed to the belief that the lessons of guerrilla warfare, where *esprit de corps,* a proper ideological outlook, and imaginative independent judgment of those at the scene of action so often proved more important than superior arms, could be applied to development of the Chinese economy. What matter, they felt, that there were imbalances and regulations were flaunted, if the economy kept on surging ahead.

The "great leap," therefore, was not a carefully organized decentralization of authority with certain powers retained in the hands of central planners and the remaining powers turned over to local levels to be used under carefully explained constraints. It was, rather, more like economic anarchy. Under the former situation prices and the market might have played a major role, but under the latter they ceased to have any function at all in areas where decision makers were Communist-trained cadres.

In 1959 and 1960, the pressure of events finally forced the Chinese Communists to abandon the "great leap" and jettison the most important aspects of the communes. Foremost among these events was a series of bad harvests beginning in 1959 and carrying through 1961. This drop in output, which had ramifications throughout the economy, was the result of a combination of bad weather and the effects of the communes. On top of this, the anarchy of the "great leap forward" caused major dislocations in industry and construction. Finally, the Sino-Soviet dispute, which had been building for several years, reached a head with withdrawal in 1960 of practically all Soviet technicians from China.

This combination of disasters led to a gradual reduction in size of the unit controlling agricultural output, reopening of free markets for certain commodities, and a reinstitution of central planning. These moves, however, did not constitute a complete return to the institutions and policies of 1956 or 1957. Many of the formal decentralization measures, some of which were not promulgated until 1958, remain in force. Most important, the cutback in the pace of capital construction in early 1961 was followed by a shift in investment funds to agriculture in recognition of the fundamental importance of a healthy agricultural sector to the whole economy. There also has been a shift in trade away from the Soviet bloc toward developed Western nations.

These measures led to a recovery in agriculture and other sectors of the economy in 1962 and a further recovery in 1963. This moderate success, however, has not bred satisfaction among party cadres with existing relatively conservative institutions. There still is much talk of reforming bourgeois thought as a prelude to another surge forward, but this may be motivated primarily by political considerations, and thus may not constitute a return to more radical institutions and policies in the economy.[10] The issues involved and their effect on price policy and the market, however, are complex, and hence are best left to more detailed analysis in subsequent chapters.

[10] Throughout 1964, for example, major ideologically oriented campaigns were in full swing (campaigns to "learn from the People's Liberation Army," "for socialist education," and the like). Even by the end of 1964, however, these campaigns do not appear to have had much effect on the economy in any way comparable to the "great leap forward."

CHAPTER III

The Market versus Centralized Controls in Agriculture before Cooperatives *

From the beginning, the major objectives of Chinese farm policy have been to raise agricultural output and the marketed portion of that output while maintaining political security and control. The importance of obtaining a substantial and increasing marketed surplus derived first from the fact that agricultural and processed agricultural products have made up approximately three-quarters of all Chinese exports. Second, although rural urban shifts in population have been small in percentage terms, the absolute number of city dwellers increased between early 1950 and the end of 1956 by over 30 million people, or 55 per cent, all of whom had to be fed.[1] Unlike the Soviet Union, however, a substantial and increasing marketed surplus could not be achieved independently of increases in farm production. Under Stalin, collectivization and heavy industrialization could be pushed without fear that the Soviet population would starve for economic reasons over the long run (in the short run many did starve). In China, a prolonged agricultural crisis such as the one that occurred in the Soviet Union, when coupled with a 2 per cent growth in population, would be economically and perhaps politically disastrous to the present regime. Therefore, where the Soviet Union could achieve most of its goals through the introduction of centrally determined compulsory delivery quotas, Com-

* Much of the material in this chapter is taken from my article "Centralization and Decentralization in Mainland China's Agriculture (1949–1962)," *The Quarterly Journal of Economics,* May 1964, pp. 208–237, copyright, 1964, by the President and Fellows of Harvard College.

[1] Breakdowns for urban and rural populations are available only for 1950–1956. Helen and Y. C. Yin, *Economic Statistics of Mainland China (1949–1957)* (Cambridge, Mass., 1960), p. 4.

munist China had to rely more heavily on control devices that had a less detrimental effect on production.

Controlling Chinese agriculture, whatever the objectives, is by no means a simple task. There are over 120 million separate farm households producing many different crops under widely varying conditions of soil and weather. The methods available for exercising control are also many and varied. In this and the following chapter, an attempt is made to analyze the role and effectiveness of one such method, market controls. The focus is not only on how prices and the market were utilized, but why, on occasion, they were rejected and replaced by centralized controls.

One deterrent to an adequate analysis of the role of prices and the market in China's agricultural sector is the poor quality of many available statistics. Difficulties with agricultural production statistics are discussed in Appendix A. Fortunately much of the data relevant to this study are not subject to the same criticisms. For a number of reasons to be discussed [2] state purchase statistics and purchase-price indexes can to some extent be relied upon. There have also been several sample surveys of rural China since 1949 where a genuine attempt was made to obtain a representative sample. The difficulty with statistics in this area, however, does not lie with their lack of reliability so much as their lack of availability. Detailed purchase-price data in sufficient quantity are difficult to obtain, and the number of large scale fairly objective surveys of rural areas is small.

For a study of the role of prices and the market, however, the need for large quantities of accurate statistics is not acute, providing the analyst has access to major directives and speeches made by Communist authorities regarding these areas. Here, the principal feature that makes for a lack of statistical data, namely the vast size (in terms of numbers of individual farming units) and diversity of Chinese agriculture, also operates to make available many important directives and speeches. Newspapers, journals, and various compilations of laws and directives published on the mainland are published in part to inform lower-level administrative personnel of what is expected of them. Although not the only channels of communication, they are among the most

---

[2] See Appendixes A and B.

important, particularly in sectors of the economy where those who need to be kept informed number hundreds of thousands and even millions. This is the case in agriculture. It is not surprising, therefore, to find that the quality and quantity of this type of material are greater than for other sectors. Directives ordering price changes in industry can be sent out to the relatively small number of factories affected directly, but a change in the purchase price of an agricultural product, if it is to achieve its purpose, must be made known in many cases to over 120 million individual households or at least to several million cadres in rural areas.

To keep the major points made in these two chapters from becoming confused by the many shifts and turns in Chinese communist agricultural policy, the material is presented historically. This chapter is concerned with the choice between market and centralized controls in the context of China's pre-1955 individual peasant agriculture. Chapter IV deals with changes in methods of control brought about by the cooperatives and communes.

Prices and Marketing in Pre-Communist China

China's agriculture throughout its long history until the winter of 1955 was based on the individual peasant's tilling his own small plot of land, and, except in Manchuria, extensive farming was virtually unknown. The Communists made many changes during their first six years of rule, but they did not change this fundamental fact. The problem that faced the central regime, therefore, was one of how to direct the production and marketing of agricultural produce under circumstances where private ownership of the land meant that the final decision on what was to be produced and marketed rested with the head of each of China's 120 million farm families. To understand this problem fully, it is necessary to have a view of China's traditional rural economy, in particular the extent to which the typical Chinese farm was tied to the market.

Probably the safest statement that can be made about the nature of agricultural production and marketing in China is that there was no single pattern. What follows, therefore, is an attempt to discern certain key features that are relevant to the question of how Chinese peasants decided what it was they would grow and how much they would market. The analysis is based on several general studies of China's agriculture before World War II, a number of studies of rural Chinese villages, and my own limited personal observation of farming methods in Taiwan and the New Territories of Hong Kong.[3]

The first and most essential feature is that the Chinese peasant farmer, in a fundamental sense, has generally been economically rational. Within the scope of his limited knowledge and given the high risks involved in almost any agricultural undertaking in China, particularly a previously untried one, he has attempted to maximize his expected return. For the relatively well-to-do, leisure was an important part of that return,[4] but this does not basically alter the assertion made about his economic rationality, particularly since only a small percentage were able to afford much leisure. In the words of Tawney, "Economy has been turned by . . . necessity into the most ruthless of religions." [5] Even the *Book of Filial Piety,* which is over two thousand years old, states that a good farmer should "suit crops to soils for profit." [6]

Given the economic rationality of the peasant's behavior, the next question is whether such behavior led to widespread production of crops and subsidiary products for the market and, if so, whether price fluctuations in the market had much effect. Statements that China is a land of subsistence farming would tend to imply that it did not. "Subsistence," however, is an imprecise term of questionable value in a study of this sort. Professor Eckstein has estimated (using official data) that in 1952 per capita crop production in China was 25 to 29 per cent above

[3] I am particularly indebted to J. R. Potter of the University of California (Berkeley) for whatever insights I may have into the economy of the New Territories and to the Joint Commission on Rural Reconstruction for Taiwan.

[4] The emphasis here is on the word "relative." As pointed out in Fei Hsiao-tung and Chang Chih-i, *Earthbound China* (London, 1948), the amount of surplus above subsistence before a peasant started substituting leisure for increased income was not necessarily very large particularly in areas where there were few opportunities to spend the surplus.

[5] R. H. Tawney, *Land and Labor in China* (New York, 1932), p. 48.

[6] Quoted in the inscription to J. L. Buck, *Chinese Farm Economy* (Shanghai, 1930). The full quotation is: "Work according to seasons / Suit crops to soils for profit / Guard behavior, spend wisely / Nurture parents with honor."

that of India.[7] It certainly does not follow from this that Chinese farmers had a large surplus, but it would seem to imply that they had some margin to work with that would allow many of them to take certain risks inherent in growing crops for the market. This argument is further buttressed by the fact that rural incomes were far from equal, indicating that those at the upper end of the scale would probably have been interested in the marketing of their produce.[8]

One does not, however, have to rely on indirect evidence. The reason for presenting the above argument is, at least partly, to explain the economic basis for the substantial degree of reliance on the market that clearly existed. Buck estimated on the basis of one survey that over half of all products raised by the agricultural sector in the late 1920's were marketed.[9] Although his sample was probably biased upward, it leaves little doubt of the importance of the market to the average farmer.[10] This statement is supported in varying degrees by several other analysts of pre-Communist agriculture in China.[11] The degree to which a farmer oriented his activities toward the market depended first on his distance from a major market, and second on the level of his

[7] Alexander Eckstein, *The National Income of Communist China* (Glencoe, Ill., 1961), p. 67. The 25 per cent figure is the one obtained when both countries' crops are valued at Chinese prices; the 29 per cent figure is obtained by valuing at Indian prices. The Indian figures are for the years 1949–50 through 1951–52.

[8] One does not necessarily, of course, have to have a "surplus" in order to market crops. Marketing is likely to be of much greater significance, however, if such a "surplus" exists.

[9] Buck, *Chinese Farm Economy*, p. 196. The term "market" as used here actually refers to a number of organizationally distinct institutions through which peasants sold their produce. For a more precise characterization of these institutions, see G. W. Skinner, "Marketing and Social Structure in Rural China, Part I," *Journal of Asian Studies*, XXIV (November 1964), 3–43.

[10] Purchases of agricultural products in 1952, prior to the institution of purchase quotas, were approximately one-fourth of the gross value of rural production according to official Chinese Communist data. Part of the difference between this and Buck's figure is due to the much greater coverage of Buck's figure (one-fifth of Buck's marketing took place in the same village where the goods were produced, for example), but as argued below, this does not appear to be the only explanation for the difference.

[11] Tawney, *Land and Labor in China*, p. 55; T. H. Shen, *Agricultural Resources of China* (Ithaca, 1951), p. 144.

income, including income from land rented out to others, particularly on the size of his reserve. If a village was within walking range of such a market or was near enough to a good road or waterway, it would market a large amount of its produce. If it was isolated from these, it would produce only what was needed in the village itself.[12] The required degree of accessibility to the market varied according to the crop. Vegetables for urban consumption had to be grown in the immediate neighborhood of the city, leading to often-described phenomena of greenbelts surrounding most of China's major urban centers. Even the comparatively modest undertaking of building concrete bicycle paths away from roads in the New Territories of Hong Kong has had a substantial effect on the ability of farmers to grow vegetables for the city.

The connection between the amount marketed and the level of the individual farmer's income and reserve was closely related to the effect of agricultural purchase prices on production and marketing. Both the general level of agricultural prices relative to those of nonagricultural products and relative prices within the agricultural sector were of importance. A rise in the general level of agricultural prices and hence of farm incomes led to use of more labor, more fertilizer, and opening of new lands, whereas a fall led to a contraction of these same inputs.[13] One would expect, therefore, that a general price increase would also tend to make it possible for peasants to take more risks and produce to a greater extent for the market, although there is no really clearcut evidence on this point.

The relation between changes in relative prices of particular crops and changes in their production was not simple, and material available does not justify an unequivocal statement. Obviously in areas where the amount marketed was small, the effect

---

[12] The most systematic study of this issue was made by Fei and Chang, *Earthbound China,* where the relative accessibility of a major market was one of the major factors behind the choice of the three villages in Yunnan to be studied. The importance of a nearby market is also analyzed in some detail by C. K. Yang, *Chinese Village* (in Kwangtung), and can be inferred from statements in M. C. Yang, *A Chinese Village — Taitou, Shantung Province* (New York, 1945), pp. 199–200.

[13] J. L. Buck, *Land Utilization in China* (Nanking, 1937), p. 347.

of relative price shifts was negligible. Even where the market took a large portion of output, many factors other than price entered into the farmer's decision. Many crops can only be grown on particular types of land, for example. Others required large amounts of capital investment beyond the capacity of many less prosperous peasants, and interest rates were usually too high to make it feasible to borrow necessary funds. A particular crop's price might be high when the farmer was deciding what to plant, but this was no guarantee of what it would be by harvest time. It was this last factor that limited the amount of vegetable growing in one area studied in Kwangtung.[14] When all qualifications are made, however, available evidence suggests that farmers were much influenced by price movements, particularly where those movements were large and prolonged. In one area in southern Hopei, for example, farmers put half of their cultivated land into peanuts after 1920 (only three or four *mow* were in peanuts prior to 1920), when the price rose from 24 to 550 cash per catty over a period of years.[15] In the case of vegetable raising, there is some evidence to suggest that farmers were influenced at least marginally by the previous year's price.[16] Moving away from specific examples, Buck states that "prices of commodities sold or purchased by farmers have an important bearing on land utilization."[17]

Further complications arose, however, from the fact that a farmer's lack of reserves; his ignorance, in many cases, of prices prevailing in other districts; the fact that most of his crop had to be sold immediately after harvest; plus violent seasonal price fluctuations combined with the fact that dealers were usually strongly organized — all tended to place the locus of market

---

[14] C. K. Yang, p. 29. A similar situation apparently exists in Pakistan, where the danger is that cash-crop prices may fall while grain prices rise; see W. P. Falcon, "Farmer Response to Price in a Subsistence Economy: The Case of West Pakistan," *American Economic Review*, LIV (May 1964), 580–591.

[15] Chi Ping, "The Effects of the Commercialization of Agriculture in Southern Hopei," in *Agrarian China: Selected Source Materials from Chinese Authors* (London, 1939), p. 163. A similar example for jasmine production is given in C. K. Yang, p. 30.

[16] Fei and Chang, *Earthbound China*, p. 212, and in the New Territories of Hong Kong (I am indebted to J. R. Potter for this information).

[17] *Land Utilization in China*, p. 311.

power in the hands of dealers.[18] Since this power was used to maximize the short-run profit of the middleman (the time horizon of the average dealer was not long), it is probable that this feature damped the farmer's enthusiasm for relying too heavily on the market. When all these various qualifications are taken into account, however, it still appears fair to say that, before the Communists came to power, Chinese farmers were heavily oriented toward the market and significantly influenced by prices paid for their produce.

The Communists, when they came to power, were in no sense ignorant of conditions in rural China. It was upon their knowledge of and ability to exploit these conditions that their success was based. That they were aware of the particular aspects of the situation described above is beyond doubt. Their principal concern during the first few years was with the land-reform movement, but considerable efforts also were made to reform marketing, tax, and credit procedures so that they would better conform to the needs of the regime. Keeping in mind the situation prior to 1949, it is desirable at this point to turn to an analysis of the effect of prices on production and sales during the relatively free market conditions of the first four years of Communist rule.

Price Policy, 1950–1953

As a result of nearly 13 years of war and civil war, agricultural production and the rural market situation in 1950 were chaotic. Production was perhaps only two-thirds of the prewar level, and the amount marketed had fallen to 25 per cent of total output.[19] The causes of the general drop in output need no elaboration, and the measures taken to restore it were primarily the maintenance of political stability, the repair of damaged irrigation systems, and other similar efforts. The fall in the marketed portion, however, was somewhat more complex. The depressed level of average per capita farm income, together with a low-income elasticity of demand for most agricultural produce, accounted for a part of

---

[18] Buck, *Land Utilization in China;* Shen, *Agricultural Resources of China;* Tawney, *Land and Labor in China.*

[19] These figures are based on official Communist data. They are rough estimates at best. All that is really known is that production in agriculture was down, probably substantially.

the reduction. This was further aggravated by the land reform, which had been completed, in the main, by the end of 1952. The available data unfortunately are not adequate for the task of estimating the effect on marketing of the elimination of the landlord class. The Communists have estimated the annual rent in China prior to 1949, but their objectivity is open to question.[20] Although rents were high, most landlords owned only a little more land than their nonlandlord neighbors. Nothing even remotely like the landed estates of Czarist Russia existed in China at this time. Nevertheless, lopping off the wealthiest class and transferring its land to the poorest group probably had a considerable effect on the market. This is supported by a 1955 survey that found that even rich peasants (a rung below landlords) marketed 43.1 per cent of their grain as compared to 25.2 per cent for middle peasants and 22.1 per cent for poor peasants.[21] Although redistribution of land undoubtedly had some positive economic benefits in the form of increased incentives toward land improvement, these may have been partially offset by the fact that landlords had formerly often rented to rich peasants, who had more capital and better knowledge of advanced techniques of farming than poor peasants.[22] In any case, land reform was primarily motivated by a desire to destroy the class most inimical to the Communists and to solidify their support from poor and middle peasants. Whatever its economic benefits, any redistribution in favor of wealthier peasants would have been unthinkable on political grounds.

There were two other causes of the decline in the marketed portion of farm produce that were not the result of political considerations or of the overall fall in farm income, and hence were more amenable to Communist economic policies. They were, first, the relatively greater reduction in the production of industrial consumers' goods, leading to a large rise in the prices of industrial products relative to those in agriculture (see Table 1); and,

[20] Chen Po-ta, *A Study of Land Rent in Pre-Liberation China* (Peking, 1958).

[21] Based on a survey of 13,245 households in 18 provinces reported in Tung Ta-lin, *Agricultural Cooperation in China* (Peking, 1959), p. 23.

[22] Fei and Chang, *Earthbound China*, p. 77; C. K. Yang, *Chinese Village*, p. 46.

TABLE 1.   Selected official price indexes

Year	Agricultural purchases (1950 = 100)	Agricultural purchases (1954 = 100)	Industrial products, rural areas (1950 = 100)	Industrial relative to agricultural products (1930–1936 avg. = 100)
1950	100.0	—	100.0	131.8
1951	119.6	—	110.3	124.4
1952	121.6	—	109.7	121.8
1953	133.9	—	108.2	109.6
1954	138.4	100.0	110.3	109.2
1955	137.7	99.5	111.9	111.3
1956	141.8	102.5	110.8	107.0
1957	148.8	107.5	112.1	103.0[a]
1958	152.1	109.9	111.4	—

Source: See Appendix B for the sources and a discussion of the degree of reliability of these price indexes.

[a] Estimate.

second, the greatly reduced market for certain specific types of products produced in rural areas.

Although the shift in relative prices back in favor of agriculture after 1950 was primarily a result of the rapid recovery of industrial consumers' goods production, the regime's policy makers contributed by making it possible for market forces of supply and demand to work freely. They did this by rapidly restoring normal channels of commerce and then by not interfering with their functioning. The first step was to bring hyperinflation under control so that the populace would have some confidence in the currency and end such practices as hoarding and barter trade. This was done primarily by bringing the budget rapidly into balance[23] and by expanding the position of state trading companies in the handling of certain key commodities, particularly

[23] Official data published several years later indicate that the budget was balanced by 1951, but data published at the time can be reconstructed to show that balance was not achieved until 1952. If foreign credits and bond sales are excluded from revenue, there were also deficits from 1953 through 1956. See Appendix C.

grain and cotton textiles. The latter measure was desirable, in part because speculative movements in China at that time tended to be destabilizing. A spiral once started was difficult to stop, particularly after the regime had automatically geared urban wages to a cost of living index based on a few major consumers' goods. Once the inflation had been brought under control, perhaps the most important of the regime's policies in this area was the negative one of refraining from using its market power over certain consumers' goods to obtain monopoly profits. This contrasts with the situation during the "scissors crisis" of 1922 and 1923 in the Soviet Union. There, industrial firms held products off the market in order to keep prices high, hence also reducing the quantity of agricultural goods that peasants were willing to market.

This reliance by the Chinese regime on the free market was due primarily to the lack of a feasible alternative. Communists in China have never felt easy about the utilization of such a market in any form, but on three separate occasions — this early period, the reopening of the free market in 1956 and 1957, and the present-day rural trade fairs — they have recognized its usefulness. Literally hundreds of articles were written during these latter two periods in attempts to show that a properly run free market, under the circumstances, was not really something capitalistic whatever its appearance. In the first period, the need for capitalists was explicitly recognized and they were encouraged to believe that they would be used over a much longer period than turned out to be the case.

The lack of a feasible alternative during the first four years was, of course, due to the absence of an already established state commercial network, combined with the need to keep the economy running somewhat smoothly while it was being established. As seen in Table 4, the state controlled only about 10 per cent of purchases from the agricultural sector in 1950 and less than 25 per cent in 1951. Since it was recognized that private traders had to make a profit to stay in business, the state allowed prices to fluctuate with changes in conditions on the market.[24] Official

[24] There were many times when the state made it a conscious policy to weaken private commerce by driving it into the red. During the "five anti"

prices were set, but they moved more or less with market prices — with some notable exceptions mentioned below.

The role of state policy in promoting the development of certain individual farm products was more active. The goods hardest hit by the war were luxury products and products whose greater part was exported or used as industrial raw materials. An example of an industrial raw material of this type would be cotton, whose output in 1949 was 47 per cent of the 1933 level, while that of a luxury product might be tea or tobacco, whose 1949 outputs were 16 and 4 per cent of their 1933 levels, respectively.[25] Silkworm production, which would come under both headings, had fallen in 1949 to only 14 per cent of its prewar peak.[26] Many other special goods and handicrafts disappeared from the market altogether.[27] Since the bulk of export earnings came from such industrial raw materials and luxury products (food grains were a relatively minor export item), any producers' goods industrialization program depended heavily on their recovery. The consumers' goods industrial sector was even more dependent on them, since they were the source of the bulk of its raw materials.

The main devices used by the state in its attempt to restore production of these industrial raw materials and luxury products to their prewar level were centrally determined purchase prices, backed up by various marketing arrangements that gave price

---

campaign the regime showed a willingness to attack private business, even at the price of a serious disruption of the economy. But this does not refute the statement in the text, if it is taken in the sense that the state allowed capitalists to make a profit when the state's desire to use capitalists overrode its desire to curtail or eliminate them.

[25] The 1949 data are taken from SSB, *Ten Great Years*, pp. 124–125, and the 1933 data are from T. C. Liu and K. C. Yeh, *The Economy of the Chinese Mainland: National Income and Economic Development, 1933–1959*, vol. II (appendixes), The RAND Corporation, Research Memorandum RM-3519, April 1963, p. 455. Both sets of data are subject to a wide margin of error, particularly the 1949 data. The point made is simply that production of these crops had dropped well below prewar levels, and that in some cases it had nearly ceased altogether.

[26] Ministries of Agriculture, Foreign Trade, Textile Industries, Forestry, and Second Commerce, "Report on the Nationwide Silkworm Production Conference" (April 30, 1958), *FKHP*, VIII, 226–227.

[27] The percentage of special local products in East China that did not enter the market because they could not be sold was 30 to 40 per cent of the total output of special local products (Shanghai Price Book, p. 385).

TABLE 2. Official cotton-grain price ratio
(catties of grain per catty of 7/8-inch middle-grade cotton)

| Year | Area's principal grain crop | | |
	Millet	Wheat	Rice
Prewar[a]	—	7.0	—
1946[b]	5.5	5.0	5.5
1950[c]	8.0	7.0	6.5
1951[d]	8.5	8.0	8.5
1952[a]	8.0–9.0	7.5–8.5	8.0–9.0
1953[e]	6.75–8.0	6.25–7.5	6.75–8.0
1954[f]	7.5–8.25	6.75–8.0	7.25–8.25
1955[g]	7.5–8.25	6.75–8.0	7.25–8.25

[a] Ho Wei, "How and Why to Compare the Present Prices of Farm Produce with the Pre-war Level," *Hsueh-hsi*, April 13, 1957, translated in *ECMM*, no. 89, pp. 20–25.

[b] Ch'en Ch'i-hsiang, "Understand Clearly the New Cotton Grain Price Ratio," *HHYP*, May 25, 1953, p. 182.

[c] *JMJP*, April 14, 1950.

[d] *JMJP* editorial, "Properly Adjust the Relative Price of Cotton and Grain and the Grain–Cloth Seasonal Price Differential," *HHYP*, May 25, 1953, p. 182.

[e] Financial and Economic Committee, "Directive on the Relative Price of Cotton and Grain in 1953" (April 1, 1953), *HHYP*, May 25, 1953, p. 181.

[f] Financial and Economic Committee, "Directive on the Relative Price of Cotton and Grain in 1954," *HHYP*, April 25, 1954, p. 166.

[g] Ministries of Agriculture and Commerce, "Directive on the Relative Price of Cotton and Grain in 1955" (April 22, 1955), *FKHP*, I, 322, states that prices in 1955 are to remain at the 1954 relative level.

adjustments greater impact. The long experience of the Chinese Communists in dealing with the rural scene apparently left them with little doubt that the Chinese peasant would respond to price incentives.

The most important state efforts in this area were directed at raising cotton production and marketing. As in a number of other undeveloped countries, the cotton textile industry was among the first industries to develop in China on a significant scale. By the 1930's the domestic industry had virtually eliminated foreign cotton textiles from the Chinese market. The majority of the Chinese population was dressed in machine-made clothing, most of which came from Shanghai. It is not surprising, therefore, that rapid recovery of this industry was a top priority target of the regime. Recovery depended on raw materials which, on the whole, had to be obtained domestically, since imports of cotton were severely restricted.[28] The primary technique used to obtain the required cotton was to raise its purchase price. This was undertaken at the earliest possible moment, in the spring of 1950 (see Table 2). Since there was still substantial inflation and state purchasing organs were too new and weak to attempt to fix a particular set of prices, directives of 1950 and 1951 were worded in terms of minimum cotton-grain price ratios to be guaranteed to cotton farmers. These regulations then were supplemented by a list of official state-set absolute prices for major cotton-producing areas, and this practice has apparently been continued ever since.[29]

These efforts probably account, at least to some extent, for the partial recovery in cotton production and sown area in 1950, but they were not executed with great efficiency. In certain areas, particularly those lacking state purchasing organs (state grain companies) the official price was below the market price, and the market price relative to that of grain was lower than the officially determined ratio. The difficult problem of setting prices properly according to quality so as to encourage the raising of higher-quality crops also existed at this time, as it apparently has ever since.[30] This is not surprising, however, since prior to

[28] The principal reason for this restriction was the desire to concentrate on importing machinery and other similar commodities as part of the general emphasis on the development of heavy industry. Cotton imports in 1950 were two and a half times those of 1949, but fell back again almost to the 1949 level in 1951 and 1952 and well below it in 1953 (*WKKT*, p. 187).

[29] For the 1951 list see *Ch'ang-chiang jih-pao*, June 2 and August 23, 1951, and *JMJP*, August 22, 1951. For 1952 see *JMJP*, August 4, 1952, and *Chieh-fang jih-pao*, August 10, 1952; for 1953, *HHYP*, September 25, 1953, p. 165.

[30] Ministries of Trade and Agriculture, "Directive on Clearly Understanding Cotton Price Policy" (October 19, 1950), *HHYP*, November 25, 1950, p. 115. How widespread the problems described were is difficult to determine. An article in *JMJP*, November 24, 1950, lists grain and cotton prices for twelve cities in cotton producing areas, and in only one case (Hangchow) was the ratio well below that specified in the directive, but it is probable that the

1949 most agricultural products in China were not graded at all.[31] The state attacked these problems not only with a strong reiteration of the intent of the initial policy, but, in addition, with the introduction of a system of advance-purchase contracts. These contracts constituted an agreement in the spring on a price and quantity of cotton to be delivered to the state the following fall. In exchange for signing the contract, the farmer was given a certain percentage or amount of the value to be purchased at the time of the signing, in effect an interest-free loan, except for "rich peasants," who had to pay a low rate of interest.[32] The advantages of this procedure were substantial. As already described, farmers in China prior to 1949 often were not influenced by purchase-price movements because they could not be sure that prices at the time of harvest would be as favorable. Advance-purchase agreements protected the farmer from adverse price fluctuations due to market forces, which individual local cadres might take advantage of even in violation of official regulations. In addition to this, these agreements provided the farmer with funds when he needed them most. The advantage to the state was, of course, that it encouraged cotton production and the sale of that production to the state. As a result of this advantage, use of advance purchase agreements was expanded from 45 per cent of total planned purchases in 1951 to 70 per cent in 1952.[33] The only major problem with their use arose because neither cadres nor farmers fully appreciated the sanctity of contracts, and difficulties arose whenever consideration of such events as natural disasters in a cotton-producing area had to be taken into account.[34]

---

problem of maintaining a proper ratio became more difficult the further away one was from these centers.

[31] T. H. Shen, *Agricultural Resources of China*, p. 108.

[32] Joint Cooperative Board, "Temporary Methods of Handling 1951 Advance Cotton Purchases," *HHYP*, April 25, 1951, p. 1338. The agreement also was to include provisions guaranteeing that a farmer plant a certain number of *mow* in cotton, the quality of the cotton to be purchased, and so forth. The statement on treatment of wealthy peasants is in Government Affairs Council, "Directive on 1954 Advance Purchase Work," *HHYP*, April 25, 1954, pp. 164–165.

[33] "Discussion of Ending the Advance Purchases of Cotton," *HHYP*, May 25, 1953, p. 183.

[34] Tientsin *TKP*, October 5, 1955.

TABLE 3. The production and marketing of cotton[a]

Year	Production[b] (million catties)	State and Private Purchases (million catties)	State and Private Purchases (per cent)[c]	Cotton-sown area[b] (million mow)
1950	1385	823[d]	59	56.8
1951	2061	—	—	82.3
1952	2607	1953[e]	75	83.6
1953	2349	1875[e]	80	77.7
1954	2130	1570[e]	74	81.9
1955	3037	2407[e]	79	86.6
1956	2890	2120[f]	73	93.8
1957	3280	2250[g]	69	86.6
1958	4200	3060[d]	73	85.8

[a] Since the bulk of the cotton crop was marketed and was ultimately transformed into textiles in plants located in a few major cities, such as Shanghai and Tientsin, there is every reason to believe that the data are reliable except, perhaps, for the early years and, of course, 1958. The 1950–1953 data, however, probably reflect the basic trends accurately.

[b] SSB, *Ten Great Years*, pp. 119, 129.

[c] Derived by dividing purchases by production. The 1956 *CCYC* article referred to in note e gives a slightly different percentage for 1955 (80.1 per cent), which must have been due to the use of a different cotton production figure for that year.

[d] SSB, *Ten Great Years*, p. 169. The figures for 1950 and 1958 include taxes in kind (that is, those paid in cotton). It is assumed that the other statistics also include taxes in kind.

[e] Tseng Ling, "The Rural Market in the Surging Tide of Agricultural Collectivization," *CCYC*, March 1, 1956, p. 13, gives the absolute figures for 1955 purchases and the absolute increase over 1954. The commodity rates (per cent marketed) are given for 1952 and 1953. The purchase figures for 1952 and 1953 were obtained from these rates.

[f] Derived from the percentage change between 1955 and 1956 (SSB, "Report on the Results of the 1956 National Economic Plan," *HHPYK*, September 10, 1957, p. 204). That the derived absolute figure is probably correct is supported by the fact that purchases during the 1956–57 cotton year (the larger part of which were made in 1956) are given as 2200 million catties (Ministry of Commerce, "To Cut Consumption in Summer Use: To Ensure Supply in Winter," *JMJP*, April 20, 1957, translated in *URS*, vol. VII, no. 17, p. 221).

[g] Derived from the percentage change in state purchases (all cotton purchases at this time were made by the state) between 1957 and 1958; see SSB, "Report on the 1958 National Economic Development Situation" (April 14, 1958), *HHPYK*, April 25, 1959, pp. 51–54. That this figure refers to the calendar (1957) rather than the cotton year (1957–58) is attested to by the fact that a different percentage is given for the cotton year (Chai Mou, "The Superiority of the People's Commune as Seen from Our Work in Finance and Trade," *CCYC*, November 17, 1959, p. 37) and that the figure was reported before the end of the 1958–59 cotton year.

The success of such measures in raising production and marketing is obvious from the statistics (see Table 3). Both production and marketing of cotton in 1952 were double or more those of 1950. The regime, in fact, felt it had been too successful. Raising of the purchase prices of some individual crops relative to those of others was never conceived by the Communists as a long-run solution to problems of inadequate agricultural production, since increases in one product could only be bought at the expense of another. The principal purpose of shifts in relative prices, therefore, was only to restore production of particular products to a more normal level (the prewar level usually being taken as the main point of reference). Once that level was reached, other methods, primarily related to increasing unit-area yield, were to be relied upon. In the case of cotton, the objective probably was some combination of the prewar cotton-sown area, the capacity of domestic industry, and the desire to reduce cotton imports. Whatever the level desired, the regime apparently felt that it had passed it in 1952, and was concerned that a continuation of policies then in existence would jeopardize the even more important goal of increasing grain output. In order to prevent further increases in the cotton-sown area, the regime lowered the cotton-grain price ratio and eliminated advance purchases of cotton, although it did make one compensatory move by changing the basis for computing the agricultural tax on cotton.[35]

As events of 1953 turned out, the state discovered that it had overcompensated, and both production and the sown area fell. In 1954, therefore, the cotton price was again raised and advance purchases were reinstituted. Natural disasters in 1954, however, led to an even greater decrease in output and purchases. Rather than further raise the price of cotton in 1955, which could have recreated the situation of 1952, the state strengthened its advance purchasing and, as will be seen later, introduced com-

[35] *Ching-chi chou-pao* editorial, "Clearly Understand the New Cotton-Grain Price Ratio in Order to Complete Agricultural Production Duties," *Ching-chi chou-pao*, no. 14 (1953), pp. 2–3. The tax on cotton was to be computed at the regular rate of 11 per cent on the basis of what the land produced when sown to grain. Since the yield of cotton in value terms was considerably above that of grain, the result was a lowering of the agricultural tax on cotton land.

pulsory purchase quotas. Nearly five times the sum issued for advance purchasing in 1954 was allocated in 1955. Along with these funds went an allocation of fertilizer and an increase in the grain and cloth ration based on the amount of cotton contracted for.[36] As seen from Table 2, these various moves, in combination with better weather, were successful in bringing about an increase in both production and marketing of cotton.

In the case of cotton, therefore, manipulation of the purchase-price structure was the principal device used to restore production to a more "normal" level. Advance purchases essentially were a device for backing up this price policy and making it more effective. From the available evidence presented here, it would appear that these measures proved to be quite successful because they were specifically tailored to the needs of the individual, economically rational farmer.

Centrally determined prices and advance purchases also were important in varying degrees to the production and marketing of peanuts and other sources of edible oils, tea leaves, certain fibers such as jute and green hemp, tobacco, silkworms, local silk, and wool.[37] Since a high proportion of each of these crops was nearly always marketed, the relatively small amounts reaching urban processing plants and export markets could only be raised substantially if production were increased above these very low levels. Marketing procedures were, therefore, as in the case of cotton, primarily an aid to implementation of the state's price policy.

Although some of the rise in prices of these products during

---

[36] *JMJP,* June 19, 1955, and SC, "Directive on the Advance Purchase of Cotton in 1955," *HHYP,* April 28, 1955, p. 141. The rule set up in the latter directive was that, along with a contract for every 100 catties of cotton, the state should issue 50 to 100 catties of fertilizer, 10 catties of grain, and 10 feet of cotton cloth.

[37] The state also set official grain prices and signed advance purchase contracts for grain. It was not, however, feasible to increase grain production by encouraging an expansion in the grain-sown area by means of price policy, since grain already used most of the land. In the case of the marketing of grain, the amounts marketed were encouraged both by grain price and advance-purchase policy, but more important was the agricultural tax and the general level of agricultural purchase prices in relation to industrial retail prices.

this period was a result of ordinary market forces, the state made special efforts in many cases to ensure that the rise was adequate to the task. A minimum ratio between the price of fibers and grain similar to that for cotton, for example, was set in 1950 and raised in 1951 for the express purpose of stimulating the sowing of fiber crops,[38] with the result that by 1952 production of some fibers was over five times the very low level of 1949.[39] The price of tea, even though in 1950 it was already greater relative to the price of rice than the 1930–1936 average, was raised from 4.9 to 5.7 times the price of middle-grade rice in 1951 and to 7.86 times in 1953.[40] Tea production recovered more slowly than either cotton or fibers, but the reason was not lack of response to price changes so much as it was the much longer time needed to rehabilitate tea production.[41] Purchases of tobacco at first suffered untimely and improper official price setting, but these problems apparently were quickly overcome, since both the production and marketing of tobacco increased very rapidly between 1950 and 1952.[42] Where efforts to raise prices were less vigorous, the response of production was equally weak. A directive in December 1953 on increasing the production of crops from which oil could be extracted was

[38] *JMJP*, April 14, 1950, and Financial and Economic Committee, "Regulations Concerning the Relative Price of Fibers and Grain and the Settling of Purchase and Grain Fertilizer Supply Problems" (March 17, 1951), *HHYP*, April 25, 1951, p. 1341.

[39] *Jen-min shou-ts'e, 1957* (Peking, 1957), p. 470.

[40] "Our Country's Development of Tea Leaf Production," *TCKT*, February 14, 1957, p. 33.

[41] Ho Wei, "How and Why to Compare the Present Prices of Farm Produce with the Prewar Level," *Hsueh-hsi*, April 3, 1957, translated in *ECMM*, no. 89, p. 23.

[42] "The Great Success of Agricultural Production Leadership in 1950," *HHYP*, March 25, 1951, p. 1068. Tobacco purchases (state and private) were 416 million catties in 1952 as against 102.8 million catties in 1950. (The 1950 figure is in SSB, *Ten Great Years*, p. 169, and the 1952 figure is derived from the absolute figure for 1955 and the percentage increases for 1954–1955 and 1952–1954. The 1955 figure is quoted in Ronald Hsia, *Government Acquisition of Agricultural Output in Mainland China, 1953–1956*, The RAND Corporation, Research Memorandum RM-2207, September 3, 1958, p. 41; the percentage increases between 1954 and 1955 are from SSB, "Communique on the Fulfillment of the First Five Year Plan," NCNA, April 13, 1959, translated in *CB*, no. 556, pp. 1–9, and for 1952 and 1954 are from *Chung-kuo chin-jung*, no. 10 (1955), p. 4. The latter source gives a percentage increase for 1956 as well, but it is only a plan figure.)

concerned with increasing output without impinging on grain acreage, and only minor price adjustments were suggested.[43] In the case of rapeseed, prices were not raised very significantly until after 1954, and before that time were probably below the prewar level in spite of the fact that production conditions for rapeseed had worsened.[44] It is not surprising, therefore, that production of rapeseed in 1956 was still only half the prewar output, and that production of other oil-bearing crops was not much greater.

As already stated, these price measures were backed up by improvements in marketing procedures, the most important of which was the institution of advance purchases. All the products mentioned so far were brought under the system of advance-purchase contracts, but not until much later than cotton had been. Although the exact timing for each product is difficult to determine, it is doubtful that advance purchases were of great significance to the production of the crops already noted until after 1954 or 1955. This technique, therefore, did not play the role in recovery of their production that it did in the case of cotton.[45]

With other crops and with animal products and subsidiary rural occupations, the government left price determination to the market. State efforts in this area were mostly confined to attempts to bring interested parties together at commodity-circulation conferences to aid in sale of various handicraft products. These conferences probably were responsible in part, at least, for the 52 per cent increase in prices of special local products between 1950 and 1952.[46] Although production statistics for these commodities are too unreliable for conclusions to be based upon

[43] Government Affairs Council, "Directive on Increasing Production of Oil Materials Crops" (December 25, 1953), HHYP, January 25, 1954, p. 157.

[44] Tsao Jui-hsiang, "Questions of Raising the Procurement Prices for Rapeseed," Liang-shih kung-tso, October 14, 1956, translated in ECMM, no. 58, pp. 25–27.

[45] JMJP editorial, "Directive on the 1954 Advance Purchase Work," HHYP, April 25, 1954, pp. 164–165; "Government Affairs Council Issues Directive on the Advance Purchase of Tea, Silk, Hemp, Tobacco, and Wool," HHPYK, March 6, 1956, pp. 129–130.

[46] TCKT data office, "Price Gaps between Industrial Products and Farm Products: Their Changes in Post-Liberation Years," TCKT, September 14, 1957, translated in ECMM, no. 104, pp. 20–29.

them, it is probable that the output increased significantly. In the case of animal products, the state took little action and prices rose by only 4.4 per cent between 1950 and 1952,[47] but production nevertheless recovered fairly rapidly. The effect of prices in this latter area, however, is complex and is best left to fuller discussion in the next chapter.

Although many products had not recovered their prewar levels by 1952, the Chinese Communists would seem to have had reason to be satisfied with the rapid rate at which rehabilitation of both output and marketing had been achieved. The marketed portion of farm production had risen from 25 per cent of gross agricultural output in 1950 to 27 per cent in 1952 and to 28 per cent in 1953 (absolute real increases of 33 and 46 per cent respectively).[48] Nevertheless, by the end of 1953 it had become apparent that affairs in the agricultural sector were not proceeding as well as the regime required. The year 1953 marked the beginning of the first five-year plan, and investment had been raised 84 per cent above the 1952 level, exports were 28 per cent higher, and the urban population had increased by 6 million persons, or 8.4 per cent, since the beginning of the year.[49] This rapid growth was sustained for a time by the good harvest of 1952, but in 1953 the weather, which had been particularly good in 1952, reverted to normal, and the production of many crops fell, while that of grain rose by only 1.6 per cent.

The most serious of the difficulties created by this situation was on the grain market, where in 1953 the state's sales of grain were running several billion catties ahead of its purchases.[50] As a result of this rapidly increasing demand for grain, the Chinese

---

[47] *Ibid.*

[48] These figures are obtained by dividing gross agricultural output by total sales of agricultural and subsidiary products. The raw data are from SSB, *Ten Great Years*, pp. 16, 168. Since the underlying data are of poor quality, these percentages are no more than rough approximations of the real situation.

[49] Yin and Yin, *Economic Statistics of Mainland China*, pp. 4, 63.

[50] Some idea of the state's deficit can be derived from the fact that state sales in 1953–54 were 80 per cent above 1952–53, whereas purchases were only up 33 per cent. Applying these percentages to the 1952–53 grain-purchase data in Table 19 and assuming purchases and sales were roughly in balance in 1952–53 one arrives at a deficit of 30 billion catties. Yang Chien-pai, *Ching-chi-chung chi-chung chu-yau pi-li kuan-hsi-te pien-hua*, p. 44.

Communists were faced with a dilemma at the end of 1953. They could alleviate the pressure on the grain market by cutting back the investment program, but substantial cuts would require acceptance of a slow rate of industrial growth. Alternatively, they could obtain the necessary grain deliveries through the market by raising grain purchase prices. The price rise would have to be so great, however, that it would force the regime to transfer a large portion of its investment resources from the producers' goods sector to consumers' goods. Since these two possibilities were unacceptable, the remaining choices were either to abandon the market and obtain the necessary grain deliveries by means of compulsory quotas or to take even more radical centralization measures in an attempt to increase the rate of growth in agricultural output.

In November 1953 the alternative decided upon was the introduction of compulsory grain-delivery quotas. This, in fact, was not the Chinese Communists' first experience with compulsory quotas. The agricultural tax, which had been in existence long before the Communists even came to power, was also essentially a compulsory quota system for grain. Before turning to the quotas introduced in 1953, therefore, it is useful to look briefly at the rationale behind the introduction of the agricultural tax and the effects that this tax had on the market and on rural production.

The Agricultural Tax

The only difference between the agricultural tax and later purchase quotas was that with the tax the state did not compensate the farmer for his produce whereas, with the quotas, it did. The compensation paid in the latter instance, however, had little effect on the amount delivered to the state.

The agricultural tax was by no means the only levy by state or local authorities on the rural population of China, and, with the exception of 1950 and 1951, it was not even the most important from the point of view of revenue. From 1952 on, tax revenue (including profits of state enterprises) from the sale of industrial products to the agricultural sector was a much greater source of funds than the agricultural tax. By 1953 income from sales of industrial products was over three times that from the tax.[51]

The original need for a tax in kind on agriculture arose out of conditions existing when the Communists came to power.[52] On the one hand, the army and the urban population had to be fed, and, on the other, inflation had to be stopped before order could be brought into the economy. Government expenditure, already swollen by demands of war, was further increased by the Communists' initial promise to take over the existing bureaucracy and maintain the salaries of those who remained at their posts. Industry and commerce, prostrate from the civil war, were in no position to contribute the needed funds. Agriculture had suffered, but relatively less than industry; in any case, it was the one major source of income left that could be taxed. The decision to make it a tax in kind probably was based on two considerations. The first was that prices and the currency were in such a chaotic state that the tax would have to be computed in terms of commodity equivalents (as were wages) in any case. The second was that the state, in addition to needing revenue, also required grain for reasons already mentioned, and it had good reason to believe that it would have difficulty fulfilling these needs if it relied on the market. The decision to tax in kind, however, was not inevitable. The Soviet Union, under similar conditions of hyperinflation in 1923 and 1924, had changed from a tax in kind on agriculture to a money tax in the hope that such a move would force peasants out of goods and into money, thus helping to stabilize prices. Although this change may have contributed, in

[51] This is based on an estimate of the burden of taxation on the rural population made by the author for another as yet unfinished study. The Chinese Communists have never explained the method of valuation of the crops collected for the agricultural tax. As a number of writers have pointed out, these crops may be somewhat undervalued, thus understating the importance of this tax.
[52] The Communists used agricultural taxes both in kind and in money before obtaining power (as early as 1938 in the Shansi-Chahar-Hopei Border Region), and this earlier experience was probably one factor determining the choice of the form of tax to be used. It is probable, however, that the major factors in the decisions were the conditions existing in 1949 and 1950. (See discussion of these earlier taxes in K. C. Chao, *Agrarian Policy of the Chinese Communist Party*, pp. 45–47, 52–54.)

TABLE 4.   Agricultural purchases and the agricultural tax

Year[a]	Purchases of agricultural and subsidiary products (million yuan)		Grain purchases[b] (million catties)	Agricultural tax[c] (million catties)	Agricultural tax (million yuan)
	Total	State			
1949	—	—	—	—	—
49–50	—	—	—	40,600	—
1950	8,000	780	66,850	—	1,910
50–51	—	—	—	35,340	—
1951	10,500	2,500	—	—	2,169
51–52	—	—	—	43,740	—
1952	12,970	5,630	—	—	2,740
52–53	—	—	61,000	38,800	—
1953	15,320	8,170	—	—	2,711
53–54	—	—	83,000	35,100	—
1954	17,360	12,070	—	—	3,278
54–55	—	—	90,270	38,000	—
1955	17,800	—	—	—	3,054
55–56	—	—	85,990	38,000	—
1956	18,400	13,330	—	—	2,965
56–57	—	—	83,430	36,800	—
1957	20,280	15,620	—	—	2,931
57–58	—	—	92,910	36,000	—
1958	22,760	19,680	—	—	3,260
58–59	—	—	111,300	—	—
1959	29,180	—	—	—	3,300

Source: For the sources and a discussion of the reliability of these data, see Appendix D.
  [a] Given in both calendar (1949) and grain (1949–50) years.
  [b] Husked grain including soybeans.
  [c] In fine-grain equivalents.

combination with other factors, to subsequent stabilization, it also increased Soviet difficulties in obtaining an adequate portion of agricultural output.[53]

Taxes on farm products in Communist China have remained in kind ever since, probably because the principal problem facing the regime in later years was not so much one of inadequate

[53] F. D. Holzman, *Soviet Taxation* (Cambridge, Mass., 1955), pp. 160–161.

revenue as one of a lack of adequate amounts of marketed agricultural produce. With over half its grain supply coming from the tax (see Table 4), it is not surprising that the regime did not consider changing its fundamental form to a money tax, particularly since elimination of the landlord class reduced the amount of grain marketed over and above the tax between 1950 and 1952–53.[54] This happened at a time when marketing of agricultural products in general was increasing by 40 per cent and the agricultural tax (in real terms) remained fairly constant. With the institution of compulsory purchases of grain at the end of 1953, the state could have switched to a money tax, but it would have served little purpose, and the administrative and educational problems of such a change, which would have had to have been explained to over one hundred million farm families, would have been considerable. For these reasons, therefore, the tax has been kept in the same fundamental form throughout Communist rule.

Detailed rates and implementation procedures of the agricultural tax have been dealt with at length by other authors[55] and need not detain us. The discussion here will be confined to an analysis of the effect of these rates and procedures on agricultural production and marketing. As a general rule, the tax was set up in a way that minimized effects on allocation of resources to particular crops and on incentives in general. By allowing the tax to be paid in the predominant crop of the area (and even in cash during crises), farmers were not required to concentrate on raising any one particular crop. The fact that most of the tax was paid in grain, however, undoubtedly did tend to encourage the peasant to grow more grain than he would have otherwise in order to meet his own demands for food. More important was the wording of the tax in a way that reduced its general disin-

[54] These statistics should be used with some care since the agricultural tax is only about 80–85 per cent grain and the 1950 figure may not be husked grain.

[55] For example, George Ecklund, *Taxation in Communist China, 1950–1959* (Washington, 1961), pp. 11–19; R. Hsia, *Agricultural Output in Mainland China*, chap. iv; K. C. Chao, *Economic Planning and Organization in Mainland China*, I (Cambridge, Mass., 1959), 188–193; K. C. Chao, *Agrarian Policy of the Chinese Communist Party*.

centive effects. This was done by setting the tax on the basis of
the so-called "normal" yield of the land, that is, the amount the
land should produce in an ordinary year. This procedure was
followed as early as 1950,[56] initially probably in order to facili-
tate administration of the tax. As one writer points out, this
administration was not an easy job, since the state met with
considerable opposition when it attempted to collect the tax, and
there is ample evidence of evasion through fixing of excessively
low yields by peasants, particularly during earlier years.[57] In
spite of these efforts, however, there apparently was considerable
unsystematic fluctuation in the "normal" yield, resulting in a
directive in August 1953 calling for a final settling of the fixed
standard, which was then to remain in effect for the next three
years without change. The order this time was promulgated for
the express purpose of stimulating farmer "positivism" (minimiz-
ing the disincentives of the agricultural tax).[58]

If the state had not fixed the tax according to normal yield, the
effect on incentives would have been significant. This would
have been less true in the "old liberated areas" (North and
Northeast China and parts of Northwest China), where the tax
was a fixed proportion of the yield. But in the "new liberated
areas," the tax was a progressive one ranging from 7 to 30 per
cent of per capita income (in terms of unhusked grain) of individual farm households. The potential disincentive of this tax
was even greater than the above percentages might suggest because the rate at each level was imposed not on the increment
above the next lowest category but on the whole income. Where
per capita income was 1000 catties, for example, the rate of tax
on total income would be 20 per cent, but on the last 50-catty
increment, the rate would be 40 per cent. Since the tax base was
fixed, however, the only function of these regulations was to

[56] See Ministry of Finance, "Regulation on the Agricultural Tax Land Area
and the Fixed Standard for an Ordinary Year's Production" (September 16,
1950), *HHYP,* September 20, 1950, pp. 1360–1361.
[57] Reiitsu Kojima, "Grain Acquisition and Supply," in E. S. Kirby, ed.,
Contemporary China (Hong Kong, 1963), V, 65–88. Mr. Kojima tells us
that a number of cadres were killed while attempting to collect the tax.
[58] Government Affairs Council, "Directive on 1953 Agricultural Tax Work"
(August 28, 1953), *HHYP,* September 25, 1953, pp. 161-162.

increase the equitability of the tax. In the tax reform of 1958, the progressive tax was eliminated altogether, although areas were given leeway in setting the rate to be applied. Since cooperatives had eliminated income differentials among individuals in a given area, arising from such things as the ownership of better land, the progressive tax made little sense.[59] Administration remained an important consideration as well, even though great numbers of cadres had been trained since 1953. Ease of administration favored the proportional tax, and was a continuing argument against calculation of the tax according to actual rather than a standard yield.[60] Although there were minor adjustments in the normal yield in 1958, the tax base has remained essentially unchanged since 1952.[61] Existence of local surtaxes during most of this period does not change the picture, since these usually were a fixed percentage of the agricultural tax.

It should not be assumed from the above discussion that the agricultural tax had no influence on production other than to encourage peasants to grow more grain to meet their own demands for food. In fact, the methods used to compute "normal yield" often tended to encourage planting of other than grain crops. The case of cotton has already been mentioned, and the same was true of other nongrain crops, at least until a special directive was passed raising the tax on these crops.[62] Since income from crops such as cotton and tobacco was relatively high, computation of the tax on the basis of what the land would produce if planted in grain tended to make the actual rate of tax much lower than the theoretical rate. Tax exemption was another similar device

[59] *Ts'ai-cheng* editorial, "Implement Agricultural Tax Regulations and Endeavor to Complete Agricultural Reform," *Ts'ai-cheng*, July 5, 1958, translated in *ECMM*, no. 139, pp. 40–44. The responsibility for payment of the tax was, of course, switched from the individual to the cooperative.

[60] Hsiao Ku, "A Preliminary Study of the Agricultural Tax in the Next Couple of Years," *Ts'ai-cheng*, December 5, 1956, translated in *ECMM*, no. 66, p. 35.

[61] For example, the normal yield in 1957 was down to 69 per cent of the actual yield (K. C. Chao, *Agrarian Policy of the Chinese Communist Party*, p. 199).

[62] SC, "Regulation on the Adjustment of the Agricultural Tax on Economic Crops the Income from Which Is Relatively Large" (December 20, 1957), *FKHP*, VI, 338–339.

used by the government to encourage such things as the opening of new lands and the planting of mulberry orchards and tea and fruit gardens. How successful these measures were is difficult to ascertain, since they were almost always carried out in conjunction with other supporting policies.

With the exception of measures described in the previous paragraph, however, the agricultural tax had relatively little influence at the margin on either the level of production or selection of crops to be planted in a given area. Since exceptions were all attempts to increase the efficiency of production, the agricultural tax appears to have been well conceived from the point of view of the goals of the regime, and it even approached the "ideal" tax (from the point of view of economic efficiency) of Western economists, the "lump sum" tax. As a result, although the tax was a conscious rejection of the market in one area, it had only a limited influence on the role of the market in other areas.

Introduction of Compulsory Quotas, 1954–1955

Unlike the case in the Soviet Union, Chinese introduction of compulsory quotas in November 1953 took place without an accompanying radical reorganization of agricultural institutions. This was probably because the rural party apparatus, which was far more highly developed in China than in the Soviet Union, made additional changes unnecessary. Even this relatively modest change in marketing technique, however, was not without cost. Compulsory quotas also had to be introduced for cotton and edible oil-producing materials and eventually for most major crops.

The specific factors behind introduction of the "planned purchase" of grain were related to both demand and supply. Absence of a recovery in the quantity of grain sold by farmers during the first four years of the Communist regime and its close relation with land reform and the role of the agricultural tax, combined in 1953 with the introduction of the first five-year plan, has already been described. The detailed reasons behind the sharp increase in demand are also described elsewhere.[63] The result was that, by the end of 1953, government purchases of grain

[63] See Chapter IX.

were running well behind target figures, whereas sales were equally far ahead of the target. This resulted in a deficit that the state could not maintain for long.[64] The basic principle laid down by the initial "planned purchase" directive was that the state was to set quotas for purchase of grain that would then be passed down through various levels of government, the share of each farmer eventually being determined in "democratic" criticism meetings. This share was supposed to take into account the needs of urban- and grain-deficit areas and farmers' own needs for food, seed, and fodder. Once the individual peasant had met this quota, he was free to keep the remainder, sell it to state grain-purchasing departments or on a state-controlled grain market, or exchange it informally with his fellow villagers.[65] The two most interesting features of this new policy, however, were the method by which grain prices were determined and that by which the concept of "surplus" was defined.

Many Western economists have implied that purchase prices of agricultural products in China were set at a very low level, especially those of grain.[66] Whether or not this is an accurate statement depends on what one means by the word "low." In the Soviet Union during the 1930's, an apparently very low level of farm procurement prices resulted from a designedly slow rise in these prices combined with a much more rapid rise in the price level of manufactured goods.[67] In the case of China, grain-purchase prices were fixed at the official level prevailing at the time the "planned purchase" directive was issued, although provisions were included that allowed for minor adjustments by lower-level government organizations. This policy does not appear to have been changed since. The 2.1 per cent rise in the average price of grain that occurred between this time and the middle of 1959 [68] probably was due mainly to minor adjustments

---

[64] See note 50.

[65] For the text of the directive see Government Affairs Council, "Order Putting into Effect the Planned Purchase and Supply of Grain," *HHYP*, April 25, 1954, pp. 158–159.

[66] Wu Yuan-li, *Economic Survey of Communist China*, p. 177; Hughes and Luard, *Economic Development of Communist China*, p. 181.

[67] Holzman, *Soviet Taxation*, pp. 166–167.

[68] *JMJP*, October 25, 1959.

such as those in Kweichow and Liaoning.[69] On the other hand, prices of industrial products sold in rural areas rose even less rapidly (0.8 per cent between 1954 and 1958), although this picture would be changed slightly if producers' goods sold in the rural areas were eliminated from the index. From this point of view, therefore, it is not reasonable to argue that purchase prices were deliberately set at a very low level.

If the actual purchase price of grain were to be compared with the price that would have existed if the increased marketing of grain had been achieved through the operation of the free market, however, the actual price would undoubtedly be much the lower of the two. Even at the lower rate of grain purchases existing in October 1953, the market price of grain in many areas was 20 to 30 per cent above the official price,[70] and, as already argued, any attempt to achieve greater purchases through the market would either have set off inflationary price increases or would have required a major shift in industrial priorities toward consumers' goods industries.

Grain prices, therefore, ceased to play much of a direct role in grain marketing, although they did continue to influence the level of peasant income. Purchase prices could not be manipulated for the express purpose of influencing peasant income, however. The purchasing power of peasant money was already rising faster than available consumers' goods, so that a rise in grain-procurement prices was not feasible. A lowering of this price, on the other hand, would have greatly increased the disincentive effects of quotas by making them appear even more like a tax.

Grain-purchase prices did not even influence the amount of grain sold over and above the quotas, largely because quotas were set so high that few farmers had any such surplus. Initially,

[69] The prices of two types of grain in Liaoning were raised about 2 per cent between 1954 and 1956 (*TCKT*, February 29, 1957, p. 22). In Kweichow the prices of grains were raised between 5 and 6.48 per cent after September 1, 1959, on the authority of the provincial government ("Unified Purchase Prices for Autumn Crops in Kweichow Province Raised," *Kweichow jih-pao*, August 30, 1959, translated in *SCMP*, no. 2142, p. 42). There is no information available to suggest whether or not this increase was confined to Kweichow.

[70] Young Po, "Planned Purchase and Planned Supply and the National Construction of Socialism," *CCYC*, February 17, 1956, p. 38.

purchasing organs must have "purchased" everything they could get their hands on. This lack of restraint undoubtedly was made necessary by the fact that fall purchasing already was underway when compulsory quotas were first introduced, and hence there was no time to go through a long process of careful quota setting. If they had not purchased everything they could get their hands on, it is difficult to see how the regime could otherwise have increased purchases in November 1953 by 85.52 per cent over October, and in December by 72.22 per cent over November (and 137.34 per cent above December 1952).[71] Subsequently, the procedure followed was more formal and in accordance with regulations, but the end result was not very different. Despite considerable attempts by individual peasants to falsify reports or otherwise avoid too severe quotas,[72] the absolute increase in purchases between the 1952–53 grain year and that of 1954–55 was over twice the absolute increase in production. The regime in fact realized that it had purchased too much in 1954–55 and, desiring also to create favorable conditions for the program of cooperatives that was about to be launched, it decided to cut back purchases and regularize purchasing procedures in a way that would take more account of individual peasant incentives.[73] The result was the "three fix" policy issued on August 25, 1955, which set purchase quotas on the basis of a "normal yield" concept similar to that used in computing the agricultural tax.[74] Purchases were to take 80 to 90 per cent of the surplus after meeting consumption and planting needs (of households having a surplus) above this normal yield (based on the actual yield of 1955), and the resulting quantity was to remain unchanged for three years. If it proved necessary to increase purchases during this time, the state could only take 40 per cent of the increased

[71] Yang Po, *Kuo-chia kuo-tu shih-ch'i-te shang-ye* (State commerce during the transition period; Peking, 1956), p. 37.

[72] Kojima, "Grain Acquisition and Supply," p. 74.

[73] For a further discussion of the motives behind the cutback in grain purchases in 1955–56 and the contemporaneous introduction of rationing in the urban areas, see Chapter IX on the consumers' goods market.

[74] SC, "Provisional Measures for the Unified Purchase and Supply of Grain in Rural Districts" (August 25, 1955), translated in K. C. Chao, *Economic Planning and Organization in Mainland China*, II, 24–31.

production of a peasant household. This policy in fact lasted in this form for only two years, but that is the subject of the next chapter.

It would seem probable that this policy would act as a considerable incentive to the individual peasant farmer, but the independent farmer in China was destined to last only a few more months. The resulting decrease in purchases, in combination with increased grain production, probably was of some help in overcoming dislocations resulting from earlier excessive purchases, but this too was complicated by many new problems arising out of the cooperatives.

Although it is difficult to prove, except in the case of hog production, the compulsory increase in grain purchases, as already mentioned, appears to have had an adverse effect on production of a number of commodities. In the case of hogs, this was due to the fact that so much grain was taken out of rural areas that there was insufficient chaff for fodder.[75] In the case of other commodities it probably was due partly to the fact that the marginal value of grain remaining in the farmer's possession was well above what it had been previously and thus also well above its official price. Relative prices of grain and other farm products had in many cases been set during the relatively free market conditions prevailing prior to the institution of compulsory purchases. This meant that in 1954, and to some extent thereafter, the state had effectively shifted relative real values in favor of grain. There was, in addition, an income effect deriving from a reduction in real retained income of farmers as a result of the tax element in compulsory quotas. This tax element may also have affected peasants' decisions of what to grow and market. The effect of these price and income effects on other products varied according to circumstances surrounding their production and marketing.

Production of soybeans, cotton, jute and kenaf, and rapeseed,

[75] For a further discussion of the factors behind the decline in hog production and the measures taken by the state to counteract this decline, see the next chapter. That the decline initially took place in 1954 and for the above-stated reasons is supported by the statistics and information in CCPCC and SC, "Decision on the Development of Live Hog Production" (February 28, 1957), *FKHP,* V, 231–235.

for example, all fell in 1954 from levels reached in 1953.[76] There is no way of distinguishing the extent to which this was due to the serious natural calamities of 1954, but it is not unreasonable to assume that the change in relative values and the income effect were at least partly responsible. It is undoubtedly part of the explanation behind the introduction of planned purchasing of cotton and oil seeds. Compulsory quotas for cotton were introduced in September 1954,[77] the wording of the directive being much like that for grain. Its purpose, however, was quite different in that, where the purchase of grain could be increased merely by the state taking a larger percentage of the existing output, cotton purchases could only be increased significantly by an increase in production. The primary function of compulsory quotas for cotton, therefore, was probably, in combination with price policy, to ensure that cotton acreage would not be reduced because of pressure from the demand for grain. The result was that cotton production and purchases rose by 43 and 53 per cent respectively during the good year of 1955 and fell back only slightly during the natural calamities of 1956. The oil-seed case is not very clear. One source states that planned purchasing of oil seeds began in November 1953, but a directive regarding oil seeds in December 1953 makes no mention of this.[78] Planned purchasing may explain the increase in soybeans, peanuts, and rapeseed in 1955, but there remains the difficulty of explaining why soybean acreage in 1955 fell by about 10 per cent.

At about the same time, and for much the same reason, the state began the "unified" purchase of a wide variety of other agricultural products. The principal difference between "unified" and "planned" purchase appears initially to have been that, in the case of "planned" purchase, the state also rationed distribution.[79] As will be seen in Chapter IX, however, this distinction

[76] See Table 5.

[77] Government Affairs Council, "Directive Ordering the Putting into Effect of the Planned Purchase of Cotton" (September 14, 1954), *HHYP,* October 25, 1954, pp. 241–242.

[78] "State Unified Purchase and Sale Situation of Edible Oils and Oil Materials," *HHYP,* October 25, 1954, p. 247; Government Affairs Council, "Directive on Oil Materials Crops," (December 25, 1953), *HHYP,* January 25, 1954, pp. 157–158.

[79] Most of the directives initiating unified purchase are not available, but

did not remain for long since a number of such products (pork, sugar, and so on) were shortly to be rationed. The system of unified purchases was really an outgrowth of advance-purchase contracts. In these contracts, as already mentioned, the state made an agreement with individual farmers on the amount to be produced and sold and the acreage to be planted. To progress from advance purchase to unified purchase all that was needed was to prohibit private commerce from dealing in the commodity and to give state purchasing agents authority to apply a little pressure at the time of signing the contract. How much compulsion was in fact applied is impossible to estimate, and it probably varied depending on the individuals involved. That contracts were not completely voluntary, however, is amply demonstrated by what happened following reopening of the free market.[80] The role of purchasing contracts, therefore, went through a transformation very similar to that of the Soviet Union in the late 1920's.[81]

The introduction of compulsory purchase quotas for grain, therefore, was obtained only at substantial cost. The role and effectiveness of purchase-price policy, a tool that had proved to be particularly useful prior to 1954, was severely curtailed. Its place, for the major crops at least, was taken by a relatively insensitive device: marketing quotas expressed in physical terms. The managerial and planning problems connected with such quotas would in themselves have reduced production efficiency. On top of these problems were the general disincentive effects of what was, in effect, a tax. Although quotas did succeed in raising agricultural marketings, production suffered. This was a situation that the Soviet Union could tolerate for over two decades, but not China.

---

the list of commodities included can be obtained from later directives published for other purposes (see, for example, SC, "Regulations on the Restrictions on Certain Agricultural Products and Other Commodities Which Are Subject to Planned Purchase or Unified Purchase by the State" (August 9, 1957), translated in K. C. Chao, *Economic Planning and Organization in Mainland China*, II, 44.

[80] See Chapter IV at note 45.

[81] Holzman, *Soviet Taxation*, p. 161.

The impact of agriculture's poor performance began to be felt fairly quickly throughout China's economy. The compulsory quotas kept the rate of increase in marketings from falling very far in 1954 (from 18 to 13 per cent), but there was very little increase in 1955 (2.5 per cent). Exports of farm and processed farm goods fell from 81.6 to 74.5 per cent of total exports between 1953 and 1955, and their absolute amount increased by 28 per cent, as compared to 37 per cent over the previous two years. More significantly, the rate of increase in industrial production of consumers' goods fell from 26.7 to 14.2 per cent in 1954, and output actually declined slightly in 1955. In the producers' goods sector the rate of increase dropped from 36.5 to 19.8 to 14.5 per cent per year during 1953–1955.[82] The lag in agriculture was by no means the sole cause of these declines. State investment in 1953 had been increased too rapidly to allow for its effective utilization, and inflationary pressures had had to be brought back under control in 1954. It is also probable that part of industrial growth in 1953 resulted from some of the same elements of recovery from wartime destruction which made 1950–1952 rates so high. Nevertheless, the main cause of the difficulties was agriculture, and the Chinese Communist leadership was well aware of this.[83]

By mid-1955, therefore, the Chinese Communists were faced with essentially the same dilemma as in late 1953, but by 1955 the option of introducing or raising compulsory quotas had been exhausted. Rejection of the market in favor of quotas had, in fact, made the more fundamental problem, that of raising farm production, more difficult. The remaining choices were to increase state investment in agriculture or reorganize controls over agriculture in a way that would benefit production.

[82] Although production data during 1953–1955 are better than for previous years, they are subject to some degree of error. These data, however, do appear to reflect basic trends accurately.

[83] See, for example, Mao Tse-tung, *The Question of Agricultural Cooperation* (Peking, 1955), pp. 22–26. Mao talks of the connection between agriculture and industry only in general terms. Specific reference to the problems of 1953–1955 and their relation to the need for agricultural cooperatives can be found in Tung Ta-lin, *Agricultural Cooperation in China*, pp. 21–22, and in Hsueh Mu-chiao, Su Hsing, and Lin Tse-li, *The Socialist Transformation of the National Economy in China* (Peking, 1960), p. 90.

CHAPTER IV

The Market versus Centralized Controls in Agriculture, 1956–1963 *

Rationale for Rejection of the Market, 1955–56

The choice made by the Chinese Communists in the winter of 1955–56 was a radical reorganization of agriculture because it appeared that farm output could not be raised in any other way except by the unacceptable alternative of an increase in state investment. The task of raising output was particularly difficult because all land that could easily and cheaply be brought under cultivation was already being farmed,[1] and the productivity of additional farm labor was well below subsistence levels of that same labor.

The choices open to the regime, therefore, were to induce peasants to invest more of their own funds, to mobilize rural labor to construct capital projects, or to introduce new technology. The first and third objectives could have been accomplished in the context of a free peasant economy through concentration of income and land in the hands of the only group with the resources and knowledge to carry these objectives out, the rich peasant class, a solution that would have been anathema to the Chinese Communists on both political and ideological grounds. Barring such a solution, there was no easy or quick way by which these aims could be accomplished through the

* Much of the material in this chapter is taken from my article "Centralization and Decentralization in Mainland China's Agriculture (1949–1962)," *The Quarterly Journal of Economics,* May 1964, pp. 208–237, copyright, 1964, by the President and Fellows of Harvard College.

[1] The Chinese Communists were so convinced that increasing the area of cultivated land was less economic than the more intensive cultivation of the existing area that in 1958 they actually reduced the total cultivated area by over 10 million acres.

market. No manipulation of the interest rate could conceivably have influenced peasants to increase their savings significantly. Equally important, mobilization of the labor of even a single village faced virtually insurmountable barriers of conflicting self-interest between those who did the work and those who benefited from it. This is evidenced by Chinese difficulties with such conflicts prior to the Communist period [2] and the failures of the community development program in India under not entirely dissimilar circumstances.[3] It is conceivable that rural underemployed labor could have been mobilized by first taxing the villagers and then paying the labor wages out of tax revenue. The efficient and equitable administration of such taxes, however, would have been so difficult that the negative effect on farm production might have more than offset any benefits accruing from the use of the underemployed labor.

Finally, the encouragement of new technology would probably have been a slow process, at least until the peasants had acquired a willingness to experiment with new techniques. This was not likely to happen soon, since they were in the main uneducated, and the consequences of a mistake could be disastrous. To the Chinese Communists, therefore, the only solution to the dilemma of how to increase agricultural output without abandoning more fundamental goals appeared to require the removal of the individual peasant's power over many key aspects of farm production and centralization of that power in hands more responsive to the wishes of the state.

The belief was that by centralizing control over the use of agricultural output in the hands of leadership cadres in cooperatives a larger portion of this output could be set aside for investment purposes than had previously been the case. Most of the difficulties in the way of effective utilization of seasonally unemployed labor for road and irrigation-works construction would also be eliminated, since the benefits would accrue to the whole village and could, if necessary, be prorated to benefit most those

[2] An example of these difficulties is described in C. K. Yang, *Chinese Village*, p. 26.

[3] One of the major problems in India was that the people who did the work did not receive the benefits of their work, or at least not proportionate benefits.

who had done the work. Finally, the introduction of new technology would not pose much of a problem, since centralized control made possible use of any technique that the party desired. In addition, putting the land under cooperatives would in itself make feasible more efficient use of the land by eliminating excessive fragmentation of plots, which, among other things, wasted land by increasing the need for boundaries. After land was pooled, crops could be planted on land best suited for them. In the past, each farmer had had to plant enough grain on his own land, whether or not it was suitable for grain, to ensure that his family would not starve if the market for his nonfood crops collapsed. Larger plots would also make possible the efficient use of various types of machinery, not so much tractors and other labor-saving devices, which would be pointless, but items such as better plows, which would improve the way in which land was cultivated.[4]

One obvious drawback to cooperatives, their effect on individual incentives, apparently was considered by the regime to be a problem of the period of transition to the new form rather than a long-run fundamental feature of the system itself. The Chinese certainly were not unaware of the experience of the Soviet Union and eastern Europe, where collectivization has proved to be a drag on all attempts by those countries to raise agricultural production. There were strong arguments, however, for assuming that Chinese agriculture was different and that, in any case, the Communist party in China had a far greater understanding of how to handle peasants than its Russian or eastern European counterparts. The very success of the Communist revolution in China, after all, had depended primarily on the party leadership's understanding and manipulation of the peasant situation. In addition, China could learn from and make a point of not repeating Stalin's mistakes. Finally, after reading through vast amounts of Communist literature on the subject, one finds it hard to escape the belief that the Chinese Com-

---

[4] One of the best listings of the advantages expected to be attained from setting up cooperatives can be found in CCPCC, "Decisions on the Development of Agricultural Producers' Cooperatives" (December 16, 1953), quoted in Robert Carin, *China's Land Problem Series* (Hong Kong, 1960), II. 87–89.

munists were convinced that socialism, if properly combined with an individual's self-interest, could provide a superior system of incentives to those of capitalism and the market.

None of the above is meant to imply that, because there seemed to be solid economic reasons for setting up Chinese agricultural cooperatives, such a step was motivated solely by economic considerations. If these promising economic elements had not existed, however, the Communists could not have risked doing what they did on purely political grounds. The political advantages of the cooperative form were obvious. By eliminating individual landholdings and placing control over the peasant's economic life in the hands of loyal party personnel, the single remaining potential source of political opposition was eliminated. Furthermore, it was desirable to carry out this political coup at an early stage, since otherwise the highly organized party apparatus in the countryside built up during the civil war and land reform was in danger of atrophying for lack of use.[5] The regime had in fact been laying groundwork for the cooperative movement ever since completion of land reform. The exact timing of the movement could have been altered slightly, but it would have been difficult to put it off or, conversely, to push it up by more than a few years.[6] Once it was under way, the speed with which it progressed probably depended mostly upon the amount of serious opposition it engendered, which by all appearances was very small.

The contrast between motives behind the Chinese and Russian decisions to collectivize is striking. Both were partially influenced by political motives, and both felt the need to achieve more direct influence over economic aspects of agriculture, but there the similarity ends. The Russian decision was a conscious rejection of the market as a means of mobilizing an already existing potential agricultural surplus. The Chinese decision was

[5] There was criticism of some cadres during this period for thinking that their job was finished once land reform was completed and that they could allow future developments to follow their natural course.

[6] Land reform and the Korean War were not ended until 1953, and some time was needed to get the country prepared for a new movement. Once decided upon, the changes had to wait until after the fall harvest so as to have a minimum impact on production.

not so much a conscious rejection of the market. Compulsory
quotas in China do not appear to have been extended to any
large degree. There was a brief attempt in 1956 at central planning of agricultural production and particularly of the acreage
sown to various crops, but this proved to be impossible and was
quickly abandoned, and the regime went back to attempting to
manipulate the relative importance of different crops by adjusting prices. The Chinese decision was instead an attempt, by
means of partial centralization of authority, to add certain functions such as promotion of technological advance, functions
which until then had not existed at all or at least had not been
controlled in any systematic way. A second reason behind Soviet
collectivization was the need to free labor from the farm so as
to provide an industrial work force. Mechanization of Russian
agriculture, which helped make this possible, was brought about
by formation of machine tractor stations.[7] These were used in
such a way as further to increase centralized control over the
production of individual collectives in addition to that achieved
by planning and compulsory quotas. Since the problem in China
was and is how to keep the population from leaving rural areas,
an institution comparable to the machine tractor stations would
have been irrational. The main thing that Soviet experience did
for China, outside of providing a case study in how not to go
about collectivizing, was to recommend use of the collective form
of organization in agriculture as something that any good socialist country should accept, rather than to reject it as a radical and
bold innovation of unknown effect.

The Nature of Cooperative Organization, 1956

Although the Chinese leadership thought they were not re-
placing the market but only increasing centralized controls in
certain specific areas of agricultural production, it fairly quickly
became apparent that they had accomplished a higher degree of
centralization than they at first realized. It was also apparent

---

[7] The mechanization of Russian agriculture became a necessity regardless of
its aid in transferring labor from the farm because of the widespread slaughter
of cattle during collectivization. Since many of these cattle were used as
draft animals, they had to be replaced by machinery.

that many of the anticipated advantages of centralization had failed to materialize. Many of these difficulties resulted from the nature of the cooperative organization that the Communists had set up.

By the end of May 1956, over 110 million families (91.2 per cent of the total in rural areas) had been organized into approximately 1 million cooperatives.[8] Initially, these were elementary producers' cooperatives, where income was distributed on the basis of both the amount of land and labor contributed to the cooperative. By the end of 1956, however, 88 per cent of all farm families had formed advanced cooperatives, where income was determined solely on the basis of the amount of labor contributed.[9]

The basic organizational forms of these cooperatives had been fairly carefully tested in a number of areas before being introduced throughout the nation.[10] Usually the cooperative encompassed an entire village of from 100 to 300 families except where the village was either too large or too small. The land, labor, and most major producers' goods were pooled (with compensation in the latter case) and each member was paid according to the amount and quality of work he contributed. In Communist terminology, "basic level" ownership was transferred from the individual peasant to a larger semisocialist organization. This organization was economically independent in the sense that it alone was responsible for any profits or losses incurred, and its members' income depended solely on what the cooperative could produce either collectively or individually. Another key feature was that a member's obligations to the cooperative were supposed to be clearly defined and limited. He was required to give a certain amount of his time, after which he was free to work on his small private plot or on subsidiary occupations in his home.[11]

[8] *Jen-min shou-ts'e, 1957*, p. 472.
[9] SSB, *Ten Great Years*, p. 35.
[10] For a Communist version of this testing period as it occurred in one *hsien* (county) of Chekiang, see Jack Chen, *New Earth* (Peking, 1957).
[11] The major directives on the organization of agricultural producers' cooperatives include Ministry of Agriculture of the Northeast People's Government, "Trial Regulations for Agricultural Producers' Cooperatives in the North-

In theory, control over management in the cooperative rested with the general meeting of members, which democratically elected the chairman and management committee. Actual practice, however, was quite different, and this difference was crucial to the mode of operation of prices and the market. If ultimate power had remained in the hands of the members, presumably the main objective of management would have continued to be to maximize income in some sense, although there might have been minor difficulties in reconciling the desires of individual members. Since power was in fact transferred without ultimate recourse to cooperative leadership cadres, the objectives of the cooperative became the objectives of these cadres.

The key issue is whether the chairman of the cooperative and his major assistants were primarily responsive to higher-level party and government organs or to the members. This question would not be important if the party and government were primarily interested in maximizing income, but, as will be seen later, this was not the case. Government and party goals, by the time they reached the cooperatives, were usually stated in terms of maximization of the rate of growth of production or sales of a few major crops. Available evidence would suggest that these basic-level cadres were torn between two forces and that most of them ended up on a not very happy middle ground, where first priority almost always went to fulfillment of the state's major goals.

In the first place, most top leadership cadres in cooperatives appear to have been Communist party members, and the intraparty control apparatus was and is a highly developed tool designed to ensure active loyalty of its members to basic aims of the party. Second, *hsiang* (rural district) and *hsien* (county) party committees were omnipresent, one of their fundamental roles being that of carefully checking on the operations of individual

---

east" (January 5, 1953), *HHYP*, March 25, 1953, p. 151; Standing Committee of the National People's Congress, "Draft Regulations of an Agricultural Producers' Cooperative" (November 9, 1955), *FKHP*, II, 624–657; "Model Regulations for an Agricultural Producers' Cooperative" (March 17, 1956), and "Model Regulations for an Advanced Agricultural Producers' Cooperative" (June 30, 1956), both translated in Tung Ta-lin, *Agricultural Cooperation in China*, pp. 93–179.

cooperatives.[12] There was some evidence to suggest that, where conflicting loyalties threatened to become serious, the party may have transferred outsiders into the area.[13] Some indication of how central authorities expected cooperative cadres to act can be seen from the wording of various draft regulations that go to some length to prevent cadres from encroaching too much on members' rights.[14]

Somewhat offsetting this influence of the party, however, was the apparent fact that, initially at least, these cadres were taken from among residents of the village[15] and thus were, to some

[12] On June 30, 1956, the party had over 6 million members whose vocation was listed as agriculture (57.88 per cent of a total membership of 10,730,000). *Shih-shih shou-ts'e,* September 25, 1956, in Kirby, *Contemporary China,* II, 141. This would make for an average of about nine per cooperative, although many of these were undoubtedly connected with other elements of the party and government apparatus and were not members of cooperatives. The total number of cooperatives reached 1,003,657 in May 1956 (*Jen-min shou-ts'e, 1958,* p. 472), and fell to 700,000 after consolidation (K. C. Chao, *Agrarian Policy of the Chinese Communist Party,* p. 293). Some further indication that heads of cooperatives were usually party members is given in a number of Communist novels and similar works about cooperatives. See, for example, J. Chen, *New Earth;* Chou Li-po, *Great Changes in a Mountain Village* (Peking, 1961), vol. I; and Chao Shu-li, *Sanliwan Village* (Peking, 1957).

[13] There is some indication, for example, that cadres in Kwangtung, a southern province whose population is not famous for its docile cooperative spirit, are sometimes composed of northerners; see Robert Guillain, *The Blue Ants* (London, 1957), p. 82.

[14] For instance, passages ordering cooperatives not to force their members to make investments in the cooperative, not to encroach upon members' free time once they have filled their work norms, and the setting of a maximum, but no minimum, on the reserve and welfare funds. Not all restrictions, however, are of this nature (such as setting only a maximum on the size of private plots).

[15] This is a very tenuous conclusion based on the way in which land reform and cooperatives were handled as shown in the works mentioned in note 12 and, in addition, Chou Li-po, *The Hurricane* (Peking, 1955); and David and Isabel Crook, *Revolution in a Chinese Village* (London, 1959). These various works are all written from the Communist point of view, but the authors have in each case made personal investigations in rural areas, and there is no reason why they should have made all the village heads party members unless this was in fact the case. The procedure described in almost all of these works was similar: land reform and cooperative movements are led by outsiders, but the heads of basic-level organizations (peasant associations, cooperatives, and the like) are taken from among more politically "enlightened" members of the village, who either are or become party members, the outsiders eventually returning to their posts at higher levels.

extent, influenced by their former ties. The village was seldom a monolithic unit whose members were fiercely loyal to each other's interests, and the Communists exploited cleavages that already existed and created new ones where necessary. Still it is hard to imagine several million cadres universally indifferent to desires of their fellow villagers, particularly in China, where family and social connections were once so all-powerful. A second element tending to create an identity of interest between cadres and members was that cadres were paid in the same way as other villagers, on the basis of the number of their work points or labor days and the income of the cooperative, one major qualification being that they did not share in income from private plots unless they themselves had one. Furthermore, the number of labor days allocated to cadres was not much greater than that of ordinary members — probably not enough to give them a different outlook on such things as the rate of accumulation on this basis alone.[16] Finally, one criterion of success in the eyes of the state was improvement of the welfare of cooperative members through increases in their income. It was perhaps not a criterion to which they gave top priority, but it was, nevertheless, of some importance.

One can also get some idea of cadre behavior from complaints about it appearing in newspaper articles and editorials and speeches by important leaders. The most frequently heard complaint was directed against cadre "commandism," the military-like ordering around of peasants, although in early years the government also criticized cadres for lying down on the job once land reform had been completed.[17] A series of party "rectification" campaigns, starting even before 1949, however, have weeded out the "capitalist" oriented members and have made it clear

[16] See individual cooperatives' regulations and Ma An, "The Relationship between the State, the Cooperative, and Cooperative Members as Seen from the Situation in Chao-szu Cooperative," *TCYC*, May 23, 1958, p. 40.

[17] There are a great number of passages regarding cadre behavior quoted in Carin, *China Land Problem Series*, vols. I and II, which include quotations from *Ch'ang-chiang jih-pao*, December 4, 1951 (I, 62); NCNA, February 28, 1951 (II, 2); NCNA, February 22, 1953 (II, 50); *Hopei jih-pao*, March 17, 1957 (II, 52–53); *Mutual Aid and Cooperation in China's Agricultural Production* (1953) (II, 48–49); and *JMJP*, June 27, 1956, and May 7, 1957 (II, vii, 272, 406).

to the remainder what the regime means when it speaks of "activists." [18] One reason for the "hundred flowers" campaign in the first half of 1957 probably arose from a need felt by the regime for further checks on excesses of lower-level leadership in the direction of commandism once the biggest single deterrent, peasant ownership and control over rural production, had been removed.

These changes in the make-up of those deciding what and how to produce in agriculture had profound and largely unanticipated effects on the output of both major crops and subsidiary farm products, and in particular on the role of the market in determining that output.

Prices, Planning, and Quotas
of Major Crops, 1956–1957

To Communists, "planning" is by definition the antithesis to the anarchy of the market. It is not surprising, therefore, that when cooperatives were established, the regime would attempt to introduce "planning."

There have been national agricultural plans since the beginning of the Communist regime. In 1950 the plan only included desired percentage increases for cotton and grain, but by 1951 most major products of agriculture were "planned." In these early years, however, the state could only rely on indirect methods, such as price policy and land reform, to achieve its goals.[19] With the advent of cooperatives the state had it in its power to turn to more direct methods. It was written into basic cooperative regulations that each cooperative should draw up a plan of production, sown area, sales, manpower, and so forth, and that it should gear that plan to production and purchase plans of the state. In theory, this regulation as written would seem to imply that the central government would pass targets for such things

---

[18] That "rightist deviations" were not completely eliminated, however, can be seen by criticism of certain cadres for first delivering grain to cooperative members (Ho Wei, "New Problems in Unified Purchase and Marketing of Grain," *Cheng-chih hsueh-hsi,* October 13, 1956, translated in *ECMM,* no. 58, p. 16.

[19] T'ien Huo-nung, "How to Determine and Put into Effect Agricultural Production Planning," *HHYP,* December 25, 1950, pp. 377–378.

as production, sown area, and purchase down through the various levels of government. At each stage the plan would be broken down further, eventually reaching the cooperative itself. In most cases, complexities in the administration of such a vast undertaking would come to require a considerable degree of flexibility on the part of lower-level government and party organizations in interpreting central plans, but this did not basically alter the end result, which was to be a set of physical-output and sown-area targets for each cooperative. Price and income effects no longer needed to be considered in these cases, because it was the duty of cadres to obey the plans.[20]

Planning as it was actually carried out, however, was quite different. Under pressure from party cadres, production targets were often set at unrealistically high levels. In other instances, an annual plan was made, but not in enough detail to be used by production brigades (the basic unit at which labor was organized), or several uncoordinated plans were made for different purposes but covering the same ground. The result was either that plans were ignored altogether or that they were applied mechanically regardless of effects on production.[21]

The low quality of planning was fully recognized by the regime by the latter half of 1956, and steps were taken to correct the situation. Stress was laid on the importance of flexibility at lower levels in adjusting targets to suit the needs of a particular area, and the number of targets set by central authorities was reduced. Furthermore, it was pointed out that these plans, once they reached the *hsien* level, were only for reference and guidance of cooperative cadres, and that no group outside the cooperative could order it to obey them.[22] This latter feature did

[20] This was roughly the picture painted by the Heilungkiang Provincial Planning Committee, for example, although they appear to be talking as much about the future as the present, in "Views on Setting Up Agricultural Producers' Cooperatives Plan Work," *CHCC,* June 23, 1956, pp. 11–13.

[21] For fuller discussion of these shortcomings, see "Several Points of View on Setting Up and Reforming Agricultural Producers' Cooperatives Plan Work," *CHCC,* October 23, 1956, pp. 16–19; speech by Sung Jen-chiung, *Eighth National Congress of the Communist Party of China* (Peking, 1956), II, 152–154; and *JMJP* editorial, "Do We Still Want to Plan?" *HHPYK,* October 6, 1956, p. 62.

[22] CCPCC and SC, "Directive on Strengthening Production Leadership and

not mean that cooperative cadres were free to ignore the plan altogether. *Hsien*-level party and government officials retained a high degree of power over cooperative cadres in many other respects, and it is doubtful that they would have looked with favor on such cavalier treatment of their efforts. The provision should be thought of more as a restraint on the worst abuses by higher levels, a restraint that also served to make clear to the cooperative leadership their fundamental responsibility for production.

Even these revisions were not sufficient, however. By mid-1958, the regime apparently decidedly to abandon direct planning of agricultural production altogether and substitute purchase quotas as the state's main method of control. The idea to abandon direct planning was brought up at the Eighth Party Congress in September 1956 [23] and was further elaborated several months later.[24] There is some question when the new system was actually put into effect, but it was probably not before 1958.[25]

This gradual abandonment of planning was accompanied by reintroduction of price policy as a basic means for controlling relative emphasis on the various major crops. For prices to have the desired effect, however, it was necessary for those making agricultural production decisions to respond to price and income incentives. This was obviously the case for individual peasants but not for cadres. Cadres, as already explained, were interested in achieving "success" in the eyes of higher party organs. "Success" in the eyes of these higher-level organs did not mean maximization of cooperative income, but involved a preference for

---

the Organization of Construction in Agricultural Producers' Cooperatives" (September 12, 1956), *HHPYK*, October 6, 1956, p. 55; "Views on Compiling the 1957 Agricultural Production Plan," *CHCC*, November 23, 1956, p. 11.
[23] Speech by Teng Tse-hui, in *Eighth National Congress*, II, 192–193.
[24] Yeh Chun, "An Inquiry into a Change in the Agricultural Planning System in China," *CHCC*, February 9, 1957, translated in *ECMM*, no. 80, pp. 15–19.
[25] The opinion of Audrey Donnithorne in "Background to the People's Communes: Changes in China's Economic Organization in 1958," *Pacific Affairs*, XXXII (December 1959), 341, was that the system went into effect sometime during the summer of 1958. This opinion is based on the fact that one writer in February 1958, in *Ts'ai-ching yen-chiu*, spoke as if the system was still being readied.

crash programs and concentration on key points, a philosophy of unbalanced growth in the extreme.

The extent of imbalance varied widely, depending on the prevailing political atmosphere, and was particularly strong during the "great leap forward," but it was always there in some form. I have not seen any document where the main goal of cooperatives is set down as the maximization of cooperative income or profit.[26] The basic planning aim is usually stated in terms of coordinating cooperative plans with those of the state, and this means concentration on key points. In agriculture this meant a crash program to increase grain output and, to a lesser extent, cotton. The statistics presented in Table 5 give some idea of the effect of such a policy on production of crops that were not the center of attention. Since individual peasants had little interest in theories of development, growth of major crops prior to 1956 was, with the aid of price policy, fairly balanced except for decreases in production of a number of crops in 1954. This exception, as already mentioned, may have had some connection with the introduction of compulsory purchase quotas. In 1956 production of a few crops fell, but this was at least partly due to the year's serious natural calamities.[27] In 1957, however, production of every crop listed—except for grain, cotton, and sugar cane—fell, in some cases very sharply, in spite of the fact that this was not a year of unusually serious natural calamities.

The shift in emphasis away from maximization of income as the goal is brought out even more clearly when one considers that this drop in production occurred in response to vigorous at-

[26] It is, of course, possible that such a document exists, but this would not fundamentally alter the point made in the text. If a goal such as this is to be followed, it must be well publicized. It should be mentioned, however, that later, under the communes, plans for subsidiary output were expressed in terms of income rather than physical output, presumably because physical output plans would have been impossible to draw up or implement for so many diverse products (Ezra Vogel, unpublished manuscript). There is some question whether these plans were ever of much significance in determining output.

[27] Overemphasis on grain and cotton, however, was mentioned by Teng Tse-hui at the National People's Congress as one of the major problems of cooperative planning in 1956 (quoted in Carin, *China Land Problem Series*, II, 256).

TABLE 5. Agricultural output data (million catties except for grain and animals)

Commodity	1933	1949	1950	1951	1952	1953	1954	1955	1956	1957	1958	1959
Gross value [a]												
1952 prices	—	32.59	38.36	41.97	48.39	49.91	51.57	55.54	58.29	60.35	—	—
1957 prices	—	—	—	—	—	—	—	—	—	53.70	67.10	78.30
Grain [b]	3,456	2,162	2,494	2,701	3,088	3,138	3,209	3,496	3,650	3,700	5,000	5,401
Cotton	1,900	889	1,385	2,061	2,607	2,349	2,130	3,037	2,890	3,280	4,200	4,820
Soybeans	23,630	10,170	—	—	19,040	19,860	18,160	18,240	20,470	20,100	21,000	23,000
Peanuts	6,690	2,536	—	—	4,632	4,254	5,534	5,852	6,670	5,142	5,600	—
Rapeseed	4,200	1,468	—	—	1,864	1,758	1,756	1,938	1,850	1,775	2,200	—
Cured tobacco	1,980	86	—	157	443	426	464	596	798	512	760	—
Tea	500	82	130	—	165	169	184	216	241	223	280	—
Sugar cane	7,860	5,284	—	—	14,232	14,418	17,184	16,220	17,332	20,785	27,050	—
Sugar beet	480	381	—	—	957	1,010	1,978	3,192	3,300	3,002	5,800	—
Jute and hemp	680	74	—	—	610	276	274	514	518	—	—	—
Silkworm cocoons												
domestic	360	62	67	94	124	119	130	134	145	136	169	—
wild	60	24	50	53	122	25	51	128	124	89	114	—
Hogs [c]	70.20	57.75	—	—	89.77	96.13	101.71	87.92	84.02	145.89	160.00	180.00
Cattle, horses, mules, donkeys [c]	65.80	60.02	—	—	76.46	80.46	84.98	87.39	87.37	83.82	85.06	85.40
Sheep, goats [c]	72.20	42.35	—	—	61.78	72.02	81.30	84.22	91.65	98.58	108.86	112.50

Source: The 1933 data are the estimates of Liu and Yeh, *The Economy of the Chinese Mainland*. The data for 1949–1959 are the official Communist estimates. The data on gross value of output are of low quality. All 1958 and 1959 figures are falsified (with the possible exception of a few of the lesser cash crops) and are included here for the sake of completeness. For a discussion of the validity of the remaining data, see Appendix A.

[a] Billion yuan.
[b] Excluding soybeans; 100 million catties.
[c] Million head.

[69]

tempts to use purchase prices to raise output of the very crops whose production fell.

After being ignored during the organization of cooperatives, price policy was reinstituted as a major policy weapon on a greatly expanded scale during and following the Eighth Party Congress. The key speech was made by Minister of Finance Li Hsien-nien, but the subject was also touched on in major speeches by Ch'en Yun and Liu Shao-ch'i.[28] Li pointed out that procurement prices for tung and tea oil, rapeseed, peanuts, sesame, tea, and silk cocoons were all too low either because they had not yet reached the prewar level relative to grain or production conditions had changed.[29] He recommended that prices of these products be raised even though, in the case of rapeseed, he realized that this measure, if successful, would lead to an expansion of rapeseed acreage at the expense of wheat. In most cases these recommendations were carried out immediately and vigorously. The price of rapeseed was raised on September 29, 1956, by from 50 to 70 per cent in the key producing areas.[30] The purchase price of tea, which in June 1956 was already 7 per cent above the same period of the previous year, was raised by another 7 per cent by year's end.[31] During the first quarter of 1957, oil-producing materials were raised again from 10 to 30 per cent and tea leaves by about 1 per cent.[32] Domestic cocoon prices, which had fallen sharply in 1953, had reached the prewar level, at least in old producing areas, by 1957, although the price of wild cocoons does not appear to have recovered by that time.[33] It is clear from this that the action taken was not halfhearted in any sense. Often considerably less dramatic shifts in the price

[28] Translations of these speeches are in *Eighth National Congress*, I, 13–112, and II, 157–176, 206–224.

[29] Li also mentioned a number of other products whose prices were out of line, but they are not relevant to this discussion.

[30] SC, "Directive on Raising the Purchase Price of Rapeseed" (September 29, 1956), Shanghai Price Book, pp. 594–595.

[31] Tientsin *TKP*, June 23, 1956; "Our Country's Development of Tea Leaf Production," *TCKT*, February 14, 1957, p. 33.

[32] *TCKT*, June 14, 1957, pp. 26–27.

[33] Ministries of Agriculture, Foreign Trade, Textile Industries, Forestry, and Second Commerce, "Report on Silkworm Production Conference," *FKHP*, VIII, 225–232.

of cotton and other crops in the past had resulted in the desired recovery in output. But in 1957 the production of every crop whose price was raised fell.

Overemphasis on cotton and grain perhaps was not the sole cause of the decline in output of these other major crops, but it was certainly the most important. Purchase quotas continued to be set in a way similar to the method used prior to the establishment of cooperatives. The one major change in the quotas did not take place until the fall purchasing period of 1957, too late to have much influence on that year's harvest. That change was a subtle one regarding the purchase of additional grain, but its effect was to undermine the principal incentive feature of the "three-fix" policy and led to substantially increased grain purchases.[34] There was at the same time a tightening up in the purchase of cotton.[35] But during the period in question, the purchase system was not fundamentally altered and could not be expected to interfere with the influence of price policy any more than it previously had, nor was there any dramatic extension of rationing of consumers' goods sold to farmers in this period.

Therefore, although the Chinese Communists had only intended to centralize certain specific activities, they also ended up losing the use of one of their most effective decentralized controls, agricultural purchase-price policy. Even after centrally planned targets proved to be no substitute for prices, the regime was unable to utilize prices to achieve its objectives. In theory, this was not a necessary result of cooperativization. Cadres could have been ordered to maximize profits, just as in the Lange-Lerner model of a socialist economy. In practice, however, this would have required a high degree of sophistication on the part of cooperative cadres and their superiors. It would also have required reliable accounting and data-collecting personnel in each cooperative. Personnel with this degree of sophistication and training simply were not available. Even if they had been, the need to choose cadres with proper political and ideological outlooks and

---

[34] SC, "Supplementary Regulation on Grain Unified Purchases and Sales" (October 11, 1957), *FKHP*, VI, 351–354.

[35] CCPCC and SC, "Directive on This Year's Cotton Unified Purchase Work" (September 7, 1957), *FKHP*, VI, 370–373.

backgrounds would have made introduction of an effective income maximization goal difficult.

Subsidiary Output and the Free Market, 1956–1957

Centralization of control in the hands of cooperative cadres, when combined with the nature of cadre success criteria, had an even more pronounced (and equally unanticipated) effect on subsidiary rural production. There are literally thousands of occupations that come under this heading. The discussion here includes everything from hog and poultry raising to household manufacture of sandals and small farm implements. Their unifying characteristic prior to the founding of the cooperatives was that they were usually handled by otherwise unproductive members of the household or in spare time between duties in the fields. They also were carried out on a very small scale, and except for vegetables, did not compete with major crops for available land. Vegetables were, of course, also a major crop or more accurately several major crops, but problems involved in both their production and marketing led them to be treated in much the same way as other subsidiary products, which is why they are included here.

These commodities made up approximately 30 per cent of gross value of agricultural output,[36] and the effect of cooperatives on their production was substantial, even though it does not show up in the figures for the gross value of agricultural production.[37]

[36] This is the percentage of over 500 subsidiary products in 1955 in Chekiang (*Chung-yang ho-tso t'ung-hsun,* no. 4, 1956, p. 1) and Szechwan (speech by the provincial first party secretary in *Chung-kuo Kung-ch'an-tang Ti-pa-tz'u Ch'uan-kuo Tai-piao Ta-hui Wen-hsien;* Eighth National Congress of the Chinese Communist Party; Peking, 1957, p. 167). Other party secretaries gave figures for Hopei (over 20 per cent), Fukien (24 per cent), and Kwangsi (44.9 per cent). The figure for the old province of Jehol is given as 40 per cent (same source as for Szechwan). It is not clear precisely which products are included, although grain and technical crops are definitely excluded.

[37] The 1956 gross value of agricultural production (at 1952 prices) was 4.9 per cent above that of 1955, whereas grain production only rose 4.4 per cent, and the production of cotton, rapeseed, and wild cocoons fell. Although output of other major crops increased (soybeans, tobacco, peanuts, and tea by a little over 10 per cent; the others by less), the gross figure would appear to indicate that subsidiary production did not fall much, if at all.

No fewer than five provincial first secretaries at the Eighth Party Congress discussed problems of subsidiary production, and one stated that output of these commodities had fallen from 5 to 15 per cent in various areas of his province (Szechwan) in 1956. The large number of articles published dealing with this problem, articles often based on investigations of a cooperative or area where subsidiary output had fallen sharply, are a further indication of the seriousness of the difficulties.[38] There seems little reason to doubt that all this attention would not have been paid if subsidiary production had not shown a substantial drop throughout the country. A high proportion of subsidiary production remained in the hands of individuals, not of cooperatives. It was carried on on small private plots and in farmers' spare time, and whatever profit they made was theirs to dispose of. The tendency on the part of cooperative leadership cadres was to look on private plots of land and spare time as just so much taken away from the cooperative. The result was that they took every opportunity to encroach on individual independence in production. Labor time owed the cooperative was set at a high level. In many cases this was combined with plans that were unrealistically grandiose, so that cooperative members were left with the impression that time given to the cooperative would earn far more than that on subsidiary production in the home. As a result, peasants in some cases even voluntarily gave up free time to the cooperative.[39] The original cooperative regulations stated that the size of retained private plots per person was not to exceed 5 per cent of total available cultivated acreage

[38] See, for example, "This Year's Spring Rural Market Situation in . . . ," *CHCC*, May 23, 1956, pp. 15–16 (the editor's preface in this article included the comment that "the fall in rural subsidiary production is a phenomenon that postdates agricultural cooperatives and is very serious."); "New Situation, New Problems," *CHCC*, August 23, 1956, pp. 14–15; Local Party Committee Investigation Team, "Management of Subsidiary Production Is Not a Small Thing; Why Is So Little Attention Paid It?" *HHPYK*, October 10, 1956, pp. 63–64; "Investigation of Subsidiary Production in . . . ," *Chungyang ho-tso t'ung-hsun*, October 1956, p. 16; NCNA, May 15, 1956; and *JMJP*, May 13 and 24, 1956. (The last three are quoted in Carin, *China Land Problem Series*, II, 238–243.)

[39] Local Party Committee Investigation Team, "Management of Subsidiary Production," *HHPYK*, October 10, 1956, pp. 63–64.

per capita, but one study based on 28 separate surveys showed that the actual size of retained plots was more commonly only 3 per cent of per capita sown acreage, with a range from slightly above one per cent to the full 5 per cent.[40] Most of these problems were not dealt with until the fall of 1957. There were exhortations to give farmers more free time, but there is some question how effective these were, since they had to be repeated only a few months later in an attempt to offset pressures of the "great leap forward," an attempt doomed to failure by the subsequent introduction of communes.[41]

In June 1957 the National People's Congress, following a proposal by Chou En-lai, revised the draft constitution of advanced agricultural producers' cooperatives, stating that the size of retained plots should be set on the basis of need for hog fodder as well as vegetables and that the maximum limit could be raised to 10 per cent.[42] Whether or not this revision had much effect in practice is difficult to say, but its effect was not very lasting, since private plots were abolished when the communes were set up in the summer of 1958. Finally, the regime also undertook to introduce a number of lesser reforms into the administration of subsidiary production at this time. For example, under private ownership, the farmer had been able to use fertilizer obtained from hogs on his own land. This fertilizer was an important part of the return on hog raising, but was of only limited use to individual farmers when land came under cooperative control.[43] The state attempted to correct this by ordering cooperatives to pay a fair price for such fertilizer. It was also directed that the

---

[40] Sung Hai-wen, "A Discussion of the Problem of Retained Plots of Land in Agricultural Producers' Cooperatives," *CCYC*, August 17, 1957, p. 13. The concern of authorities with this problem is illustrated by the fact that 25 of these surveys were taken from different publications (mainly provincial newspapers) from January 1956 to April 1957.

[41] CCPCC and SC, "Directive on Doing Vegetable Sowing Work Well so as to Strengthen Vegetable Production and Supply Work" (July 17, 1958), *FKHP*, VIII, 239.

[42] Standing Committee of the National People's Congress, "Decision on the Increase of the Retained Plots of Members of Agricultural Producers' Cooperatives" (June 25, 1957), *FKHP*, V, 263.

[43] "Our Cooperative Wants to Raise 20,000 Hogs," *Jen-min shou-ts'e, 1957*, p. 487.

boundary between what was to be collectively managed and what was to be handled by individuals be clearly demarcated, and cooperatives were generally ordered to pay more attention to collectively run subsidiary activities.[44]

The most dramatic and important measure undertaken by the regime to solve this problem, however, was a direct attack on difficulties of marketing by reopening a free market. The state had never consciously closed down the free market, but it had accomplished roughly the same thing when it socialized most of commerce in 1955, although farmers continued to exchange a certain number of goods among themselves. The effect on subsidiary production, described by Vice Premier Chen Yun at the Eighth Party Congress,[45] was particularly stifling. Prior to the socialization of commerce the state had not really seriously attempted to control prices of the myriad commodities in this category. With most purchasing channeled through state commercial organizations, however, official prices took on a new significance, one that was often detrimental to production. Previously, if the state's prices were unfavorable, the producer could always sell his wares to a private party. The problem was further aggravated by mutual exclusiveness in purchasing on the part of many purchasing organs (that is, a particular crop in any one area could only be sold to one previously designated purchaser). This made it impossible for producers to deal with other state purchasers if one paid too low a price or generally lacked interest in the product.

The free market was reopened primarily and explicitly because of these bureaucratic and price-setting difficulties.[46] The exact timing of the opening is not clear, but it undoubtedly varied considerably depending on the area. In most cases outside of urban areas, it probably involved little more than the relaxation

[44] See note 39 and SC, "Notification on the Unification of the Management of Village Subsidiary Production" (October 22, 1957), *FKHP,* VI, 447–449.

[45] Chen Yun, speech, in *Eighth National Congress,* II, 157–176.

[46] Pan Ching-yuan, "Why Is It Necessary to Have a Free Market?" *Cheng-chih hsueh-hsi,* no. 11, November 13, 1956, translated in *ECMM,* no. 61, p. 32. A third factor was also given considerable attention as well. This third factor was the problem of efficiently supplying these commodities to the consumer (see discussion in Chapter IX).

and change of administrative rules of already existing market arrangements.[47] By December 1956, however, the free market had been in operation long enough for its major difficulties to become manifest.[48] The most serious of these, from the point of view of the state, was the entry onto the free market of agricultural products subject to planned and unified purchase by the state. Lines between what was and was not supposed to be sold on the free market had not been clearly demarcated. There is some question whether or not the state intended peasants to market these goods on the free market once they had fulfilled their compulsory purchase quotas.[49] When it was discovered that farmers were selling these goods on the free market before completing their purchase quotas, the state issued a directive prohibiting their sale to other than authorized purchasing agents.[50]

The extent of the free market also was restricted by the state's desire to take a more active role in promotion of certain key subsidiary products. Hogs, for example, remained subject to unified purchase,[51] and hog prices were rigidly controlled by the state. Because hogs were raised primarily by individual peasants and not the cooperative as a whole, state purchase-price increases

[47] One source puts the size of the free market as 10,340 million yuan in 1955 and 11,520 million yuan in 1956. (Wang Ping, "The Free Market in China: Its Scope and Changes," *TCKT*, June 14, 1957, translated in *ECMM*, no. 92, p. 26). This, however, is somewhat misleading, since the writer includes all goods sold directly by industrial and agricultural producers other than those channeled through state and cooperative commercial organizations. Many such goods were probably sold under conditions where tight control was implemented.

[48] See Sun Yi-min, "Strengthen Leadership over the Free Market," *CHCC*, December 23, 1956, translated in *ECMM*, no. 77, pp. 14–20.

[49] It was stated in one article that it was an objective of reopening the free market to raise peasants' production ardor by allowing them to sell these goods on the free market once their quotas were filled (Ch'i Liang, "What Advantages Are There to Opening a State Led Free Market?" *Shih-shih shou-ts'e*, November 10, 1956, translated in *ECMM*, no. 64, p. 29).

[50] SC, "Regulations on the Restrictions on Certain Agricultural Products and Other Commodities Which Are Subject to Planned Purchase or Unified Purchase by the State" (August 9, 1957), translated in K. C. Chao, *Economic Planning and Organization in Mainland China*, II, 43–47.

[51] SC, "Directive Ordering Various Areas Not to Raise on Their Own Authority Purchase Prices of Agricultural Subsidiary Products Which the State Unifiedly Purchases" (November 14, 1956), *FKHP*, IV, 333.

in 1956 and 1957 (by 13.9 per cent in 1957)[52] still had significant effects on hog production. Live hogs, after reaching 101 million head in June 1954, had fallen to 84 million by June 1956. It is reasonable to assume that purchase-price increases and other above-mentioned steps were responsible for raising the number to 145.9 million head by the end of 1957.[53]

Unlike excessive centralization of control over major crops, therefore, control of subsidiary output could still be handled through the market without a major reorganization or abandonment of cooperatives. This was true because production of these items remained in the hands of individual income-maximizing peasants. In Communist eyes, however, this economic success was seriously marred by political and ideological distaste for revival of "capitalist" forces. The more vigorous "capitalist" activities were, the more the regime feared these activities would undermine the effectiveness of "socialist" agriculture.[54] It is not surprising to find, therefore, that despite the apparent success of peasant initiative in handling subsidiary output, the regime, when it set up the communes a year later, tried to incorporate much of this production under "socialist" control.

Effectiveness of Intended Centralization, 1956–1957

Even for activities over which the regime had purposely centralized authority there were complications, though none so serious as those cases already mentioned where centralization was unintentional. Local construction projects were carried out on a much greater scale, but were still limited by conflicts of interest at the village level and above. It is also probable that rates of savings and investment by individual cooperatives were raised.[55] Control over the rate of savings was achieved merely by

[52] SC, "Notification of an Adjustment in the Purchase Price of Live Hogs" (February 15, 1957), *FKHP*, V, 181–182.
[53] CCPCC and SC, "Decision on Live Hog Production," *FKHP*, V, 231; SSB, *Ten Great Years*, p. 132.
[54] Pan Ching-yuan, "The Struggle between the Road of Socialism and the Road of Capitalism on the Free Market," *Hsin chien-she*, March 13, 1958, translated in *ECMM*, no. 136, p. 33.
[55] One relatively reliable survey of 228 cooperatives shows a significant increase in the cooperatives' capital in 1957 over 1956, which, if true, tends to

setting a maximum percentage of total income that could be saved and then letting pressure from cooperative cadres ensure that that maximum would be reached. There was also a limited amount of funds issued to cooperatives by the central government in the form of loans, which influenced the cooperatives' rate of investment (see Table 6). It is worth noting, however, that in 1956 and 1957, when the central government wished to increase its direct investment in the cooperatives,[56] it relied less on budget allocations or loans and more on price reductions on agricultural producers' goods sold to the cooperatives.

During the early years of the regime, prices of fertilizers and plows, in terms of grain, commonly were twice what they had been before the war.[57] Starting in 1955, the state began to cut the prices of a wide variety of producers' goods, often quite substantially. At times this was accomplished by directives issued by the central government,[58] and at other times factories were told to lower their prices as they were able to reduce costs.[59] No general index of the prices of these goods is available, but the cuts for those commodities where cuts were made were commonly as high as 30 to 40 per cent. In spite of the size of the reductions, however, prices remained above cost. Generally speaking, cuts were not made where the commodity was in particularly short supply relative to demand.[60] The state could have financed

confirm the belief that the rate of savings and investment was raised (*TCYC* data office, "Research Materials on Income Distribution in 228 Agricultural Producers' Cooperatives in 1957," *TCYC*, August 23, 1958, pp. 10–11).

[56] Most state investment in agriculture went to such things as major water conservation projects, which were not handled through the cooperative organization.

[57] *Nan-fang jih-pao*, February 19, 1953, quoted in Carin, *China Land Problem Series*, I, 90.

[58] Two of the major national directives were "Nationwide Lowering of the Retail Prices of 13 Types of Important New Model Agricultural Tools," *JMJP*, September 10, 1955; and SC, "Report on the Lowering of the Prices of Farm Pumping Power Machinery" (April 8, 1958), *FKHP*, VII, 310–315.

[59] See *Chieh-fang jih-pao*, October 11, 1955; Tientsin *TKP*, October 29, 1955; and *Nan-fang jih-pao*, October 16, 1955. A number of these prices began to be cut prior to 1955, but it was in 1955 that this cutting appears to have been widespread.

[60] Most of the cuts appear to have been for various types of farm machinery and insect sprays. There were exceptions, however. At least two sources stated that fertilizer prices in their provinces were reduced (*Yunnan jih-pao*, January 6, 1956; and *Chungking jih-pao*, January 17, 1958).

TABLE 6. The financing of agriculture[a] (million yuan)

| Year | State agricultural credit[b] | Cooperative agricultural credit[c] | State investment in agriculture, forestry, water conservation, weather | | Agriculture as percentage of total state investment[d] | Sales of capital goods to agriculture[d] |
			Total[d]	Water conservation[d]		
1950	95	—	—	—	—	730
1951	205	—	—	—	—	1,030
1952	482	—	600	410	13.8	1,410
1953	666	—	770	480	9.7	1,920
1954	783	120	420	220	4.6	2,500
1955	1,001	470	620	410	6.7	2,820
1956	3,029	1,210	1,190	710	8.0	3,700
1957	2,760	—	1,190	730	8.6	3,260
1958	—	—	2,630	1,960	9.9	6,680
1959	—	—	2,400	—	—	8,100
1960[e]	—	—	3,910	—	—	11,000

[a] Since all of the above items were under the direct control of the central government, there is every reason to believe that the data in this table are reliable with the probable, but not necessary, exception of 1958 and 1959.

[b] Year-end remainder. Young Pei-hsin, "The Road to Raising the Agricultural Development Fund," *CCYC*, January 17, 1958, p. 32, for years 1950–1956, and *TCYC* data office, "The Domestic Market Commodity Circulation Situation in 1957," *TCYC*, April 23, 1958, p. 24, for 1957.

[c] Young Pei-hsin, p. 33.

[d] Years 1952–1958 for investment and 1950–1958 for sales of capital goods to agriculture are in SSB, *Ten Great Years*, pp. 57–58, 170. The 1959 and 1960 (plan) statistics are from Li Fu-chun, "Report on the Draft 1960 National Economic Plan," *Second Session of the Second National People's Congress of the People's Republic of China* (*Documents*) (Peking, 1960); and Li Hsien-nien, "Report on the Final State Accounts for 1959 and the Draft State Budget for 1960" (March 30, 1960), *ibid.*, pp. 35, 63.

[e] Plan data.

the large increase in producers' goods sold to agriculture from 1956 on through budget allocations and loans. The absence of a highly developed planning apparatus, however, would have meant that the goods would have gone to the cooperatives with the swiftest-acting or most persuasive cadres, and not to those who could afford and use them effectively. As it was, the central authorities had no easy time getting these cadres to use their own investment funds efficiently. The temptation to build unproductive or inefficient showcase projects was great.[61]

One of the best-documented examples of the difficulties involved in getting cadres and the central government to make efficient use of resources earmarked for agriculture is the case of the double-wheeled double-bladed plow. This case also has the advantage of pointing up the fact that the state's ability to carry out rapid technological change in agriculture was not an unmixed blessing. These plows had worked well in a number of areas in 1954 and 1955, and, with the upsurge of cooperatives, the authorities decided that every well-equipped cooperative needed a full quota of such tools. Production and sales plans were raised first from 400 thousand to 5 million plows and then scaled down to around 2 million. The leadership cadres of the cooperatives had either been forced to buy plows they did not want or did so because they felt no cooperative was complete without several double-wheeled double-bladed plows. As things turned out, the plow was unsuitable to many areas of the country, so that by the middle of 1956, although 1.4 million plows had been produced (at considerable cost in terms of disruption of other industries), only 800 thousand had been sold, and of those 40 to 50 per cent were not being used. The result was that their production was stopped entirely and was not renewed on any significant scale until 1958.[62] This was an extreme case, but similar lesser occurrences must have happened frequently, particularly since so much emphasis was placed on a cadre's party loyalty and ideological purity, qualities perhaps only coincidentally possessed by the better farmers. The Communist leadership on occasion has recognized this difficulty by calling on the cadres to

[61] One of the more revealing passages in Felix Greene, *Awakened China* (New York, 1961), is one in which the head of a commune pointed out the reasons why movie projectors, libraries, and X-ray equipment took precedence over more food for the commune's members (pp. 166–167).

[62] This account is based on "Why Is There a Stopping of Production and an Obstruction of Sales of Double-wheeled Double-bladed Plows?" *CHCC*, September 23, 1956, pp. 1–4.

pay more attention to the views of the older, and hence more experienced, peasants.

Finally, one cannot leave this discussion of centralization without some mention of its effects on individual incentives (general income incentives to work as contrasted with specific incentives to respond to price changes). The importance of these effects is often exaggerated, but it was nevertheless real. The key problem was that, as the unit controlling production and incomes got larger, the connection between work and reward became more remote. Elaborate bonus systems were set up to overcome this, but these were not complete substitutes for the incentive of knowing that one's own effort or lack of it affects one's own income and no one else's. Cadre supervision may have overcome some disincentive effects, but certainly not all. In recognition of these problems, the regime at the end of 1957 took steps to decentralize the authority within the cooperatives by delegating some of it to the production brigades (a subsidiary unit of the cooperatives).[63] In addition, existing duties were clearly defined so that they would not be interfered with or usurped by higher authorities and so that responsibilities and rewards of an individual would be more closely tied to his job performance. It is probable that these steps were taken not only to overcome the general disincentive effects but also to enhance the effect of market and price controls and thus overcome some of the overemphasis on grain and cotton.

The fruits of attempting to supplement the market with centralized control in 1956 and 1957, therefore, were not very impressive. Over-all agricultural production continued to creep upward, but only very slowly.[64] The problems that had existed in 1955 had not been resolved. The attempt in 1956 to raise the rate of investment and industrial growth significantly had to be abandoned. Industrial growth in 1957 was slower than in any year except 1955. Advantages of centralization had proved illusory for

[63] CCPCC, "Directive on Doing Agricultural Producers' Cooperative Production Management Work Well" (September 14, 1957), *HHPYK*, October 10, 1957, pp. 136–137.

[64] The official estimates show a rise of 4.9 and 3.5 per cent respectively (SSB, *Ten Great Years*, p. 118), while the Liu–Yeh estimates are 3 and .5 per cent (Liu and Yeh, *Economy of the Chinese Mainland*, p. 560).

three basic reasons. First of all, it turned out to be impossible to centralize certain functions without interfering with the proper carrying out of others. Some of these problems were only the result of the unforeseen difficulties that are bound to occur when any fundamental change in an organization takes place in so short a time. There was no necessity for difficulties with subsidiary production to continue once the problems of the transition had been overcome, for example. The excessive concentration on grain and cotton, however, was more fundamental. Second, it proved difficult to find an adequate substitute for the incentive provided by the knowledge that one's reward depends solely on one's own effort and skill. Finally, the advantages of centralization in raising the rate of investment and promoting technological change did not prove to be great. This was largely because rural cadres were not sufficiently skilled to carry out these efforts efficiently.

At the beginning of 1958, therefore, the regime was, in a sense, in worse shape than in 1955. The same conflict between the basic goals of the regime and the inadequacy of agricultural production existed as before, but in addition the regime had brought its major weapon (the cooperatives) to bear and had found it wanting. Perhaps given time and a willingness to move further toward more genuine cooperation rather than "commandism," the Chinese Communists might have found a way out that would not have involved substantial reduction in the emphasis on heavy industry. Instead, they attempted in 1958 to solve the problem by an even bolder and more radical reorganization of agriculture: the communes.

Communes and Anarchy, 1958–1959

The commune movement, which got under way in the summer of 1958, was hailed as one of the most revolutionary developments in the history of mankind by both Communists and anti-Communists alike, although the adjectives used differed. The rural communes were in fact considerably less radical than the publicity about them, but they did make several profound changes. To understand fully why communes were set up in the first place,[65] one would have to go deeply into the inner dynamics of the Chinese Communist Party.[66] The leadership's disillusionment with greater relaxation of control in general as a result of the abortive "hundred flowers," or free-speech campaign, for example, made any further relaxation, even if confined to the economic sphere, out of the question. The answer to the problem of the sluggish development of agriculture, therefore, had to be found elsewhere. It could not be found by centralizing economic decisions in Peking; even the modest attempts in this direction with regard to planning had proved unworkable.[67] The solution decided upon, which was applied to industry as well as agriculture, was to tighten the grip of party personnel at the local level and then to remove practically all constraints except ideological ones, which emanated from the central government. Pressure was then put on these local party cadres to achieve spectacular economic results through exercise of their own energy and ingenuity. A combination of decentralized decision making together with a maintenance of ideological reliability on the part of those making the decisions had proved successful in guerrilla warfare, and was fully expected to do as much for the economy.

The stated reasons for expanding the basic unit in agriculture from an average size of 200 families (the cooperative) to 4000 to 5000 families (the commune) were linked with the added func-

[65] A discussion of the decision to introduce communes involves the implicit assumption that their introduction was led and was not fundamentally a spontaneous development. I agree with the opinion expressed by Audrey Donnithorne that "the initiative . . . lay with Mao and the Party, though they probably acted in tune with the hard core of cadres in the countryside," but reasons for the belief would take us too far afield ("Background to the People's Communes, p. 348).

[66] Some of the political elements of the "great leap forward" are discussed in Roderick MacFarquhar, "Communist China's Intra-Party Dispute," *Pacific Affairs,* XXXI (December 1958), 323–335. For a general discussion of the development of the communes, see Richard Hughes, *The Chinese Communes* (London, 1960).

[67] Planning, in the sense of setting physical output targets for major crops (and income targets for subsidiary output), did take on greater importance under the communes than it had previously under the cooperatives, but the key planning unit was the *hsien* (Ezra Vogel, unpublished manuscript). What influence Peking really had on these plans is not clear, but it was certainly in no way comparable to that of planning in industry.

tions that a larger unit could undertake.[68] An unstated reason probably was that it was easier to ensure proper party control when only 26,000 units had to be staffed, instead of the previous 700,000. The most important economic function that a larger unit could undertake was organization of much larger quantities of labor for work on water-conservation projects and in local industries. The larger unit also was big enough to exercise control over local commercial, credit, and industrial establishments, which previously had had to be controlled on a nationwide or provincial basis. Cooperatives, as already mentioned, were limited in the size of water-conservation projects that they could undertake by the need to reconcile the interests of each village involved. Furthermore, no single cooperative could hope to find enough surplus labor or managerial skills in its own small group to staff anything but an extremely small industrial firm, even on a seasonal basis.

This move to increase the size of the basic administrative unit in rural areas was not as much in conflict with the attempts in 1956 and 1957 to reduce the size and authority of cooperatives over agricultural production as it appears. At least in theory it was not. According to the commune regulations,[69] control over agricultural production itself was to remain where it was. As in the case of the cooperatives, centralization was carried out with the idea of increasing the number of activities handled at the local level rather than centralizing control over already-existing activities. Once again, however, theory and reality were far apart. The major problem was that, when control over a few activities was centralized, it was difficult to prevent a gravitation of all

---

[68] See, for example, a brief discussion of what the communes were supposed to achieve in K. C. Chao, *Agrarian Policy of the Chinese Communist Party*, pp. 163–164. See also Donnithorne, "Background to the People's Communes"; and Edgar Snow, *The Other Side of the River: Red China Today* (New York, 1962), chap. lvi.

[69] The most important of these are CCPCC, "On the Question of the Establishment of People's Communes in Rural Areas" (August 29, 1958), *FKHP*, VIII, 1–5; CCPCC, "Resolution on Some Questions Concerning the People's Communes" (December 10, 1958), and "Draft Regulations of the Weihsing People's Commune" (August 7, 1958), both translated in Kirby, *Contemporary China*, III, 213–252; and "Draft Regulations of the Ch'i-li Ying People's Commune," *HHPYK*, September 25, 1958, pp. 76–80.

other decision-making powers to the center. This tendency of gravitation toward centralization occurred partly because of the difficulty of coordinating decisions at different levels within the commune and partly as a result of the atmosphere within which the communes' party leadership operated. There was no hard and fast rule that would have allowed commune heads to plan for use of labor on large water-conservation projects without in some way coming into conflict with demands on that same labor from production-brigade heads (the heads of the old cooperatives) for use in farming. Since the commune leadership contained the more senior party personnel, they invariably won out — whatever the economic merits of their case.

This situation was made even worse by extreme pressure on commune leaders to achieve spectacular results, together with the removal of all restraints on their exercise of initiative. Decentralization of almost all authority for organizing communes down to the commune itself effectively removed all constraints on cadre interference in subsidiary production, in determining the rate of savings and consumption, and in the planting and harvesting of major crops. Even where there were specific regulations against such interference, as in the case of responsibility for planning major crops, it was safer to deviate toward the left, that is, toward greater centralization and reduction of individual control, than to follow regulations literally.[70] Pressure from the top was by no means the only cause of overzealousness by lower-level party cadres. Their own thorough indoctrination in Communism, together with their relative youth, undoubtedly gave them overconfidence in their own ability plus faith in the inherent superiority of more "Communist" forms of organization. All the propaganda put out by the central party organs on the general theme of the rapidly approaching "Communist" millennium certainly did nothing to discourage such views.[71]

Whatever the causes, the result of the commune movement was

[70] Even on something as fundamental as the size of the communes the deviation was toward a size much bigger than what was recommended (4600 families versus the recommended size of 2000 families per commune).

[71] For a discussion of the spate of articles on the approach to Communism, see "Transition to Communism (I) and (II)," *China News Analysis*, nos. 278–279 (May 29 and June 5, 1959), pp. 1–7.

a vast increase in rural construction work combined with a severe accentuation of all the problems created by the cooperatives. Private plots were abolished altogether, and along with them went the free market, since it no longer served any function. The time that peasants had to devote to crops grown on these plots had been encroached upon by pressures from the "great leap forward" even before the introduction of communes.[72] After communes had been established, this encroachment was carried to such great lengths initially that the peasant's time for family subsidiary occupations was eliminated, and even his time for sleeping was reduced.

Perhaps even more serious than the centralization of authority in the heads of communes and the removal of limits on cadre encroachment on the private sector was the concurrent removal of all external means of guiding the commune leadership toward rational economic decisions. Even under the cooperatives, cadre success had tended to be reckoned only on the basis of ability to increase grain and cotton output. In 1958 and 1959 decentralization of the State Statistical Bureau's power to collect agricultural production statistics down to the commune organization itself and the resulting falsification of all farm data[73] made it impossible for higher-level organs to know whether a particular measure was successful, even within the narrow scope of their emphasis on grain and cotton. Statistics could no longer be used to appraise performance. Rational planning in accordance with any criteria at all was made even more difficult for the commune leadership by the competition in target raising carried on among individual communes and the resulting need for constant plan revision. No sooner would a particular commune raise its grain-output target than one of its neighbors would set an even higher goal, and the whole process of planning in the first commune would have to be started all over again. It is not surprising, therefore, that agricultural purchase-price adjustments played an

[72] The regime had to urge the cooperatives to make special arrangements to see that enough vegetables were grown because of this pressure. CCPCC and SC, "Directive on Vegetable Sowing Work," *FKHP*, VIII, 238–239.

[73] For a full discussion of the changes in state statistical organization in 1958, see C. M. Li, *The Statistical System of Communist China* (Berkeley and Los Angeles, 1962).

even smaller role than previously. Under the cooperatives, cadres commonly had come from the village they were responsible for and were probably somewhat influenced by the membership's desire to maximize their income. Commune heads were too far removed from individual peasant's reactions to feel any such pressure directly,[74] and the falsification of statistics made it difficult to obtain information through administrative channels even if they had so desired. What is surprising is that the central government and party organs reacted to the continuing poor performance of most industrial crops by raising their purchase prices even further, in the belief that this would somehow raise their output.[75] Some indication of the results of these efforts can be surmised from the fact that in 1959 the regime ceased publication of all crop-production figures, except for those of grain, cotton, and soybeans.

In addition, financial restraints operating through limits on the availability of funds were undermined by the huge influx of money into rural areas in the form of large increases in agricultural credit and budget allocations directly to communes.[76] In

[74] Greene, *Awakened China,* p. 129, states that most, but not all, of the commune directors whom he met were Communist party members. The one whose brief life history he reports was from the same area, but not from a village, of his particular commune (p. 162). Greene visited 15 communes in various parts of China (p. 177). Snow, *The Other Side of the River,* chaps. viii, lviii–lix, points out that communes are usually run by party members, who need not be local residents. In one commune 80 per cent of the party members were local people, for example. Even where the administrative head of the commune was a local man promoted from below, real power rested with the branch party secretary, who was apt to be a *hsien* political officer (Ezra Vogel, unpublished manuscript). For a more detailed analysis of the structure of party control in communes, see J. W. Lewis, *Leadership in Communist China* (Ithaca, 1963), chap. vii.

[75] The purchase prices of soybeans, sugar cane, sugar beets, and peanuts were raised. SC, "Directive on Adjusting Several Types of Commodity Prices" (October 16, 1959), *Jen min shou-ts'e, 1960,* p. 388.

[76] *China News Analysis,* no. 258 (January 2, 1959), p. 5, states (on the basis of *JMJP,* December 18, 1958), that agrarian loans made by banks in 1958 were equal to the total amount made during the first five-year plan. The magnitude of loans by the state to agriculture in 1958 and 1959 can also be seen from the fact that total loans to agriculture from 1950 to 1959 were 27.5 billion yuan. Subtracting 9.5 billion yuan made by credit cooperatives and 9 billion yuan for loans from 1950 to 1957, there remain 9 billion yuan for loans in 1958 and 1959 ("Credit Work's Role in the Promotion of Production," Peking

agriculture, as elsewhere, this easy-money policy further accentuated the tendency to ignore income and profit goals and to concentrate on a few key physical output targets. The cooperatives had to pay their own way, and this limited how far cadres could go in building nonproductive establishments or ones that would not become productive until some time far in the future. It also provided them with an incentive to respond to purchase-price adjustments. Such financial restraints were not effective for the communes.

Finally, one cannot ignore the effect that commune organization had on incentives of individual peasants to put forth their best effort. Some features relevant to the question of incentives, however, were not as significant as publicity made them appear. The "part wage part free supply" distribution system, for example, was in reality not very different from the procedure existing under the cooperatives. There, peasants had been paid both in money and in kind, with payment in kind being determined partly by work done and partly by need. Communes took this same food, plus that which had once been grown on private plots, served it in mess halls, and called it free supply. The wage portion was something of an innovation in that peasants were probably paid at more regular intervals, rather than having to wait until the harvest was sold before their shares could be divided up.

In the area of individual incentives, the most significant change brought about by communes was that the basis upon which wages were calculated was the income of the whole commune, rather than that of the cooperative or production brigade. In effect, this removed the reward given to the individual peasant one step further from direct connection with the amount of work he performed. Elaborate bonus systems for brigades, teams, and individuals were set up just as they had been under cooperatives, but these were far from adequate substitutes for the built-in bonus system that exists when the individual depends completely

---

TKP, May 24, 1960, translated in *JPRS,* no. 3869, p. 2). For a regulation on how credit to commune run enterprises was handled, see SC, "Regulations on the Work of the People's Commune Credit Department and State Enterprise Circulating Capital" (December 20, 1958), *FKHP,* VIII, 158.

on his own performance for his reward. Of equal importance were the egalitarian tendencies of rural cadres. Although the spate of articles and speeches on how China was on the verge of making the transition from socialism to communism were not meant to have immediate practical application, they could not help but influence the decisions of rural cadres. Their success depended not only on obedience to the party directives of the moment, but on anticipation of future directives as well. Even prior to 1958 the regime had had to make special efforts to get cooperative cadres to make sufficient allowances for disincentive caused by leveling of incomes both within and among cooperatives. Part of the motive behind reduction in the size of cooperatives had been that this would automatically take better account of incentive differentials in income. In 1958 the further separation of work from reward was at least partly responsible for the subsequent agricultural crisis.

The commune movement, therefore, proved first of all that more centralized control of labor allocation could not work effectively. There were economic advantages to increasing the number of hours worked by making individuals work longer and during seasons when they would otherwise have been idle. These advantages, however, were more than offset by the decreased quality of labor resulting from the many disincentives attached to this form of organization and the inefficiency with which the labor was used because of inadequate managerial skills of rural cadres and removal of basic market guidelines without finding an adequate substitute. Communist ideology and party pressures accentuated these disadvantages, but they probably would have existed to some degree in any case. The commune movement also proved that the authorities in Peking could not abandon all responsibility for setting basic guidelines within which lower-level cadres could operate. Cadre self-interest in such areas as subsidiary production and objective reporting was bound to be in conflict with the best interests of the state.

The Chinese Communists paid a heavy price for this knowledge, but the price was obscured for a time by the good harvest of 1958. When the central authorities finally realized that the net effect of communes on agricultural production had been deleteri-

ous, they were forced to face the fact that their ambitious industrialization program was, at least for the time being, up against
basic and unpostponable requirements of agriculture.

Revision, 1960–1963

The time that it took the central authorities to realize the
seriousness of the crisis they had helped create and to act on
this knowledge was longer than usual. This was in part the result of the decentralization of most controls formerly exercised
at the center down to the commune, although deep ideological
commitment to the commune movement was also an important
factor. The most serious loss of central control in this respect was
that of means of attaining accurate information about what was
really going on at lower levels. Without the accurate reporting
of the State Statistical Bureau, the top leadership was probably
unaware that a crisis was brewing until it was well under way.[77]
The leadership was also unable to ascertain fully the true causes
of the crisis. To accomplish this latter objective they would have
had to require detailed seasonal and area breakdowns in data
so that they could separate out the effects of poor organization
from the effects of the bad weather that affected most of China
between 1959 and 1961.

The decentralization of authority also prolonged the time
needed to deal with the difficulties in agriculture. The leadership
not only had to decide what needed to be done but it had also
either to convince commune cadres to do it or else re-establish
central lines of authority so that they could be ordered to do it.
The latter method was quicker but on the whole inefficient. From
the beginning of the Communist regime the system of agricultural controls was based on the principle that any central directive must be applied with considerable flexibility and imagina-
tion at the operational level so as to take local conditions into
account. It was generally assumed that in order to ensure that
this would be the case, convincing cooperative and commune

[77] If the leadership had been fully aware of the impending difficulties, it
would presumably have taken measures to avoid or soften the effect of negative
propaganda by such measures as not giving so much publicity to grossly falsified production data.

cadres of the advisability of taking a particular action was superior to putting it in the form of a military order. Under the communes cadres had been given even greater leeway to take initiative, particularly in the direction of more radical moves. As a result, it was difficult to get them to move in the opposite direction, especially when the central authorities themselves seemed reluctant to put their full weight behind reversing the trend. The first move back was the gradual reintroduction of a semblance of a free market in rural areas in the form of trade fairs.[78] By early 1959 the regime was aware that subsidiary production had suffered heavily, at least partly because of overtight commercial controls. It initially attempted to cope with the problem by a renewed emphasis on contracts and special meetings where such contracts were drawn up, but met with considerable reluctance on the part of commune cadres, who felt that such contracts would merely reduce their freedom of action. Because of this, the authorities began experimenting with reopening of rural markets in particular areas, which culminated in a directive of September 25, 1959, calling for their nationwide adoption.[79] Prices, however, were to be kept under much tighter control than in the previous free market, and state commercial organizations were told to keep a sharp lookout for a resurgence of capitalism.

By the summer of 1960 the regime went a step further by encouraging restoration of small private plots and of limits on the amount of labor time which the commune could require of its members. That these measures were not met with complete enthusiasm by local cadres is evidenced by the fact that the authorities still found it necessary to explain why they were restored and to answer criticism of them well into the middle of 1961.[80]

[78] For a fuller discussion of the various administrative changes involved in the reintroduction of rural trade fairs, see Audrey Donnithorne, "The Organization of Rural Trade in China since 1958," The China Quarterly, no. 8 (October–December 1961), pp. 77–91; and "Changes and Muddle," China News Analysis, no. 299 (October 30, 1959), pp. 1–7.

[79] CCPCC and SC, "Directive on Organizing Rural Market Trade" (September 25, 1959), Jen-min shou-t'se, 1960, pp. 380–381.

[80] See, for example, "The Nature of Private Plots of Land and Family Subsidiary Production of Commune Members," Peking TKP, March 15, 1961, translated in SCMP, no. 2478, pp. 17–19; Shih Hsiu-lin, "Some Views on the

As was the case with restoration of rural markets, the role of private plots was conceived in a much more limited way than it had been under the cooperatives. Rather than making private plots the basis of hog and vegetable raising, the state continued to rely on various collective expedients. Hog raising was still to be conducted by collective units, although large hog farms were de-emphasized and private hog raising was just something that was also to be encouraged.[81] There is evidence, however, that by the beginning of 1962 the authorities had almost come full circle and private hog raising was again spoken of as more important than public hog raising.[82] Considerable emphasis, on the other hand, continued to be placed on various enterprises' and institutions' raising their own subsidiary foods.[83] The army, for example, was said to be completely self-sufficient in vegetables.[84] During 1961, the authorities made efforts to activate rural trade fairs so that they would become a more positive incentive to subsidiary production. This did not involve changes in regulations so much as it did an attempt to overcome the reluctance of local

---

Nature of Land Retained for Private Use," Peking *TKP*, June 21, 1961, translated in *SCMP*, no. 2547, pp. 13–17.

[81] See three articles appearing in *Hung-ch'i*, April 16, 1961, translated in *ECMM*, no. 260, pp. 28–42; "On Raising Hogs and Accumulating Manure," Peking *TKP*, August 31, 1961, translated in *SCMP*, no. 2595, pp. 21–24. Two refugees who left Kwangtung in 1961 state that some individuals were raising hogs in their area but not many ("Who Is Mao Tse-tung? Four Answers," *Current Scene*, vol. I, no. 22, January 5, 1962, pp. 2, 7).

[82] "A Production Brigade in Kwangtung Province Is Successful in Developing Hog Breeding," *Nan-fang jih-pao*, February 23, 1962, translated in *SCMP*, no. 2711, pp. 7–10. The article refers to the policy of "developing both public hog raising and private hog raising, with the latter as the more important" (p. 7). The policy in early 1960, for example, was: "Public raising is the main, private raising gives support" ("The 1960 Agricultural Battle Line," *Hung-ch'i*, no. 2, 1960, reprinted in *Jen-min shou-ts'e, 1960*, p. 423). In 1961, the regime spoke of the simultaneous public and private raising of hogs (*JMJP* editorial, "Develop Undertaking of Hog Rearing by Rearing Hogs Privately and Publicly at the Same Time," *JMJP*, December 2, 1960, translated in *SCMP*, no. 2425, p. 12).

[83] See Ch'i Liang, "Carry Out More Properly Production of Non-staple Foodstuffs in Organizations and Enterprises," Peking *TKP*, March 20, 1962, translated in *SCMP*, no. 2720, pp. 16–20.

[84] "Chinese People's Liberation Army Self-sufficient in Vegetables," NCNA, November 14, 1961, translated in *SCMP*, no. 2622, p. 18. The article also speaks of a partial self-sufficiency in meat.

cadres to permit any really free trading. They were encouraged to allow prices to fluctuate more freely in response to conditions of supply and demand and to expand the amount of trade taking place on these markets.[85] In spite of all these efforts, however, one is left with the impression that most were half measures. Local cadres, at least, appear to have been thoroughly sold on the advantages of collective production and planning even if the central authorities were not.

Finally in 1961 the regime also began to take a number of measures aimed at correcting the general disincentive effects of communization by passing control over production and incomes down to lower-level units. In a sense, this emphasis on the role of lower-level units began with a resolution of December 10, 1958, reaffirming that it was the brigade that was to organize agricultural production and the team that was to arrange labor allocation.[86] It was not until the beginning of 1961, however, that ownership and hence the calculation of profit and loss and wages had been passed down to production brigades.[87] In early 1962, this was carried a step further by the transfer of basic-level ownership down to the production team.[88] By 1963 all vestiges of the

[85] See, for example, Kuan Ta-t'ung, "Firmly Enforce the Policy of Activating Rural Trade Fairs," Peking *TKP*, January 26, 1961, translated in *SCMP*, no. 2456, pp. 1–6; Jen Ching-lu, "Prices in Trading at Rural Fairs and the Role of the Law of Value," Peking *TKP*, May 12, 1961, translated in *SCMP*, no. 2508, pp. 1–5; Kuo Chih-chun and Ouyang Tou, "Some Questions of How to View Trade at Rural Fairs," Peking *TKP*, December 25, 1961, translated in *SCMP*, no. 2660, pp. 18–22; Ho Cheng and Wei Wen, "Discussion of Rural Market Trade," *CCYC*, April 17, 1962, pp. 11–15.

[86] CCPCC, "Resolution on Some Questions Concerning the People's Communes" (December 10, 1958), translated in Kirby, *Contemporary China*, III, 213–234.

[87] See JMJP editorial, "The Three-Level Ownership System with the Production Brigade as the Basic Level Is the Basic System for People's Communes at the Present Stage," *JMJP*, December 21, 1960, translated in *SCMP*, no. 2408, p. 10; *JMJP* editorial, "Conscientiously Implement Policies of Rural People's Communes," *JMJP*, April 2, 1961, translated in *SCMP*, no. 2476, pp. 24–27.

[88] This was mentioned first in the New Year's editorial in *JMJP*, January 1, 1962, p. 1. The major document detailing the changes to be made, "The Sixty Theses," was apparently transmitted to rural cadres in April or May of 1962 (Ezra Vogel, unpublished manuscript). One indication that control over agricultural production was decentralized even further than statements for nationwide consumption would indicate can be found in "Party Bulletin of Pao An

part wage part supply system had disappeared and been replaced by the old piece-rate system of the cooperatives.[89] Thus after four years of experimenting with larger units, the regime was back to a unit that may have been even smaller than the one with which they had started. These adjustments were brought about more by changes in the level of ownership than by reducing the size of communes and brigades.[90] This was probably because the regime could accomplish the same ends either way; and unlike most farm-related actions, the second could be carried out quickly and easily by an administrative order. It also had the added advantage that it allowed the regime to claim that communes were still very much in existence.

Although generally successful, these moves only managed to restore the situation to conditions that had prevailed in 1957, if that. There was nothing about these policies that could have been expected to do any more toward solving the fundamental dilemma facing the regime. The 1962 harvest apparently was quite good and the 1963 harvest even better.[91] Vegetables and similar free-market commodities again were plentiful, and pork, which had virtually disappeared from the diet of most Chinese, was again available at precommune levels.[92] But this performance

Hsien, Kwangtung," September 22, 27, 30, and October 6, 8, 1961, translated in *URS*, vol. XXVII, nos. 7–8, April 24, 1962, p. 114. The article discusses how the cultivation of rice was in some cases contracted out to individual peasants.

[89] See Andrew Nathan, "China's Work-point System: A Study in Agricultural 'Splittism,'" *Current Scene*, vol. II, no. 31 (April 15, 1964), pp. 1–13.

[90] Certain levels of organization (e.g. higher-level brigades) were sometimes abolished altogether and some adjustments in size were made (e.g. the number of communes was increased substantially). But most changes in size were made by such devices as shifting several lower-level units from one brigade to another (Ezra Vogel, unpublished manuscript).

[91] In an interview with Edgar Snow on January 23, 1964, Chou En-lai stated that the grain harvest of 1962 had been more than 10 million tons over that of 1961 and that the 1963 harvest had been higher than that of 1962 by a comparable amount, yet production had not reached 190 million tons (the 1957 harvest was 185 million tons). One Hong Kong estimate puts 1963 grain output at 179 million tons ("Agriculture in China, 1963," *Current Scene*, vol. II, no. 27, January 15, 1964, p. 4).

[92] See "'Plain Living and Hard Struggle': An Economic Assessment," *Current Scene*, vol. II, no. 28 (February 15, 1964), p. 3; Colina MacDougall, "Modernising Farms," *Far Eastern Economic Review*, XLII (November 21, 1963), 382–383.

was nowhere near good enough to sustain a substantial and lop-sided investment in industrial producers' goods. As a result, the basic conflict between the needs of agriculture and those of rapid industrialization had to be resolved, temporarily at least, by shifting resources from the latter to the former.

Centralization versus the Market

It should be clear from the above discussion that almost from the beginning the Chinese Communists have faced a basic conflict between their desire to build a heavy industrial base as rapidly as possible and China's low level of per capita agricultural output. As early as 1953 the regime was forced to abandon the market in favor of centrally determined compulsory quotas for major crops. Where for Stalin a similar centralization of control over marketed agricultural output had provided a long-run solution of over twenty years' duration, the relative poverty of China made these quotas only a temporary respite of little more than two years in length. In fact, by harming individual farmers' incentives they probably hastened the need for measures that would get at the real problem, that of agricultural output. From 1955 on the key question was how to raise agricultural production without in any way reducing the state's investment in the producers' goods industry. This was a goal that ultimately proved to be beyond China's capacity, but between 1955 and 1959 both within China and without there was a belief that it could be achieved by a partial centralization of authority over certain aspects of agricultural production. Guided by this belief, the Chinese Communists first tried cooperatives and then communes.

In a limited sense both types of organization accomplished what they were set up for. Centralization made possible utilization of rural underemployed labor in various construction projects. Furthermore, the greater the degree of centralization the larger the size and number of projects that could be undertaken. The communes were even large enough to build and staff various industrial and commercial establishments. In addition, the more that decision making was centralized, the easier it was to encourage the trial of new techniques and to raise the rate of rural savings. The accomplishments along these lines, however, were not very great. Cadres were too often insufficiently skilled or overly doctrinaire to use the added resources or new techniques efficiently.

Even these advantages of centralization, however, were bought at heavy cost. A serious but by no means the only cost was the decline in peasant incentive, which accompanied the removal of the direct connection between individual effort and the produce of the land. This decline was more serious the larger the unit that controlled agricultural output and the larger the unit on the basis of whose income individual wages were determined. The efficient use of resources in controlling farm production was also more difficult as decision making became more centralized. The Chinese Communists recognized this latter danger, but failed to take account of how difficult if not impossible it was to centralize control over labor and financial allocation for one purpose (construction) and not for another (farm production). This problem was further complicated by the lack of adequate criteria by which cadres could hope to plan their unit's activities successfully. This, too, got worse as the unit became larger and the connection between villagers, who could be counted on to encourage maximization of income, and cadres became more remote. The tendency to concentrate on grain and cotton at the expense of other crops might have been somewhat reduced if it had been possible to centralize planning all the way up to Peking, but the lack of adequate and timely data made the one move in this direction a complete failure. The lack of response by cadres to price changes made it impossible for the central planners to achieve indirectly what they could not accomplish directly. In theory the market and prices could have continued to play a role, but in practice centralization of control in Communist China proved to be a substitute for, and not a supplement to, the market and price controls.

The one area where centralization had no merit whatsoever was in subsidiary production and marketing. The regime had to learn twice over that these commodities could only be handled efficiently by individual peasants working on their own under the stimulus of a free market. The problems with subsidiary output also illustrate one of the major dilemmas facing the authorities in Peking, whenever they attempted to reorganize agriculture: if reorganization were to be effective, plenty of leeway had to be allowed for adjustment to local conditions by lower-level cadres. Because these same cadres were under extreme pressure to prove their enthusiasm and ideological purity, however, the adjustments made were often more closely related to the political atmosphere of the times than to local economic conditions. Moreover, even without these pressures, there were real conflicts of interest between cadres and the central government, of which private plots and free time were the most conspicuous example. Therefore, although the central authorities could not become too involved in the details of the various reorganizations, they could not afford to decentralize all of their authority to lower-level party cadres as they had in 1958.

By 1960 and 1961 the Chinese Communists finally became aware of this conflict between the advantages of centralization and its costs. During the entire course of their experimentation in the rural areas they had failed to discover any combination of centralized and decentralized control that, on economic grounds, was any better than the combination that had existed prior to the cooperatives. As a result, they were ultimately forced to make the decision that these reorganizations had been designed to avoid — to cut back investment in the producers' goods industry and shift it to agriculture.

The difficulties that the Chinese Communist have run into in their attempts to make either the cooperatives or communes work effectively cast doubt on whether there are any realizable advantages from centralization in agriculture, even in overpopulated and labor-intensive countries such as China. Political and ideological considerations aside, there appears to be little that centralization accomplishes that cannot be done better through extension services, taxes, and market and price controls in the context of a free peasant economy. In Communist China, however, political and ideological considerations cannot be put aside. The political and ideological advantages to the regime of the collective form of organization in agriculture have been too great for this organization to be abandoned except under the most desperate circumstances. The real question for China, therefore, is not whether cooperatives or communes work better than a market-controlled free peasant economy, but whether they can be made to work well enough so that agricultural output and marketing rise fast enough to support the industrialization program and perhaps modest increases in the standard of living as well.

One measure that probably would increase cooperatives' chances of success would be greater use of the market and prices to determine what is to be produced. To date, however, there is no real evidence to suggest that the Chinese Communists will abandon their penchant for crash programs and "planning" and substitute income maximization as the basic target. Barring such a step, perhaps with time the skills of cadres will improve sufficiently to reduce many of the costs of centralization. It may also be that political and ideological pressure on rural cadres will be reduced and that a number of minor adjustments will result at the local level which will damp down disincentives. Always working in the opposite direction, however, will be the need of the totalitarian state to maintain tight political control together with a genuine aversion to anything smacking of capitalism. Even if a modified form of the cooperative does prove workable, there is no assurance that the Chinese Communists will abandon their attempts to find a more radical solution to their basic dilemma. The retreat in agriculture has yet to be talked of as a permanent or long-run solution, and there is much talk of reforming the bourgeois thought of the population and then having another go at reorganization. This may be only to keep the party itself from losing its ideological drive, but it may also mark the beginning of another attempt to find some dramatically effective substitute for the market.

CHAPTER V

The Theoretical Role of Wholesale Prices and Profits in Industry

Central planning, enforced by means of centralized controls, has been assumed by many to be the only effective way of attaining rapid industrial development. The Chinese Communists, therefore, have not been alone in this belief, but differ primarily in that they have put it into effect more thoroughly and systematically. In the first half of this chapter, the basic features of this system of controls are described along with the rationale that has been, in fact, or could be, used to support such a system for an economy such as China's.

Powerful factors, however, have also worked to undermine the effectiveness of the Chinese regime's network of centralized controls. The authorities have found it desirable to decentralize a number of important functions in the industrial sector. These decentralized controls, in certain circumstances, have involved extension of the role of prices and the market, and in others have involved transfer of administrative duties from higher- to lower-level decision makers in ways that have ignored the market altogether or have reduced the effectiveness of market controls. These formal moves toward decentralization, the rationale behind them, and their effect on the role of wholesale prices and other market forces are discussed in the latter half of this chapter.

Formal laws and regulations, however, give only a very incomplete picture of the Chinese system of industrial controls, particularly with respect to the function of the market. Two major elements, ideology and the inexperience of Communist cadres, have undermined both centralized and decentralized controls. The discussion of these elements in the next chapter points up the difficulty of operating any system of controls efficiently, whether heavily market-oriented or not, over a large number of state-owned industrial enterprises.

The Structure of Control, 1950–1963

As studies of factory management in the Soviet Union have shown,[1] an understanding of the theoretical or legal structure of controls over industrial firms is only one step toward understanding the actual operation of the system. It is, however, a necessary first approximation. The basic pattern is familiar to any student of economies of the Soviet type. Central planners in China compiled a list of production goals for each industry and enterprise, which, although stated to be realistic targets, were in fact meant to be minimum objectives that well-run enterprises were expected to exceed. Prior to November 1957 each industry was given twelve such targets, of which five could be classified as physical goals upon which price and financial policy, in theory, had little or no influence. These five included the output of major products, total number of employees, trial manufacture of new varieties of products, total number of employees on the job at year's end, and certain important technical and economic quotas. If the last are broken down into their component parts — consumption of raw materials, level of mechanization, and rate of equipment utilization — the number of physical targets is increased to seven. There were similar sets of physical targets for capital-construction enterprises including such targets as production capacity utilized, progress of construction projects, volume of building and installation work, and the like, and for transport and commercial enterprises.[2]

To back up these targets, the Government Affairs Council's Financial and Economic Committee began, as early as 1950, rationed or unified distribution of certain key raw materials or

---

[1] J. S. Berliner, *Factory and Manager in the USSR* (Cambridge, Mass., 1957); David Granick, *Management of the Industrial Firm in the USSR* (New York, 1954).

[2] Fang Fa, "Some Common Knowledge of the National Economic Plan," *Hsueh-hsi,* October 2, 1956, translated in *ECMM,* no. 65, pp. 38–41; Shigeru Ishikawa, *Chugoku ni okeru shihon chikuseki kiko* (Capital formation in China; Tokyo, 1960).

major equipment. In 1952 the number of commodities so distributed was only 28, but rose to 96 in 1953, and 235 by 1956.[3] These goods were distributed to departments concerned on the supposed basis of requirements in their production plans. Where a portion of the products was used by consumers or widely scattered handicraft cooperatives, the state would set aside a certain percentage that was then sold on the market, though still largely under some form of *de facto* rationing. Private factories either obtained their raw materials from this market or, more commonly in later years, by direct allocation from state enterprises in accordance with special contracts drawn up to bring private businesses directly under state control without actually taking over ownership. Rationed distribution of these commodities not only backed up the explicitly stated plan targets, but in addition made it possible to enforce various priorities implicit in the Soviet type of planning, that is, priorities that were made necessary by planning for over-full utilization of resources.

Individual enterprises also were limited by having control over their major expansion placed in the hands of others. Construction projects, except for very small ones, commonly were placed under the control of special construction enterprises until completed. Thus a factory manager always was limited by his existing plant and equipment and by whatever additional plant central authorities deemed necessary.

Finally, imposed on this system of physical controls was an additional and separate set of financial controls. Financial targets (which before November 1957 included such items as profits, cost reduction, and wage bill) were conceived of partly to back up physical goals and partly to fill in gaps that could not easily be filled without an excessive proliferation of physical targets. Thus it was simpler to put a limit on the total wage bill than to specify the number of workers in each salary grade, for example.

The key element of financial control, however, was not financial targets but controls over the sources and uses of enterprise funds. The most important were sales and profits taxes. These taxes took away a large portion of the funds coming into an individual en-

[3] "A Brief Description of the State Distribution of Commodities during the Past Year," *TCKT,* July 14, 1957, translated in *ECMM,* no. 97, p. 21.

terprise and turned them into the state treasury where central planners could reissue them or not as they saw fit.

The regime's control over the availability and use of enterprise funds was by no means simply confined to their authority to remove these funds by means of sales and profits taxes. There were elaborate rules governing how enterprises could obtain funds for their own use and how they could use them once obtained. In the first place, enterprises' funds for use in meeting everyday expenses (working capital) were clearly separated from funds for expansion. The latter were financed out of the budget, and actual payment of funds was handled by a special bank, first the Bank of Communications, and after 1954 the People's Construction Bank, except in the case of joint enterprises, where the Bank of Communications retained control. This rule was not without exceptions. Below-norm projects,[4] for example, could be undertaken on the enterprise's own initiative, but the size of investment not subject to centralized planning was not large, at least not until after authority was somewhat decentralized in 1958, as can be seen from data in Table 7. Even basic construction investment, which was financed out of the small portion of total profits that an individual enterprise was allowed to retain, had to be used according to the central plan and under supervision of the Construction Bank.[5]

Sources of working capital were somewhat more complex. In the first place, each enterprise had income from sales of its output after deductions were made for profits and sales taxes. Taxes were paid into the central or provincial treasuries several times a month so that funds from income above cost were not retained by enterprises long enough to be of great significance. This latter feature was important because otherwise the very high rates of

---

[4] "Below-norm" projects are those basic construction projects on which the total expenditure is less than a fixed amount that varies depending on the type of enterprise. For specific figures, see SC, "Provisional Regulations on the Examination and Approval of Plans and Budgetary Estimates for Capital Construction" (July 12, 1955), translated in K. C. Chao, *Economic Planning and Organization in Mainland China*, I, 77–81.

[5] SC, "Regulation Putting into Effect the Enterprise Retained Profits System" (May 22, 1958), *FKHP,* VII, 239–242; Ministry of Finance, "Regulation on the Distribution and Use of 1956 State Enterprise Profits in Excess of the Plan" (October 11, 1956), *FKHP,* IV, 267–268.

TABLE 7. Proportion of investment centrally planned (million yuan)

Year	Total state investment	Centrally-planned investment	Not centrally planned
1950	1,130	1,040	90
1951	2,350	1,880	470
1952	4,360	3,710	650
1953	8,000	6,510	1,490
1954	9,070	7,500	1,570
1955	9,300	8,630	670
1956	14,800	13,990	810
1957	13,830	12,640	1,190
1958	26,700	21,440	5,260
1959	31,700[a]	26,700	5,000
1960[b]	38,500[a]	32,500	6,000

Source: SSB, *Ten Great Years*, pp. 55–56; Li Fu-chun, "Report on the Draft 1960 National Economic Plan" (March 30, 1960), and Li Hsien-nien, "Report on the Final State Accounts for 1959 and the Draft State Budget for 1960" (March 30, 1960), both in *Second Session of the Second National People's Congress*, pp. 2, 61–62.

[a] Derived by adding capital-construction outlays by localities and departments to budget allocations for investment.

[b] Plan data.

profit on both consumers' and producers' goods would have provided firms with so much working capital that serious financial discipline would have been virtually impossible. With private firms, financial discipline was maintained by a combination of taxes and price squeeze. Contracts between state and private firms were drawn up in which the state firm agreed to supply the private firm with raw materials (which otherwise would have been unobtainable) at prices above those paid by state companies.[6] These prices were explicitly set so as to allow capitalist enterprises a return of 10, 20, or 30 per cent on their capital (only one-fourth of which could be paid out in dividends).[7]

[6] For a more detailed discussion of the various forms that this took, see Kuan Ta-tung, *Socialist Transformation*, chap. v.

[7] Profit of private enterprises averaged 20 per cent of capital, according to Ch'en Yun, "On Commercial Work and Industrial Commercial Relations," speech to the National People's Congress, June 30, 1956, translated in *CB*, no. 398, p. 2.

State enterprises also retained a portion of their profits, but until 1958 the sum involved was small, only 40 per cent of profits in excess of the plan target. If budget data are an adequate indicator of the extent of overfulfillment, income from this source would have been negligible in 1955 and 1956, less than 3 per cent of total profits in 1957, and less than 9 per cent in 1954.[8] In 1958 retained profits were changed to a fixed percentage of total profits, which averaged out to be about 10 per cent,[9] or about 5 per cent of cost. Thus even in 1958 enterprises had little more than enough funds to match costs. Since sales revenue was seldom exactly synchronized with outlays, enterprises were in need of funds over and above what they could get from their own sales. For some firms the need was mainly seasonal, while in others, particularly in rapidly growing firms, revenue might regularly lag behind outlay.

These needs were met out of a combination of allocations from the budget and loans from the People's Bank. The allocations were made without interest or need to repay, whereas the loans had to be repaid and carried an interest charge. Interest charges on industrial loans varied over time but were approximately 5 or 6 per cent per annum. In 1959, faced with a need to tighten up financial control, the state abolished appropriations for working capital from the central or local budgets and determined that all enterprise working-capital needs, above what could be met out of their own revenue, would be provided in the form of loans from the People's Bank.[10] This system, however, proved to be unsatisfactory, and in 1961 was replaced by one where 80 per cent of

[8] These estimates are probably too low, since they were obtained by taking 40 per cent of total profits actually paid into the treasury in excess of the planned amount. In fact, many enterprises exceeded the target, while others fell below it, but the latter did not have 40 per cent of profits below plan taken away from them.

[9] This is the estimate for 1958 given by Li Hsien-nien, "The Implementation of the State Budget for 1957 and the Draft State Budget for 1958" (February 1, 1958), NCNA, February 12, 1958, translated in *CB*, no. 493, p. 17. The percentage for each enterprise was fixed on the basis of the enterprise's past expenditure on such items as new-product testing and labor safety.

[10] SC, "Revised Regulations Putting State Enterprise Circulating Capital under the Unified Management of the People's Bank" (February 3, 1959), *FKHP*, IX, 121–125.

an enterprise's working funds come from the Ministry of Finance and only 20 per cent from the bank.[11]

Individual firms never had much freedom in the use of these funds, according to regulations, whatever their source. Not only could they not use the funds for financing capital construction except in certain limited instances, they also could not use them to increase the wage bill beyond the target figure. Even more important, enterprises had to draw up detailed income and outlay plans that had to be approved by higher-level authorities. This plan then formed the basis upon which loans were given and budget allocations made. Even the enterprise's own deposits (it was only allowed enough cash for three days' operations) were, according to the regulations, not to be used for other than approved purposes.[12] Additional funds from the bank or budget were allocated in a rationed manner on the basis of an income and outgo plan, and, in the former case, after provision of collateral (usually commodities that the funds were used to purchase). The interest rate was set much too low to have had a significant effect on demand for working capital. Its influence was further reduced because interest charges were a part of cost, and hence could be easily met out of revenue, except in a relatively small number of enterprises where profits were too low. Furthermore, interest charges, because they could be included in costs, were mostly paid by the state through reduction in the enterprise's profits tax liability.

The enterprise did retain a limited capacity even in theory (in practice, this ability was far from limited, as will be seen in the next chapter) for easing its own financial situation to the extent that it could readjust the inflow and outflow pattern of its funds. The major areas where this could be done, through such activ-

[11] Ministry of Finance and People's Bank, "Several Regulations Reforming Methods of Supplying State Enterprises' Circulating Capital" (May 17, 1961), *FKHP*, XII, 74–78.
[12] Financial and Economic Committee, "Methods of Enforcing Currency Management and Compiling Currency Income and Outgo Plans" (December 25, 1950), *HHYP*, January 25, 1951, pp. 610–615. This was the basic regulation setting up cash control. For more detailed discussion of these procedures, see Cheng Chu-yuan, *Monetary Affairs of Communist China* (Hong Kong, 1954), sec. vi.

ities as delaying of payment and purchases on credit, were, however, declared illegal from the beginning. The remaining possibilities were largely in the nature of slow long-run improvements in the flow of funds, which could not be made to respond quickly to short-term fluctuation in credit needs.

The proliferation of financial controls prior to 1957, therefore, really did not much enhance the role of prices and the market, although some notable exceptions will be mentioned below. Most of these controls were too specific to allow much latitude to factory managers. Instead, as already mentioned, the primary purpose of these measures was to backstop the physical targets.

Generally speaking, the Chinese Communists have never really felt the need to justify this system of centralized, essentially physical, controls on pragmatic grounds. It is a basic tenet of Marxism that planning is an essential feature of a socialist system, in contrast with the "anarchy" of capitalism. Furthermore, the Soviet Union had already set the pattern for practical application of this tenet. Nevertheless, there also were pragmatic grounds upon which one can justify such a system for China, and it is not unlikely that they had some influence on the regime's choice.

Outside the Communist bloc, the argument in favor of centralization and extensive use of physical controls starts, not by accusing capitalism of outright anarchy, but of creating serious distortions in the price structure in underdeveloped countries that in turn lead to serious misallocations of investment funds. These same underdeveloped countries are presumed to be capable of remedying these distortions through central planning backed up by a system of centralized controls. Although these countries obviously lack the technical proficiency necessary to plan effectively in a developed country, it is argued that the problem for an underdeveloped country is much simpler. Specifically, there are far fewer commodities and investment projects to plan and fewer interdependencies among sectors. Thus the skills required to attain adequate timely information (statistics) and effective coordination, the two major problems of centralization, are within reach of at least a number of underdeveloped countries. Furthermore, new technology can be borrowed from the developed countries and put into operation with minimal adaptation to local conditions. In addition, since so many key inputs are imported, shortages caused by planning can be offset simply by importing more of the short commodity.[13] Finally, and perhaps most important, the initial stages of economic development today commonly require major structural changes in the economy. Such structural changes can, it is argued, be accomplished much more rapidly by central planning and allocation than by comparatively slow responses to market forces.

If, however, information and coordination problems are not simply a function of the number of commodities produced, major adaptations in technology do have to be made, and imports cannot be manipulated at will, the argument for centralization and extensive use of physical controls is weakened considerably. The Chinese Communists, in fact, recognized several of these difficulties from the outset, while other circumstances forced them to make changes at a later date. These difficulties and changes are the subject of the latter half of this chapter.

Formal Decentralization and the Market, 1950–1963

The main features of the industrial sector in mainland China, which made centralized control anything but a simple task, were the number of firms involved and the diversity of techniques used in the production of any given commodity. The image of industry in China is usually that of the steel mills of Anshan and Wuhan, but a large portion of industrial output was produced by individual handicraftsmen or in factories employing fewer than fifteen workers. Even a factory employing a hundred or more persons was often little more than a piece of land with trays for drying and vats for pickling food. If they had machinery, it was often of a primitive kind. In Table 8 an attempt has been made to estimate gross value of industrial output in other than modern large-scale enterprises. Although the estimates are crude, the picture portrayed is clear enough. Not only do such enterprises account for about half of industrial output (probably less if ex-

---

[13] For further discussion of these points, see J. M. Montias, "The Soviet Economic Model and the Underdeveloped Countries," in Nicholas Spulber, ed., *Study of the Soviet Economy* (Bloomington, 1961), pp. 66–67.

TABLE 8. Proportion of industrial output in small- and medium-scale enterprises (million yuan)

Year	Gross value of industrial enterprises[a]	Gross value of non-modern enterprises[a]		Gross value of small-scale[b]	Gross value of small- and medium-scale[c]	
		Value	Per cent		Value	Per cent
			1952 prices			
1949	14,020	6,110	43.6	—	9,500	67.9
1950	19,120	8,230	43.1	—	—	—
1951	26,350	10,440	39.6	—	—	—
1952	34,330	12,280	35.8	10,939	—	—
1953	44,700	15,890	35.5	13,890	23,800	53.2
1954	51,970	17,990	34.6	14,791	—	—
1955	54,870	17,790	32.4	13,999	—	—
1956	70,360	20,020	28.4	—	—	—
1957	78,390	22,760	29.1	—	33,300	42.5
			1957 prices			
1957	70,400	20,730	29.4	—	—	—
1958	117,000	29,730	25.4	—	—	—

[a] SSB, *Ten Great Years*, pp. 87, 91. Modern industry is defined as industry (both large- and small-scale) that uses modern technique and equipment. It is industry whose main processes use machinery, but it does not include production processes that only use very simple machinery; see State Planning Commission, *Fa-chan kuo-min ching-chi-te ti-i-ko wu-nien chi-hua-te ming-tz'u chien-shih* (A simple selection of terms used in the first five year plan for the development of the national economy; Peking, 1955), p. 2.

[b] *TCKTTH* data office, "The Situation with Respect to Our Socialist Industrialization," *HHPYK*, January 25, 1957, p. 58. Small-scale industry is defined as any industry with 15 or fewer workers unless the industry lacks mechanical power, in which case it is defined as any enterprise with 30 or fewer workers (State Planning Commission, p. 2). Data on the output of these enterprises are crude approximations at best.

[c] These figures represent crude attempts at a minimum estimate of the gross value of production of all enterprises employing 500 or fewer persons. The estimate is made up of four parts:

(1). The gross value of output of handicraft industry. Although the average handicraft cooperative in 1956 had 51 employees, according to Chao I-wen, *Hsin Chung-kuo-te kung-yeh* (New China's industry; Peking, 1957), p. 109, it is doubtful that a significant number had over 500 persons. This was certainly true before 1956, as indicated by materials in Handicraft Industry Team of the Economic Research Office of the Chinese Scientific Institute, *Yi-chiu-wu-szu-nien ch'uan-kuo kuo-t'i shou-kung-yeh t'iao-ch'a tzu-liao* (Research materials on the individual handicraft industry in the entire country in 1954; Peking, 1957).

(2). Eighty-six per cent of the gross value of private industry in 1949 and 1953. In 1953 only 0.1 per cent of all private industrial enterprises had over 500 employees; see Kuan Ta-tung, *The Socialist Transformation of Capitalist Industry and Commerce in China* (Peking, 1960), pp. 24–25. Even if one makes the somewhat extreme assumptions that the average number of employees in this group was 1000 and that their productivity was twice that of other private industrial employees, the output of these large enterprises was only 14 per cent of all private industry. It is doubtful that the percentage in 1949 was any higher, since the average number of employees per enterprise was slightly lower.

(3). In joint public-private industry, it is assumed that all output in 1949 was in enterprises of over 500 employees (the average was 544), and in 1953 it is assumed somewhat arbitrarily that the percentage was 70 per cent (the average number of employees per enterprise had dropped to 261). In 1957, after all private industry had come under joint public-private management, the average number of employees per enterprise dropped to 74, even though a large number of private enterprises had been merged. It is assumed that these mergers and socialization lowered the percentage of private and joint enterprises over 500 persons to 25 per cent.

(4). It is assumed that 10 per cent of socialist industry was produced by small and medium enterprises. This percentage is a little over half the percentage of workers in such socialist enterprises in 1949. It is conservatively estimated that this percentage did not rise, even though the average number of persons per enterprise dropped from 520 to 300.

TABLE 9. Number and average size of industrial firms by type of ownership

Type of ownership	1949	1950	1951	1952	1953	1954	1955	1956
Socialist								
No. of firms	2,677[a]	—	—	10,671[b]	12,295[b]	13,666[b]	15,190[b]	—
Avg. no. of employees per firm	281[a]	—	—	236[c]	—	—	—	—
Gross value output per firm (1000 yuan)[d]	1,390	—	—	1,420	1,660	1,910	1,990	—
Cooperative[b]								
No. of firms	—	—	—	6,164	12,799	17,938	18,282	—
Private								
No. of firms	123,165[a]	133,018[a]	—	149,571[b]	150,275[b]	134,278[b]	88,809[b]	112,000[e]
Avg. no. of employees per firm	13[a]	14[a]	—	14[f]	15[f]	13[f]	15	—
Gross value output per firm (1000 yuan)	55[a]	55[a]	—	70[g]	87[g]	77[g]	82	—
Joint public-private[a]								
No. of firms	193	294	706	997	1,036	1,744	3,193	32,166
Avg. no. of employees per firm	546	445	236	249	261	306	246	74
Gross value output per firm (1000 yuan)	1,140	1,410	1,140	1,370	1,940	2,930	2,250	590
Total no. of firms[b]	—	—	—	167,403	176,405	167,626	125,474	—
Large- (and medium-) scale[b]	—	—	—	27,527	31,379	31,187	—	—
Small-scale[b]	—	—	—	139,876	145,026	136,439	—	—

[a] Chao I-wen, *Hsin Chung-kuo-te kung-yeh*, pp. 35, 64, 75. The number of socialist employees per enterprise in 1949 is for production workers only.

[b] *Jen-min shou-ts'e, 1957*, p. 428.

[c] The total number of workers and employees in socialist industry in 1952 is given in *First Five Year Plan for Development of the National Economy of the People's Republic of China in 1953–1957* (Peking, 1956), p. 190.

[d] SSB, *Ten Great Years*, p. 37, gives the total gross value of socialist industry.

[e] Hsueh Mu-chiao and others, *Socialist Transformation*, p. 217. This figure antedates socialization.

[f] Yin and Yin, *Economic Statistics of Mainland China*, p. 70.

[g] *Ibid.*, p. 44.

[109]

pressed in value added terms), they also have accounted for a substantial if declining portion of the increase in industrial output.

A by-product of this smallness of scale has been a large number of individual enterprises, as shown in Table 9. With over 170,000 firms in 1953 and, even after many consolidations, approximately 125,000 in 1955, the problem of centrally directing and controlling industry no longer appears as simple relative to agriculture or to the industrial sectors of more developed countries as it might if one's focus were on Anshan.

One effect of the backwardness and smallness of scale of Chinese industry was to necessitate the continued use of a certain amount of decentralized control through manipulation of wholesale prices. During 1950–1952, industrial wholesale prices were determined almost solely by the market, and these prices in turn determined distribution. As a result of the Korean War and industrial-recovery demands, coupled with the United States embargo, industrial prices in this period rose sharply relative to prices in other sectors. Gradually, however, the state gained control over markets for a number of major producers' goods. In Shanghai, for example, the state initially only controlled 9.8 per cent of the market supply of metals and machinery, but control had risen to 56.2 per cent by the final quarter of 1952.[14] As state control increased, price formation became a function controlled by the central authorities,[15] and the rapid introduction of rationing for key producers' goods[16] greatly reduced what little effect the market still had on prices.

Once the Chinese Communists had attained control of producers' goods prices, instead of following the Soviet practice of pricing producers' goods at 3 to 5 per cent above average cost, they froze these prices at the levels prevailing during the Korean War. Even after a major reduction in these prices in 1955–56, their level in 1957 was still 43 per cent above average cost and presumably remained at or near that level through 1963. For

[14] Shanghai Price Book, pp. 380–381, 395.

[15] Once the state gained control of prices there was no longer a single wholesale price for each commodity. There also were "transfer" and "ex-factory" prices. For a discussion of the minor differences, if any, between these concepts, see Appendix B.

[16] See note 3.

TABLE 10. Tax plus profits as per cent of average cost on individual commodities

Commodity	Per cent
All commodities (1957)[a]	50
Consumers' goods	
Cotton cloth (1957)[b]	107
rate on yarn	43
rate on cloth	52
Cigarettes[c]	160–335
Sugar[c]	40
Grain[d]	15–20
Average of light industry (including commerce)[e]	47
Producers' goods	
Electric power (1956)[f]	101
State iron and steel enterprises[f]	25
Average of heavy industry[e]	43

[a] This is a crude estimate based on budget data and the gross value of industrial production (in 1957 prices). First, total revenue from the profits of state-owned enterprises was added to the total of the industrial and commercial tax. Enterprise profit not paid in to the treasury was approximately 2 billion yuan (derived from 1958 total and percentage increase over 1957, Ministry of Finance, "Report on Questions Pertaining to Present Enterprise Finance Work," February 25, 1959, *FKHP*, IX, 132), which was somewhat larger than estimated depreciation expenses of 1.5 billion yuan (5 per cent of fixed capital). If one assumes, to be conservative, that half the planned paid-in profit of transport and commerce was not from the transport and sale of industrial products and deducts this sum from the original total, one arrives at a figure which is approximately 50 per cent of total cost.

[b] Profit on yarn (standard 21-count) in 1957 was 42.88 per cent of cost in Shanghai, the major production area (Chin Liu-fan, "A Preliminary Analysis of Cotton Yarn Prices in Our Country," *CCYC*, December 17, 1959, p. 46). This figure is consistent with other cost and price data for Shanghai (*WKKT*, p. 173; Shanghai Price Book, pp. 490–491) for years when the rate of utilization of spindles was low and cost was relatively high (it rises to 57 per cent in good years). The cost of yarn used in producing one bolt of cloth (36.576 meters) can be derived from data in *WKKT*, p. 170. If one assumes that yarn makes up 85 per cent of the cost of making standard 12-lb. cloth, whose average price in 1957 was 35.7 yuan per bolt (Huang K'o, "How We May Settle the Disequilibrium between Social Purchasing Power and the Supply Volume of Goods in 1958," *CHCC*, November 9, 1957, translated in *ECMM*, no. 119, p. 33), one arrives at the figures in the table. The profit rate on both yarn and cloth is consistent with data on the amount of net income derived by the state from a bale of yarn and a bolt of cloth (Chia To-fu, "Speech at Outstanding Workers' Conference," *Kung-jen jih-pao*, May 9, 1956, translated in *URS*, vol. III, no. 17, p. 236).

[c] The amount of profits plus sales taxes per unit of output of cigarettes and sugar is given in *TCKTTH* data office, "Questions Concerning Socialist Industrialization," *TCKTTH*, no. 21, November 14, 1956, translated in *ECMM*, no. 69, p. 33. The price used for sugar is the estimate in Appendix B. There are a wide variety of price quotations for cigarettes (Tientsin *TKP*; *Ching-chi chou-pao*; Shanghai Price Book, pp. 542–543), but the standard price appears to be about 2 yuan per box of 200, which would yield a profit of 335 per cent. The 160 per cent figure is derived using a price of 2.5 yuan per 200.

[d] Liu Yuan, "Food Grain Prices Fixed by the State Are Reasonable," *Liaoning jih-pao*, September 20, 1957, translated in *SCMP*, no. 1658, p. 18, states that the profit margin on the planned purchase and supply of grain was 20 to 25 per cent. Ma Feng-hwa, "The Financing of Public Investment in Communist China," unpub. diss., University of Michigan, 1959, p. 66, states that he believes that this does not include storage, handling, and transport charges even though Liu Yuan states that it is gross profit. I, however, believe it is safer to assume the figure represents what Liu says it does. Another source (*JMJP*, October 25, 1959) states that the purchase sales differential was 8 per cent. This appears to be low and may be net of taxes, which would bring the figure closer to 15 per cent.

[e] Fan Jo-yi, "A Brief Discussion of the Profit Rate on Capital," *CHCC*, August 23, 1958, p. 28, gives the profit rate of light industry as 32 per cent and that of commerce as 11 per cent. Adding the two gives a very crude estimate of the total rate. This rate presumably includes the tax, since Fan is talking about comparing returns from investment in different types of enterprises. The estimate may be biased downward, both by the exclusion of transport profits and by the assumption that the profit rate refers mainly to sales of consumers' goods. The heavy-industry profit rate is that given by Fan without any addition for commercial profit.

[f] *WKKT*, pp. 28, 30–31, 73. The iron and steel figure may be biased downward because of its being derived from total profits of metallurgical industries belonging to iron and steel enterprises and the gross value of production of state iron and steel enterprises, which may include other enterprises.

many individual commodities, the level was much higher (see Table 10).

Wholesale prices in the consumers' goods industrial sector, of course, could not be priced at or near cost unless the regime either wanted to ration all consumers' goods distribution or abandon its emphasis on producers' goods. Except during the first few years when producers' goods were sold on the market, however, similar reasoning for such goods does not apply.

There apparently were two principal reasons, other than inertia or the need to deal with a private sector, why high wholesale prices for industrial producers' goods were retained. In the first place, average costs varied greatly among enterprises in a given industry. The difference in average cost between a large- and small-scale copper-ore-dressing plant, for example, was 32 per cent.[17] These differences were partly the result of more backward technique in some firms and partly due to unavoidably different conditions under which production took place (for example, the different depths at which coal seams were found). Newly constructed enterprises and mines also tended to operate with high costs for several years, so that disparities in costs were a function of the industry's growth rate as well.[18] If prices were set at the average costs of the industry as a whole, many firms would have had to operate at a loss, thus necessitating widespread subsidies. Given the number of firms involved and the prevailing crude state of data pertaining to the less modern firms, this would have been a formidable administrative task. Even the extensive use of subsidies in the Soviet Union (for different reasons)[19] had, at best, been a necessary evil.

[17] Secretariat of the National Conference for Small Scale Ore Dressing Plants, "A Small Copper Dressing Plant Built and Put into Operation in Only 21 Days," *Yu-se chin-shu*, February 18, 1959, translated in *JPRS*, no. 1080D, p. 9. Other examples of cost disparities are for 21-count yarn, wheat flour, grade "C" cigarettes, and matches, which were 70, 100, 50, and 150 per cent respectively (*Kung-jen jih-pao*, May 9, 1956, translated in *URS*, vol. III, no. 17).

[18] For example, costs of newly constructed coal mines were 100 per cent higher in the first year of operation and required three to five years to reach full capacity. Chang Meng-tseng, "The Problem of Product Prices in the State Coal Industry," *Ts'ai-cheng*, March 5, 1958, pp. 14–15.

[19] Soviet subsidies were made necessary because producers' goods prices were held constant during periods when wage inflation was driving up costs.

Second, high producers' goods prices were maintained because they still played some distributive function. The 235 rationed commodities (in 1956) were not the only industrial producers' goods, and even portions of the 235 could not really be handled by central planners in a systematic way, and hence were sold on the market. After the Eighth Party Congress in 1956, in particular, distribution procedures were loosened considerably.[20] There even was a debate in the economic journals over what level heavy industrial prices should be in which proponents of a lower price policy argued that it would tend to encourage adoption of new techniques. The argument, however, was not completely convincing because it was admitted even by its proponents that demand for such goods already exceeded their supply.[21] Nevertheless, low prices for items such as abundant raw materials undoubtedly encouraged their use in a marginal way even when these materials were rationed. Given a choice between two substitutes, a factory manager probably put more pressure on the authorities to obtain the cheaper of the two. There also is evidence that the transport price structure existing prior to 1955 and poorly determined area price differentials tended to encourage irrational transport.[22] Even in the sectors most subject to central planning, therefore, prices continued to play a significant if subordinate role.

Large numbers of small-scale, backward enterprises also dictated the nature of enterprise taxation and for reasons similar to why a high price policy was pursued. In the Soviet Union, most state revenue from enterprises came from the turnover, or sales, tax, not the profits tax.[23] In China, in contrast, profits taxes surpassed sales taxes in importance by 1954, and by 1959 had grown to twice the level of sales taxes.[24] The reasoning behind this em-

[20] See speech by Ch'en Yun, *Eighth National Congress*, II, 157–176.
[21] See Fan Jo-yi, "More on the Price Policy for Heavy Industry Products," *CCYC*, June 17, 1957, translated in *ECMM*, no. 93, p. 14; Nan Ping and So Chen, "The Value of the Means of Production and the Function of the Law of Value under the Socialist System," *CCYC*, February 17, 1957, pp. 38–51.
[22] *JMJP* editorial, "Reform of the Railroad Price System," *HHYP*, June 28, 1955, pp. 128–129; and Fan Jo-yi, p. 28.
[23] Holzman, *Soviet Taxation*, p. 222.
[24] Yin and Yin, *Economic Statistics of Mainland China*, p. 85; Li Hsien-nien, "Report on the Final State Accounts for 1959 and the Draft State Budget for 1960" (March 30, 1960), *Second Session of the Second National People's Con-*

phasis was relatively straightforward. Since sales taxes were a fixed percentage of price, given the wide disparities in costs in particular industries, a high sales tax would have caused many firms to make losses, whereas a low tax would leave low-cost firms with large profits that could then be taken away by a profits tax. The former thus necessitated subsidies, while the latter did not. It was possible with a high-tax policy to allow special tax reductions for less efficient firms, and this on occasion was done,[25] but such a procedure had little to recommend it over the use of subsidies.

The major advantage of high sales taxes was that they enhanced financial discipline. High profits and profits taxes tended to reduce pressures to lower costs, since higher costs could always be taken out of profits and profits taxes in such a way that the state ended up paying the bill. By making it easier to obtain funds, therefore, the central authorities actually reduced the significance of profits and hence of the market in the eyes of factory managers. This, however, was a burden the state, consciously or otherwise, was willing to pay to avoid the administrative burden of centrally determined subsidies or tax rebates.

Other decentralization measures taken in 1957 and 1958, on paper at least, tended to enhance the role of prices and the market. The major formal changes were reduction in compulsory plan targets from twelve to four, enhancement of the profits target, and reduction of the portion of investment that was controlled through the central plan. The intended increase in the role of market forces can be seen from the fact that two of the remaining four targets were profits and the total wage bill, and that retained profits were raised and control over the purposes for which retained profits could be used was relaxed.[26] In addition, the amount of investment not coordinated through the central plan, when expressed as a percentage of total investment,

gress of the People's Republic of China (Documents) (Peking, 1960), pp. 50, 59.

[25] Lo Keng-mo, "The Question of the Turnover Tax on Heavy Industrial Products," CCYC, June 17, 1956, p. 28.

[26] SC, "Regulation Putting into Effect the Enterprise Retained Profits System," FKHP, VII, 239–242; Ministry of Finance, "Regulation on 1956 State Enterprise Profits," FKHP, IV, 267–268.

doubled in 1957 over 1956 and was doubled again in 1958.[27] Construction units were given greater independence in handling funds allocated to them, although the principle of separating working capital from investment funds was retained.[28] The net effect of these measures, together with the relaxation in procedures for allocating industrial products and raw materials and the already-existing high price policy for industrial producers' goods, should have been to enhance significantly the role of market forces in directing industrial firms. In fact, the role of the market, from 1958 through 1960 at least, was greatly reduced. This was because the system of controls, in practice, was very different from what it was supposed to be in theory, but this is the subject of the next chapter.

In their search for formal decentralization measures, the Chinese Communists by no means relied solely on directives involving greater reliance on the market. A major effort was made in 1958, for example, to transfer responsibility for directing a large number of enterprises from Peking to provincial governments. Only the largest firms and those producing key materials remained under direct authority of the central government. For most others, responsibility for coordination of distribution and other important functions passed down to provincial authorities.[29] This was possible because these enterprises' major inputs were locally grown or manufactured, thus requiring little or no coordination with enterprises in other provinces. In 1958, authority to determine prices in many cases also was passed down to provincial authorities, probably mainly on the theory that they would be closer to the actual situation and thus could set prices

[27] Derived from data in Table 7.

[28] SC, "Regulations on Reforming the Basic Construction Financial Management System" (July 5, 1958), *FKHP*, VIII, 123–124. This regulation proved to be too liberal and was revised: SC, "Revised Regulations on Changing the Basic Construction Management System" (May 20, 1959), *FKHP*, IX, 135–137.

[29] CCPCC and SC, "Several Regulations on Advancing the Commodity Distribution System" (September 24, 1958), *FKHP*, VIII, 100–101; "Why Are Supply Plans for Certain Commodities under Unified Distribution and Ministry Control To Be Placed in the Hands of Provincial and Municipal Governments?" *Shang-yeh kung-tso*, September 12, 1957, translated in *ECMM*, no. 118, pp. 44–46; CCPCC and SC, "Regulation Changing the Method of Examining and Approving the Plans for Above Limit Basic Construction Items" (September 24, 1958), *FKHP*, VIII, 102–105.

more accurately.[30] This may have improved such things as setting prices according to quality, but it is doubtful that it introduced any real flexibility into pricing, since provincial authorities probably were more afraid to allow price increases than the central authorities. It is doubtful, therefore, that this move had much effect on the role of the market. Chinese Communist attempts to develop small-scale industries under the auspices of communes and even schools and army units also involved little increased reliance on the market.

The large number of industrial enterprises, deficient data pertaining to all but the largest and most modern of those enterprises, and the desire to avoid the high costs of wholesale adoption of capital-intensive Western and Soviet technology, therefore, all encouraged the Chinese Communists to experiment with modifications in their essentially centralized system of planning and control. These considerations partially offset the advantages of centralization deriving from the relatively small number of investment projects to plan and the limited interdependence between sectors. It was the relative lack of interdependence, in fact, which made possible the decentralization of authority to provincial and commune cadres. It was the same lack of interdependence, however, that allowed the regime to think of decentralization and market control as something other than synonymous concepts. On the other hand, this consideration was only one of several reasons why the market was not the major decentralization device formally promulgated, and, more important, why market control was not very effective even in areas where its intended role was significant. These other reasons are the subject of the next chapter.

[30] CCPCC and SC, "Regulation on Spheres of Price Control and the Commercial Management System" (April 11, 1958), *FKHP*, VII, 315–318.

CHAPTER VI

Ideology and Inexperience
in the Control of Industry

Success Criteria for Plant Managers

Extralegal and illegal moves at lower levels of authority constantly frustrate the workings of the formal control structure. These nonlegal factors not only affect the issue of centralization versus decentralization or physical versus market controls, but, in addition, the issue whether it is possible at all to direct efficiently socialized industries in an underdeveloped country such as China, whatever the controls used.

The major source of difficulty arose out of the nature of the Communist party control apparatus and the people who manned it. The essence of minority Communist control in China is that all key positions, whether military, political, or economic, be held by party members of demonstrated loyalty. The effect of this system in the agricultural sector was discussed at length in Chapter IV. On occasion in industry and elsewhere, high formal titles are bestowed on nonparty personnel, but in all such cases a subordinate party member exercises real control. Party members of sufficient standing to be appointed factory managers, heads of factory party committees, and to higher positions, however, have usually built their reputations in guerrilla warfare against Japan and the Nationalists.[1] Although thoroughly indoctrinated in Communist ideology, they generally have had little

---

[1] This information was obtained from interviews by the author with refugees in a position to know; from miscellaneous published sources such as plays and novels about factories — for instance, Hsia Yen, *K'ao-yen* (The test; Peking, 1959), and Ai Wu, *Steel and Tempered* (Peking, 1961); and foreign visitors — see Sripati Chandra-Sekhar, *Red China: An Asian View* (New York, 1961), pp. 62, 65–66, and Snow, *The Other Side of the River,* p. 207.

or no formal education.[2] This combination of Marxism and lack of sophistication together generated attitudes incompatible with the efficient use of such tools as financial and market controls and even with the rational allocation of resources in general.[3] Reality and Russian experience and advice forced modifications in these attitudes, but did not submerge them completely.

Party leadership, if anything, has tended to increase over time, although there also have been major retreats from excessive party control. In early years the state had to depend heavily on management skills in private industry and on older, and hence often non-Communist, employees in state industry. From 1956 through 1960, however, the position of factory party committees in control of firms was greatly enhanced, as was the importance of party personnel in the enterprises in general.[4] It was this move, in fact, that made possible the various decentralization measures of that period. The state felt it could not decentralize authority without first ensuring that those upon whom the new authority fell were completely under the direction and influence of the party. This policy had a number of undesirable effects whose reasons are discussed below. These effects led in 1961 and 1962 to a partial restoration of the authority of factory managers.[5] In late 1963 and throughout 1964, however, the pendulum seemed to

[2] In September 1955, only 5.73 per cent of the top leadership personnel of industrial enterprises had graduated from universities or specialist schools of a comparable level, as contrasted with 56.03 per cent for the engineering and technical personnel of the same enterprises. *TCKTTH* data office, "The Breakdown and Organization of the Number of Workers and Employees in Our Country in 1955," *HHPYK,* January 25, 1957, p. 89.

[3] Aside from its political implications, resource allocation has little or no place in Marxist ideology. See P. J. D. Wiles, *The Political Economy of Communism* (Cambridge, Mass., 1962), pp. 50–56.

[4] See speech of Li Hsueh-feng, *Eighth National Congress,* II, 304–317. In addition to discussing the enhanced role of party committees, Li also states that in 1956 most of the cadres in enterprises were party members (p. 315).

[5] See, for example, Basic-level Organization Section, Finance and Trade Department, Chinese Communist Party Tientsin Municipal Committee, "Further Implement the System of Responsibility of Directors under the Leadership of Party Committees," Peking *TKP,* November 20, 1961, translated in *SCMP,* no. 2643, pp. 8–12; and Chinese Communist Party Committee of the Commerce Bureau, Kingtechen Municipality, "Thoroughly Enforce the Party Committee System in Enterprises and Fully Develop the Role of Collective Leadership" (the title is misleading), Peking *TKP,* March 28, 1962, translated in *SCMP,* no. 2725, pp. 1–8.

be swinging back with the renewed advocacy of more party control in industry.[6]

The party committee was, of course, an important element in Soviet plant management, too, and in theory played a similar role to that of party committees in Chinese factories. In both countries the committee was supposed to be a supervisory organization that was not to interfere directly with management, but in China, particularly after 1956, this distinction was not clearly made in practice, probably to a greater degree than was the case in the Soviet Union in the 1930's. Furthermore, the Chinese Communist Party remained much more of a revolutionary party than its Soviet counterpart of the 1930's. Not only party committees, but factory managers themselves, appear to have identified themselves more closely with this spirit than with the technical and administrative aspects of their enterprises.[7]

Attitudes generated by this system of party control manifested themselves, first of all, in a tendency on the part of factory managers to ignore all plan targets other than those for the physical output of major products or the gross value of output (before 1957). This ignoring of financial targets, such as profits, was not only the result of attitudes of factory managers, but also, to some degree, of attitudes held by central planners themselves.[8] This may have resulted partly from the fact that Chinese planners were trained by their Soviet counterparts (as were factory managers), and thus acquired much of the same scale of priorities. Planners also were out of the same mold as factory managers and could therefore be expected to hold some of the same ideas.

[6] See "Political Work Is the Lifeline of All Work," *Hung-ch'i*, March 31, 1964, translated in *Current Scene*, supplement, vol. I, no. 1, pp. 1–10. For a further discussion of some of these issues prior to this tendency for the pendulum to swing back, see Franz Schurmann, "Economic Policy and Political Power in Communist China," *The Annals of the American Academy of Political and Social Science*, CCCXLIX (September 1963), 49–69.

[7] For a discussion of the role of the party committee in the Soviet firm, see Granick, *Management of the Industrial Firm in the USSR*, chap. xii.

[8] Ishikawa, *Chugoku ni okeru shihon chikuseki kiko*, pp. 92–93. His sources were Hsueh Mu-chiao, "Preliminary Views on the Present Plan Management System," *CHCC*, September 9, 1957, p. 27; Sun Yeh-fang, "A Discussion of 'Gross Value of Output,'" *TCKT*, July 14, 1957, pp. 8, 10; and Yu Tai-ch'ien, "Can We Use 'Profit' in Place of 'Production Value?'" *TCKT*, March 14, 1957, p. 16.

Too much emphasis should not be placed on the effect of central planners' attitudes, however. The problem of enforcing financial targets was a part of the more general problem of getting enterprises to work according to plan, any plan, rather than to expand indiscriminately with whatever resources were at hand. In the initial period, central authorities concentrated on getting a rational calculation system into all major enterprises and in getting some semblance of obedience to plans sent down from higher authorities. At that time, plans were changed fairly frequently well after work on the projects had begun, and, in the financial field, many enterprises even lacked sufficient data from which to calculate production costs.[9] Planning at the national level was equally crude. The state began working out basic plan targets in 1951 and 1952, but the actual introduction of annual plans did not begin until 1953,[10] and the first five-year plan (1953–1957) did not come out until 1955. Even after planning became more sophisticated, however, the tendency remained to put primary emphasis on fulfilling production targets whatever the effect on other targets.[11]

Nevertheless, throughout this period and into 1958 the state continued to put pressure on enterprises to pay more attention to financial matters in general and profits and cost targets in particular. The principal effort was placed on increasing the importance of the profits target in the eyes of plant managers. In 1954 the Ministry of Finance issued a directive stating that enterprises could keep 40 per cent of profits that were in excess of the plan's profit target, and these funds could be used to meet shortages in circulating capital and a number of other items.[12] In 1956 this

[9] Fu I-kang, "Raise the Financial Work of State Enterprises One Step," *HHYP*, September 20, 1950, p. 1377; "No Work Should Be Begun without Planning," *JMJP*, June 16, 1951, translated in *CB*, no. 119, p. 3.

[10] Li Fu-chun, speech, *Eighth National Congress*, II, 292.

[11] Chou En-lai, "Report on the Work of the Government" (September 23, 1954), *Documents of the First Session of the First National People's Congress* (Peking, 1955), p. 84; Statistics Unit, Department of Planning, Ministry of Heavy Industry, "The Execution of Production Plans in 1955," *Chung-kung-yeh t'ung-hsun*, no. 1, January 1, 1956, translated in *ECMM*, no. 35, pp. 21, 23; Po I-po, speech to National People's Congress, *Nan-fang jih-pao*, July 31, 1955, translated in *CB*, no. 353, p. 5.

[12] Ministry of Finance, "Methods of Dividing and Using Profits of State

regulation was liberalized slightly in that funds from this source could be carried over into the next year and bonuses were to be given specifically for exceeding planned profits.[13] Both directives stated that all enterprise bonus funds were to be taken out of profits in excess of the plan's profit target before making the 40–60 split. Bonuses, however, do not appear to have had the significance in China that they have had in the Soviet Union. There does not appear to have been, for example, anything comparable to the bonuses paid to factory managers in the Soviet Union.[14] In China, leadership cadres in enterprises theoretically were not supposed to receive bonuses at all. There were various perquisites which went with high office, such as homes, cars, servants, and vacations at special resorts, but these appear to have been related to position rather than the fulfillment of goals — though the evidence on this point is far from conclusive.[15]

Bonuses paid, therefore, went to workers and technical personnel. Although it was undoubtedly desirable for a manager to have a large fund available for this purpose, it will be argued in the next chapter that bonuses helped to promote diligence among employees but were not needed to attract new workers. Hence they probably were less important than in the Soviet Union for this reason as well.

Other measures taken to enhance the role of financial targets,

Enterprises in Excess of the Plan in 1954" (October 18, 1955), *FKHP*, II, 523–524.

[13] Ministry of Finance, "Regulation on 1956 State Enterprise Profits," *FKHP*, IV, 267–268.

[14] Berliner, *Factory and Manager in the USSR*, chaps. iii and iv.

[15] This information is derived from discussions with long-term residents of China in a position to know, from the fact that bonus laws seem always to be worded such that they do not apply to managers, and criticisms of bonuses given to enterprise cadres, in *JMJP*, May 5, 1957. There is also some evidence to the contrary. One source published in January 1952 — *Shanghai kung-shang tz'u-liao* (Shanghai industrial and commercial materials), p. 192, referred to in Ishikawa, *Chugoku ni okeru shihon chikuseki kiko*, pp. 93–94 — includes a bonus system for plant managers. This, however, is the only such directive of which either I or Professor Ishikawa are aware, and it may only reflect the tendency to copy Soviet practice *in toto* in those earlier years. There is also a later directive that may have applied to factory managers, though there is nothing in it that specifically says so: SC, "Temporary Regulation on Bonuses for the Working Personnel of State Administrative Organs" (October 26, 1957), *HHPYK*, November 25, 1957, pp. 88–90).

and thus of price and market influences, were the already-mentioned reduction in number of targets to four and the increase in the portion of profits retained by the firm. None of these measures had the desired effect, however, not only because of the attitudes of plant managers, but also because of the state of financial controls in general, not just financial targets.

Control of Enterprise Funds, 1950–1963

The ease with which enterprises could obtain funds for just about any purpose undermined Chinese Communist efforts to enhance the role of profits targets as well as market controls in general. This lax control of funds resulted partly from a tendency on the part of plant managers to ignore most financial regulations, not just financial plan targets, and partly because of lack of sympathy with tight financial control even at the highest levels within the party.

First of all, it should be pointed out that lax financial policies did not exist because financial authorities lacked sufficient legal power to carry out their duties, or sufficient political power to exercise their legal authority. Furthermore, unlike the Soviet Union, the interests of financial authorities were not intertwined with those of the enterprise itself.[16] The legal financial structure was described in detail in the previous chapter and need not detain us here.

Something further needs to be said, however, about the political power and relative independence of the banking and financial authorities. The Minister of Finance, first Po I-po, and later Li Hsien-nien, was always among the top echelon in the Communist hierarchy. Li Hsien-nien, for example, was later placed on both the Politburo and the Secretariat of the Chinese Communist Party. In the Politburo he was one of only four who could be classified as being primarily concerned with economic affairs.[17] The head of the People's Bank, Nan Han-ch'en, and later Ts'ao Chu-yu, did not have anything approaching comparable status, but both he and his deputy directors were Communist party mem-

---

[16] Holzman, *Soviet Taxation*, p. 37.
[17] The others were Ch'en Yun, Li Fu-chun, and T'an Chen-lin.

bers.[18] Furthermore, the Bank had the same authority as that of a ministry, so that it was directly subordinate only to the State Council and not to the Ministry of Finance, for instance. The independent attitude of financial authorities can also be seen from criticisms of its independence that appeared during the "great leap forward." [19]

Nevertheless, political independence and power led only sporadically to tight control of enterprise funds. Analysis of this phenomenon is best facilitated by a detailed account of the timing and degree of financial control and the reasons why control was lax or tight in particular periods.

An overabundance of funds during certain periods arose, first of all, from radical increases in direct budget appropriations. Investment in economic departments showed an increase of 65 per cent in 1953, 66 per cent in 1956, and 112 per cent in 1958, increases that undoubtedly outstripped the availability of construction materials and labor requirements. Appropriations for working capital also were erratic (see Table 11), but are a less useful indicator of the availability of such funds, primarily because the budget was only one of several sources of working capital.

A more important source of working capital came in the form of bank loans. Chinese Communist banking policy was not very sophisticated. At least through 1956 the relation between credit, budget expenditure, and revenue and the conditions of commodity demand and supply do not appear to have been fully recognized.[20]

---

[18] *Directory of Chinese Communist Leadership* (Hong Kong, November 1960), p. 40, and revised version (May 9, 1962), p. 42. The vice-ministers and sometimes even the ministers of less crucial ministries such as Forestry, Water Conservancy and Electric Power, Light Industry, and the like were not party members.

[19] See, for example, Tseng Chih, "To Handle Well Some Interrelated Matters of Fiscal Work," *Ts'ai-cheng*, May 24, 1959, translated in *ECMM*, no. 176, pp. 26–27; Chang Ch'uan-shu, "The Anshan Financial Office on How to Strengthen Enterprise Financial Overseeing Work," *Ts'ai-cheng*, January 5, 1958, pp. 25–27; *JMJP* columnist, "The Correct Way of Settling Industrial Circulating Capital Problems," *HHPYK*, September 10, 1958, pp. 122–123.

[20] Jung Tzu-ho, "The Question of Equilibrium for the State Budget, for the State Credit Plan, and for Supply and Demand of Commodities," *Ts'ai-cheng*, June 5, 1957, translated in *ECMM*, no. 90, pp. 11–16; Young Pei-hsin, "A

TABLE 11.   Budget allocations to economic departments (million yuan)

| Year | Economic construction | | |
	Total	Investment	Difference (working capital)
1950	1,740	—	—
1951	3,510	—	—
1952	7,630	3,330	4,300
1953	8,650	5,500	3,150
1954	12,360	6,790	5,570
1955	13,760	7,600	6,160
1956	15,910	12,430	3,480
1957	14,910	11,630	3,280
1958	26,270	29,900	1,630
1959	32,170	24,640	2,270

Source: For the years 1950–1958, the source is SSB, *Ten Great Years*, pp. 23, 57–58. The investment figures were obtained by subtracting investment in administration, culture and education, health, city public works, and other from total within-plan investment. The 1959 total for economic construction is from Li Hsien-nien, "Report on the Final State Accounts for 1959," *Second Session of the Second National People's Congress*, pp. 49–73, and the investment figure was obtained by assuming that non-economic investments and basic construction investment outside the plan were the same as in 1958 (total investment was the same as 1958). The difference between the first two columns is probably, but not certainly, working capital.

Loans apparently were issued to anyone with a legitimate economic purpose provided the total did not exceed some limit, probably mainly determined by the level of deposits. Since deposits were inflated by inclusion of the previous years' accumulated budget surpluses, banks did not lack for funds. For the Soviet Union, Professor R. P. Powell has argued that such a "commercial loan" credit policy was inherently inflationary.[21] Prior to 1958 in China, however, these policies may have contributed to laxity in financial control, but they do not appear to have been

Study on the Problem of Balance among the Financial Revenue and Expenditure, Cash Income and Outgo, and the Supply and Demand of Commodities," *CCYC*, October 17, 1957, pp. 50–63, which attempts to refute "rightist" accusations regarding the lack of recognition of these relationships.

[21] As quoted in Holzman, *Soviet Taxation*, p. 27.

inherently inflationary. In 1953 through 1956, for example, circulating capital of state industrial enterprises increased at approximately the same rate as the increase in gross value of industrial production.[22] Even in 1954, when surpluses of that year plus previous years of over 6 billion yuan were deposited in the People's Bank,[23] the increase in state industry's circulating capital was only 11 per cent.

In 1958 and 1959, however, there was a radical change in loan policy. Restraint that had been exercised up to then was at least partially removed. Part of the increase in loans that took place merely was a result of a changeover from providing circulating capital through the budget to providing it by loans. This process began in 1958 [24] and completely replaced budget appropriations in 1959.[25] That the increase was not only due to changes in procedure is indicated by the fact that total deposits in the People's Bank in 1958 increased by an amount equal to the increase during the entire first five-year plan. In 1959 these deposits rose by another 35 per cent over 1958.[26]

It does not follow that banking and financial authorities changed the principles upon which loans were granted. Increases in funds were less than reported increases in industrial output during these two years.[27] Ready availability of finances, therefore, probably resulted from the fact that credits were issued on the basis of spurious production data. By 1961 the regime recog-

[22] Jung Tzu-ho, "The Question of Equilibrium for the State Budget."

[23] Li Hsien-nien, "The 1954 Final Accounts and the 1955 Budget," Hong Kong *TKP,* July 1955, translated in *CB,* no. 336, p. 5.

[24] Li Hsien-nien, "The Implementation of the State Budget for 1957," *CB,* no. 493, p. 14.

[25] SC, "Revised Regulations Putting State Enterprise Capital under the Unified Management of the People's Bank," *FKHP,* IX, 121–125.

[26] Ch'en Hsi-ya, "The 1958 Banking Work and the 1959 Tasks," *Chung-kuo chin-jung,* May 25, 1959, translated in *ECMM,* no. 178, p. 29; Li Hsien-nien, "Report on the Final State Accounts for 1959," *Second Session of the Second National People's Congress,* p. 51. The switchover to loans would, if anything, have tended to reduce the size of total deposits since loans had to be paid back.

[27] The exact percentage increase in funds is not available but it can be deduced from the above-mentioned increases to be substantially less than 170 per cent, a figure derived by assuming that deposits at the end of 1952 were nonexistent, which was obviously not the case. The larger were deposits in 1952, the smaller is the percentage increase for 1958–59.

nized that the issuance of loans had been excessive. Articles re-
appeared rehashing the arguments in favor of maintaining a
balance between the budget, credit, and material supplies.[28] It apparently even was necessary to reiterate the fact that previous
years' surpluses could not be freely used.[29]

Easy access to legitimate sources of working capital was not
the only reason why control of such funds was lax. Financial
regulations were among the least obeyed of centrally issued legis-
lation. When the Communists established ownership and control
over certain key industrial and mining enterprises in 1949 and
1950, the financial system was in chaos. Even in the Northeast in
the middle of 1950, finances of state industrial enterprises were
in sufficient disorder that there must have been little or no effective financial control over them. Actual prices often were higher
than accounting prices, giving enterprises profits that they did
not have to turn into the treasury. Cost computations were extremely confused, thus also leaving considerable margin for expansion of circulating capital.[30] The regime at that time moved
swiftly to bring about some semblance of order by promulgation
of a whole series of financial directives. These measures did stop
the inflation and put some system into enterprise financial behavior, but their success should not be exaggerated. For example,
1950 regulations setting up many important aspects of financial
control specifically stated that state enterprises were not to obtain credit from each other in any form (and the various forms
were spelled out in detail) and could only obtain such credit
from the People's Bank.[31] Yet in the second quarter of 1954, this

[28] Ke Chih-ta and Wang Cho, "On Several Interrelations in Finance and
Banking," Peking *TKP*, November 17, 1961, translated in *SCMP*, no. 2650,
pp. 3–11; Ch'eng Yuan-yeh, "Strengthen the Concept of the Integral Whole,
Manage Credit Funds Properly," Peking *TKP*, June 13, 1962, translated in
SCMP, no. 2771, pp. 4–8.

[29] Wu Sheng-kuang and Ts'ai Jung-shu, "A Cursory Discussion of the
Previous Year's Surplus," Peking *TKP*, April 9, 1962, translated in *SCMP*, no.
2756, pp. 1–4.

[30] Fu I-kang, "Raise the Financial Work of State Enterprises," *HHYP*,
September 20, 1950, pp. 1376–1377; "Northeast Ministry of Industry's In-
vestigation of the Financial Situation in State Factories and Mines," *HHYP*,
September 20, 1950, pp. 1376–1377.

[31] Financial and Economic Committee, "Methods of Enforcing Currency
Management," *HHYP*, January 25, 1951, pp. 610–613.

type of credit made up 17.2 per cent of total circulating capital of enterprises under the jurisdiction of the five industrial ministries. Moreover, the directive ordering abolition of this credit only foresaw its gradual, not its immediate, abolition.[32] One of the key features of the entire financial situation was that funds were to be earmarked for specific purposes and to be used only for those purposes.[33] But five years later there were still complaints that funds were not sufficiently earmarked or were being used in ways other than had been intended. Various devices, for example, were still being used to inflate costs so that a larger portion of profits could be retained by enterprises than was authorized by the state.[34]

These deviations, on the other hand, should not be overemphasized. They were, it is true, widespread, but the fact that they were talked about so much is an indication that the central authorities were making considerable effort to bring financial behavior of enterprises into line. Since they started from almost total chaos in this area, one could not expect them to be completely successful in a short period of time, but successes that were achieved in these earlier years were largely dissipated by subsequent financial policies. Large increases in budget allocations in 1956 and 1958 have already been mentioned. At the same time, there also was a relaxation in the enforcement of financial regulations. Enterprises on a broad scale reverted to their former practices of ignoring limitations on the scope of use of particular funds, channeling substantial amounts of circulating capital into capital construction investment. Many items that did not belong there were included in costs of production, and prices used in

[32] People's Bank of China, "Report on Eliminating the Use of Commercial Credit between State Industries and between State Industries and Other State Enterprises as a Substitute for Bank Balances" (March 30, 1955), *FKHP*, I, 270–273; Ministry of Commerce and People's Bank of China, "Regulation Eliminating Commercial Credit within the State Commercial Network and between Various Departments" (May 28, 1955), *FKHP*, I, 278–286.

[33] *E.g.*, Northeast People's Government, "Temporary Regulations on the State Enterprise Financial System" (August 27, 1950), *HHYP*, September 20, 1950, pp. 1378–1379.

[34] A. M. Pilmin, "The Role of Public Finance in the Enforcement of the Economy and Austerity Program," *CCYC*, October 17, 1955, translated in *ECMM*, no. 21, p. 37.

calculating profit to be turned over to the state were set below prices at which the goods were actually sold.[35]

This relaxation allowed individual enterprises to accelerate turnover of funds greatly, and, together with the generally greater availability of funds, considerably eased their financial position. In the first half of 1956 the velocity of circulation of working capital increased by almost 20 per cent over the first half of 1955, and, after falling during the deflationary policies of 1957, rose again sharply in 1958 by about 30 per cent.[36]

The central authorities took a number of steps to correct this situation as early as the beginning of 1959, but since the 1959 and 1960 budgets provided for allocation of large sums of money for various purposes it is doubtful that there was much tightening up, at least in 1959. Furthermore, turning over all circulating capital to the People's Bank helped only to the extent that the bank felt that it would not be politically inexpedient to exercise its legal authority.

It does not appear likely that serious financial discipline was re-established until the decision was made at the ninth plenary session of the Eighth Party Central Committee (January 1961) to reduce the scale of capital construction and lower the rate of industrial development. This move appears to have been combined with a general attempt to re-establish effective financial control. How effective these measures have been it is not possible to say, but there is evidence that circumvention of regulations continued to some degree at least into 1962.[37]

The underlying causes of periodic laxity of financial control,

[35] SC, "Report on Several Questions Regarding Present Enterprise Financial Affairs Work" (February 25, 1959), *FKHP*, IX, 131–134. These latter two procedures could be thought of as increasing the quantity of working capital rather than accelerating its velocity, but since these items would not appear in official circulating-capital statistics, they would have the effect of increasing the velocity of circulation figures.

[36] Tseng Chih, "To Handle Matters of Fiscal Work," *ECMM*, no. 176, p. 29; *TCKT*, August 14, 1956, p. 6. The concept used by the Communists is the number of days needed for the turnover of funds.

[37] *TKP* editorial, "Satisfactorily Control and Use the Circulating Funds of Industry," Peking *TKP*, June 20, 1961, translated in *SCMP*, no. 2543, pp. 5–6; Investigation and Study Team, Canton Municipal Bureau of the Chemical Industry, "Spend Less Money and Do More Work," *Nan-fang jih-pao*, June 2, 1962, translated in *SCMP*, no. 2780, pp. 13–16.

both at central and enterprise levels, were similar in nature to the reasons why factory managers tended to ignore financial targets. When party control was strong, financial discipline was weak. This can best be illustrated by the events of 1958, an extreme example of forces that were always present.

The disappointment with economic performance in 1957 has already been described (see Chapter IV). This, together with the avalanche of criticism during the brief "hundred flowers," or free-speech, campaign, led, in the latter half of 1957, to strong counteraction by the party in an attempt to restore party discipline and the pre-eminence of Communist ideology. This attempt was so successful that it effectively cowed the voices of caution and restraint. Financial authorities, in particular, were intimidated by criticisms to the effect that, by maintaining tight financial discipline, they were ignoring Communist principles and placing too little faith in the masses.[38]

Direct attacks on financial authorities were not the only means whereby financial control was weakened. The basic idea of the "great leap" was that tremendous economic advances could be achieved if party cadres in factories and communes were given free reign to exercise initiative. Any constraints not just financial ones, on this initiative would simply hamper progress. In the light of this reasoning, even central planning was considered excessively restrictive. Plan targets, as a result, no longer had to balance out with each other, but only had to be set high enough to give cadres a really "great leap" to shoot at. This process lost all touch with reality when statistics were subjected to similar considerations, that is, grossly falsified to show that any procedure recommended by the cadres had, in fact, achieved the predicted results. The "great leap," therefore, was not a decentralization of authority at least partially through the market, as some of the formal regulations discussed in the previous chapter seem to indicate, but a decentralization subject to no constraints other

---

[38] The senior financial cadres, like other cadres, held the positions they did because of their contributions to the revolution, not because of their financial skills. Like factory managers in large enterprises, they commonly lacked much formal education. Because of this and their party affiliations they could be expected to respond willingly to party pressures (Ezra Vogel, unpublished manuscript).

than those of party discipline and ideology. Chinese Communist ideology had little to say about problems of allocation, so that the not surprising result of this decentralization was economic anarchy.

The situation prior to and following the "great leap forward," with respect to financial controls and the market, was no different in nature, only in degree. Factory managers tended to ignore financial targets and controls whenever possible. As a result, they also tended to ignore most market influences, even in the comparatively limited areas where one would have expected, from formal regulations, that the market would have had some effect. When the market did have influence, it was because authorities at higher levels were able to overcome political and ideological pressures and exercise reasonably tight control of enterprise finances. Tight financial control meant that factory managers had to pay some attention to market forces in order to conserve financial resources.

Effect of Financial Control on Industrial Output and Cost, 1950–1963

Determining the periods when financial control was tight and when it was lax is not difficult. Appraising the effects of financial control or lack of it on industrial output and costs of production is another matter. Unlike agriculture, in the industrial sector there have been no dramatic increases or decreases in the production of key commodities that are directly and solely related to the availability of enterprise financing. The slowdown in industrial development in 1957 and the sharp drop and only partial recovery in factory output in 1960 through 1963 resulted in part from "easy money" policies toward industry. Of greater importance, however, were the performance of agriculture, the withdrawal of Soviet technicians and plans in 1960, and the abandonment of planning of all kinds.

Nor do data on labor productivity and unit costs of production provide one with much greater insight. Labor productivity rose rapidly through 1958, not because of greater efficiency necessarily, but because the amount of capital per laborer also increased substantially.[39] It is worth noting that the profit rate on capital fell at least from 1955 to 1957,[40] but this too is to be expected whenever manufacturing processes rapidly become more capital intensive.[41] Such data indicate that the balance between the use of capital- and labor-intensive technique may be less than ideal, a fact the Chinese Communists recognized and tried to deal with by emphasis on small-scale industry during the "great leap forward," but in themselves they tell little about the efficiency with which these techniques were being used.

Statistics on costs of production are not of much greater help. From 1953 on, the Chinese Communists opened many new plants. New factories, particularly those of a type with which a country has had no previous experience, tend to operate at very high costs for a few years. Such costs are bound to fall rapidly, even under conditions of considerable inefficiency. In longer-established industries the meaning of cost data is not much clearer. Per-unit costs in consumers' goods industries dependent on agriculture fluctuate widely, not so much the result of changing attitudes toward efficiency, as the level of the previous year's harvest. Because imports of agricultural raw materials are severely restricted, a bad harvest in cotton, for example, causes the textile industry to operate below capacity, thus raising per-unit fixed costs.

It is not impossible to sort out the underlying causes of changes in labor productivity and costs, but the effort would take us well beyond the scope of this book.[42] Nevertheless, it is desirable to attempt a cursory and somewhat impressionistic appraisal in order to put the effects of lax financial control in perspective.

For 1954 and 1955, there is evidence to suggest that increasing centralized control over finances and supervision of enterprise

---

[39] *E.g.*, between 1953 and 1955, fixed capital per worker in industry rose from 6060 to 8000 yuan. Fan Jo-yi, "A Brief Discussion of the Profit Rate," *CHCC*, August 23, 1958, p. 22.

[40] The rate dropped from 23.1 per cent in 1955 to below 20 per cent in 1957 (*ibid.*, p. 23).

[41] Technological improvements can offset a tendency for the rate of profits to fall as processes become more capital intensive, but they are less likely to be sufficient when the move toward more greatly capital-intensive processes is particularly rapid as it was in China.

[42] A work on labor productivity is presently being undertaken by R. Michael Field.

activities in general was beginning to have an effect. Iron and steel enterprises that met or surpassed all four major plan goals (value of output, labor productivity, cost, and profit) rose from 50 per cent of all such enterprises in 1953 to 81.3 per cent in 1955. Iron and steel firms meeting only one target (presumably output in most cases) fell from 16.7 per cent to zero.[43] Economization of electricity throughout the country rose by 22 per cent in 1954 over 1953, and by another 55 per cent in 1955, bringing about savings of 10 million yuan in 1955.[44] In 1953 only 30 per cent of enterprises under the Ministry of Heavy Industry met all four major plan targets,[45] a figure that probably rose substantially in the next two years.[46] Most industrial growth in this period still came from new investment, but a part, perhaps as much as 2 or 3 per cent a year, came from increased efficiency (out of a total increase of over 10 per cent per year). Financial discipline was not the sole cause of increased efficiency, but it is doubtful that any increase would have been possible without it.

In 1956, impressionistic evidence suggests that financial laxity together with a general boom psychology led to decreased efficiency in industrial production. Coal mine costs (per metric ton) in Liaoning in 1956 were 16 per cent above 1955;[47] 32-count yarn costs rose nearly 2 per cent in 1956 even though the cotton-yarn utilization rate rose from 77 to 94 per cent and raw cotton prices were steady;[48] the amount of wood used in making wood pulp rose in 1956 by 1 or 2 per cent after falling steadily from 1953 through 1955;[49] and raw materials used per unit of output in five types of edible oils, with one exception, increased in 1956 after falling between 1953 and 1955.[50] In the producers' goods sector the Ministry of Heavy Industry failed to meet its cost reduction

[43] *WKKT*, p. 27.

[44] *WKKT*, p. 62. It is not clear just how this figure was arrived at.

[45] Chou En-lai, "Report on the Work of the Government," p. 84.

[46] In 1954, for example, the various industrial ministries as a whole surpassed the cost-reduction target, as did at least 11 major individual industries. SSB, "Report on the Results of 1954 Economic Development and State Planning," *HHYP*, October 28, 1955, p. 166.

[47] *TCKT*, March 14, 1958, p. 21.

[48] *WKKT*, pp. 169, 173.

[49] *WKKT*, p. 221.

[50] *TCYC*, February 23, 1958, p. 18.

and profits targets in the first quarter of 1956 largely because of excess consumption of raw materials.[51] Economization of electric power in 1956 had fallen back to the level of 1954 and profits of metallurgical industries belonging to iron and steel enterprises, after rising to 622 million yuan in 1954 and 806 million yuan in 1955 (from 522 million yuan in 1953) fell back to 801 million yuan in 1956, even though output in 1956 rose sharply.[52] There were some exceptions: tobacco used by the cigarette industry per unit of output continued its downward trend in 1956, although the trend was reversed in the first half of 1957,[53] perhaps a delayed reaction resulting from enterprises' ability to disguise waste for a short period at least.

The 1956 boom, therefore, was not simply a process whereby extra growth in one year reduced industrial growth by a comparable amount in some other year or years. Wastage of materials, in effect, meant that industrial development in the nonboom years would have to be reduced by a greater percentage than it had been increased in the boom.[54] It was not just agriculture, therefore, that caused industrial growth in 1957 to be the slowest of any year since 1949 except 1955.

Although material wastage and high costs apparently were brought under control in 1957,[55] all attempts at cost reduction were abandoned during the "great leap forward," at least through 1960. More serious than raw-material wastage was the sharply reduced quality of output. Decline in product quality unfortunately is not something which can be measured accurately by out-

[51] Statistics Unit, Department of Planning, Ministry of Heavy Industry, "Analysis of Results of State Plans Administered by the Ministry of Heavy Industry during the First Quarter of 1956," *Chung-kung-yeh t'ung-hsun,* May 1, 1956, translated in *ECMM,* no. 42, pp. 19–26.

[52] *WKKT,* p. 28.

[53] *TCYC,* February 23, 1958, p. 18.

[54] "Percentage" as used here refers to a percentage above or below what the annual average rate of growth would have been if growth had been steady rather than fluctuating. There is the implicit assumption that nothing in fluctuating or cyclical growth would in itself tend to raise the annual average growth rate.

[55] In 1957, for example, state revenue from enterprise profits and industrial and commercial taxes (which are really a part of profits) rose at a rate almost as fast as that of industrial output, unlike 1956, when revenue grew only about half as fast as industrial production.

side observers. Even the Chinese Communist leadership has difficulty knowing what is happening in this regard.

The problem of maintaining quality was not unique to the "great leap." It was part and parcel of the whole question of efficiency for earlier years as well. Poor quality can be thought of as having two aspects: the first is the decline in quality of a given item (a shovel which lasts for two years instead of three); the second is a shift in production from useful items to those of little or no use, usually because the less useful item is easier to produce and hence production targets can more readily be surpassed. In 1958 and 1959, industrial output did rise very rapidly, but it is now clear that much of what was produced was worthless or nearly so. This was not just a problem for small-scale factories, but for all enterprises, large and small. By 1960 industry was in such a state of disorganization, with enterprises unable to get needed materials of the required quality, that the regime had to turn all its efforts to re-establishing balance and control. The decline in industrial output in 1960–1962 and only partial recovery in 1963 were a direct result, therefore, not only of the agricultural crisis and the Russian withdrawal, but also of this disregard for the whole question of efficiency. Financial controls were not the only means whereby the state maintained an interest in problems of efficiency on the part of factory managers, but they were among the most important. Disregard of tight control over enterprise funds during the "great leap," therefore, was bought at a high price.

Control of the industrial firm in Communist China would have run into fewer basic problems if the Soviet system of centralized planning and emphasis on output targets had proved as suitable for China as it was for the Soviet Union in the 1930's. The backwardness of Chinese industry, the large number of firms involved, and the desire to develop and exploit more labor-intensive techniques all pushed the regime toward consideration of various decentralized controls. Although central planning retained its position in the forefront of the various controls utilized by the regime, the need for decentralized controls was felt to be too important to the system to be ignored. In practice, partial decentralization was carried out both through the market and by means of administrative reorganization.

Decentralization of economic decision making, however, was usually combined with a transfer of power to the party — in effect, political centralization. Any alternative, such as turning over authority to nonparty economists and technicians, would have been considered undesirable, except as a temporary measure, because it would have threatened the paramount role of the party, a role fundamental to the existence of Chinese Communism. Party influence, however, meant control by cadres inexperienced in economic matters and imbued with an ideology that was, to a degree, incompatible with market forms of decentralization and was not sensitive to problems of allocation in general. Party authorities in the industrial firm thus tended to ignore market constraints on their economic decisions, constraints which would have made those decisions work more efficiently for the development of the economy. In fact, during periods of extreme political control, as during the "great leap forward," the system degenerated into economic anarchy.

One possible way out of these difficulties was to emphasize technical and economic training for party personnel. This, however, would eventually transform the party itself from a revolutionary body to a party of technical bureaucrats, a transformation that has, in fact, progressed quite far in the Soviet Union and for which the Chinese Communists have shown considerable distaste. There is no obvious way out of this dilemma, and one has certainly not been found on the mainland of China.

CHAPTER VII

Wage Determination

Of the payments to the three factors of production, only wages have been of real significance in Communist China. For both ideological and practical reasons, neither interest nor rent payments have been allowed to play any role whatsoever in the allocation of resources. Rent is paid for individual housing, but the rates set are so low that they play no role in housing allocation. Interest payments are placed on all loans by banks and credit cooperatives to the agricultural, commercial, and industrial sectors, but the rates set there are also too low to have much influence over allocation of capital. This is particularly true in the case of industry, where tax regulations made it so that the state in effect paid 90 per cent of interest costs on any given loan.[1]

Although the role of wages in the urban sector is considerably more important than that of rent and interest, it too is severely circumscribed by direct physical controls over the labor market and by Chinese Communist use of various nonmonetary incentives. The major objectives of wage policy as a control device that could be manipulated by central authorities have been to provide employees with incentives to work harder and attain advancement and higher skills, to influence allocation of labor, and to maintain control over the size of the total wage bill so that urban demand would not outstrip the available supply of consumers' goods. These objectives could not, of course, be pursued independently of each other. One potential source of conflict among objectives is that the desire to maximize incentives might interfere with minimization of inflationary pressure on the consumers' goods market. Another possible conflict is that between control over inflation and the role of wages in labor allocation.

[1] See Chapter V.

This incompatibility of objectives has in fact existed to some extent in China, but the major areas of conflict have not been so much the result of incompatible objectives as of the less than completely efficient pursuit of those objectives.

The discussion here starts with an analysis of the nature and degree of centralized control over allocation of the urban labor force and the effect that policies pursued by the regime in this area have had on the total urban wage bill.[2] This will be followed by an analysis of the principles underlying Chinese Communist wage determination. Control over labor allocation and wage determination are, of course, closely related, but the proliferation of direct controls over the labor market makes a division along these lines both possible and useful.

Labor Allocation and the Size of the Wage Bill

One of the most important differences between China today and the Soviet Union on the eve of its first five-year plan was the dissimilarity in the two countries' labor markets. In the Soviet Union by the 1930's the government had begun to experience a shortage of industrial labor and undertook several measures in an attempt to alleviate this situation. These measures included the promotion of migration of workers from rural areas and the use of female labor.[3] Nevertheless, the shortage continued, making recruitment of labor one of the prime concerns of the Soviet plant manager. Since the labor market remained relatively free from direct controls over allocation until just before the Second World War, competition among enterprises was keen and there was a high rate of turnover of Russian industrial labor, over 100 per cent during most of the first five-year plan.[4] This competition generally took the form of an offer of higher wages and greater side benefits, especially housing. These competitive offers of higher wages would not have been possible if it had not been for state financial policy, which was so lax that heads of enterprises seldom had much difficulty getting needed

[2] The analysis in this section owes a considerable debt to Ishikawa, *Chugoku ni okeru shihon chikuseki kiko,* chap. iii.

[3] Warren Eason, "Population and Labor Force," in Abram Bergson, ed., *Soviet Economic Growth* (Evanston, 1953), pp. 112–113.

[4] Holzman, *Soviet Taxation,* p. 32.

funds. There was a provision for a 10 per cent overexpenditure in any month following one when no such outlay was made; this was compounded by allowing wage overexpenditures whenever the output plan was overfulfilled. The result was an increase in average wages of nearly six times and in the total wage bill of over fifteen times between 1928 and 1940, while real wages fell.[5] During the war and until early 1956 the government attempted with some success to deal with this problem through restrictions on labor mobility, including such measures as imprisonment or fines for unauthorized absence from work or leaving a job. Abolition of these measures in 1956 did not lead to a restoration of the prewar wage spiral, largely because by that time general financial controls had been tightened considerably and improvement in planning technique had taken some of the pressure off factory managers.[6]

In China, on the other hand, there has never been anything remotely close to a labor shortage. Although it is doubtful that there has been much truly underemployed labor in the sense of having zero labor productivity, particularly given the techniques of labor organization employed by communes and cooperatives, productivity of a large sector of the population has been extremely low. Talk of labor shortage during the "great leap forward" of 1958, to the extent that it was more than mere propaganda, must be thought of in this light. There undoubtedly were and continue to be unending opportunities for building irrigation and other works involving removal of large quantities of earth with little or no machinery, but the rate of return on most such activities must be so low that their undertaking could only be justified on economic grounds if there were great numbers of at least seasonally unemployed farmers. Barring some unforeseen and successful radical reorganization of agriculture and rural small-scale industry, this surplus of labor appears destined to continue into the indefinite future. The approximately 2 per cent annual increase

---

[5] Holzman, pp. 39–40, and Janet Chapman, "Real Wages in the Soviet Union, 1928–1952," *Review of Economics and Statistics,* XXXVI (May 1954), 134–156.

[6] D. R. Hodgman, "Soviet Monetary Controls through the Banking System," and F. D. Holzman, "Comment," in Gregory Grossman, ed., *Value and Plan* (Berkeley and Los Angeles, 1960), pp. 105–131.

in population has added between 12 and 15 million to the population each year, of which only between 1 and 6 million have been either born in or migrated to cities.

The availability of large pools of labor in rural areas did not necessarily imply that this labor was readily available to the industrial labor market. In many underdeveloped countries the rural work force often has proved too undisciplined and unskilled to be of much use even in fairly simple industrial jobs, but this was not the case in China. Although there have been relatively minor problems of labor discipline, Chinese farmers once were exported to Southeast Asia in large numbers for the very reason that they could be relied on to work steadily and hard. Furthermore, there has been a long history in China of migration to the cities, particularly during periods of famine and lesser natural and man-made disasters. Even in good times for agriculture, there has been a steady flow into urban centers of people hoping to make their fortune. These people are seldom possessed of industrial skills, but this is not crucial, because a high proportion of industrial construction jobs have involved little more than the use of a shovel and a bamboo carrying pole.

Even among long-term residents of cities there has been at least some unemployment during most of the period since 1949. The figure for 1951 was over 3 million, and by 1957 was still slightly over 1 million. These estimates, however, are not very reliable. It is doubtful that in early years the regime had the capacity for making anything but very rough estimates, while the figure for 1957 was only the number of registered unemployed. Registration of unemployed really began in July 1952, although certain special groups had been registered previously. The definition of being unemployed was so loose that it covered people too old or physically handicapped to work. Even so, it was restricted to people with permanent addresses in urban areas, so that the statistics excluded the often substantial numbers of recent arrivals from rural areas. Thus cities probably have always had significant numbers of people looking for work from which factories in need of workers could draw. Professor Ishikawa argues that government measures in 1954 to open new channels for people to get employment may have indicated a decrease in the size of urban unemployment.[7] On the other hand, it appears to have been the case that such unemployment has never completely ceased to exist and, if anything, has increased since the slowdown following the "great leap forward." [8]

This endless supply of unskilled labor at subsistence wages has been far from an unmixed blessing for the regime. Population increase in rural areas can be handled by local people, but in the city it necessitates provision by the government of both housing and food, with various supplementary expenditures on sanitation, transportation, marketing, and so forth. The major problem facing the Chinese Communists, therefore, has been how to control growth in urban population. To accomplish this the regime has resorted to a wide variety of measures including both physical and market controls.

The key physical controls are those which were directly aimed at preventing rural people from moving to urban areas. To leave his cooperative or farm an individual first of all has to obtain permission from local authorities. Once having arrived in the city he has to obtain further permission to stay, for without it he not only cannot legally remain but also cannot receive his basic food rations. To back these measures up, organizations have been set up at strategic communications points to "persuade" people to return to their farms and provide them with means of doing so.[9] In theory, therefore, all the central government has to do is issue a directive stating that permanent migration to the cities is thenceforth illegal, but this in fact is not the case. In the first place permission of local rural authorities is often quite per-

[7] This discussion of unemployment is based on Ishikawa, pp. 44–47. The principal primary sources include Government Affairs Council, "Decision on the Labor Employment Problem" (July 25, 1952), *HHYP*, August 25, 1952, pp. 29–30; Labor Employment Committee of the Government Affairs Council, "Methods for the Unified Registration of Unemployed Personnel" (August 27, 1952), *HHYP*, September 25, 1952, pp. 42–43; and Hsing Yu-hung, "In Order to Continue to See Clearly the New Objectives and Struggles of Labor Employment," *HHYP*, July 25, 1954, p. 141.

[8] A large number of the people entering Hong Kong from Canton in the exodus of May 1962, for example, were those who had recently become unemployed and had little prospect of finding work.

[9] Directives on the prevention of the blind outflow of rural labor were issued every year between 1950 and 1957 except for 1951 and 1955. For the list, see Ishikawa, p. 53.

functory and in many other cases it is ignored altogether by those wishing to leave.[10] Even in the cities control has been far from tight, and it has often not been difficult to become eligible for food rations.[11] Thus the regime has found it necessary to make considerable additional efforts to transfer surplus urban personnel back to the countryside. These efforts began as early as 1955[12] and have since reached substantial proportions. Initially, the policy appears to have concentrated on unemployed workers, particularly those who still had close connections with their villages, but in recent years it has been broadened to include large numbers of city students who, having completed their education, cannot or are not likely to find factory work.[13] There has often been considerable compulsion in this transfer, but exactly how much is impossible to say.[14] There has always been a tendency in China for people to return to their native villages during hard times, but today, when the situation in the cities has been bad, that in rural areas has usually been worse.[15]

Although these measures when employed with vigor have enjoyed a considerable degree of success, they have at times been at least partially undermined by activities of industrial and construction enterprises, which have been subject to a number of controls over their freedom to employ additional workers. In the first place, as already mentioned in the previous two chapters, there have been plan targets for the total number of employees

[10] See CCPCC and SC, "Directive on Prohibiting the Blind Outflow of the Rural Population" (December 18, 1957), *HHPYK*, January 25, 1958, pp. 119–120.

[11] "Surplus Labor in Canton Should Return to the Countryside to Participate in Rural Production," *Nan-fang jih-pao*, December 30, 1955, translated in *SCMP*, supplement, no. 1261, p. 6.

[12] Lin Chiang-yun, "Certain Problems in the Control of Labor Power," *Lao-tung*, November 15, 1955, translated in *ECMM*, no. 27, p. 26.

[13] *E.g.*, Hsing Ch'ung-chih, "Carry Out Properly the Work in Connection with Youths Returning to the Rural Areas," *Chung-kuo ch'ing-nien*, June 1, 1962, translated in *ECMM*, no. 322, pp. 16–21.

[14] Arrivals from Canton in 1962 gave the impression that few regular urban residents went to the countryside voluntarily.

[15] This is largely because industrial conditions depend heavily on the size of the agricultural harvest. When the harvest falls industrial production also falls, although to a lesser extent, partly because heavy industry does not depend on agriculture very heavily and partly because purchases of agricultural products fluctuate less than production.

and the total wage bill and, prior to the 1957 reforms, for the average wage and total number of employees at the end of the year. Furthermore, a factory or construction firm is not supposed to employ labor directly but is required instead to apply to the local labor department, which sends workers if it considers the request a suitable one. These measures have not been without effect, but like so many other plan targets, compliance with labor targets is to some degree ignored whenever the pressure is on to fulfill the output plan, and much recruitment of labor is done through direct contact with rural areas.[16]

As a result, compliance with labor targets depends to a large degree on the availability of funds to individual enterprises, that is, as with so many other targets, on the tightness of financial policy.[17] This relation can be seen clearly from Tables 11 and 12. The key figures are those for total employment in production departments rather than the more commonly quoted ones for the total number of workers and employees. Both sets of data must be used carefully, since they were subject to fluctuations that were due solely to changes in organization. Socialization of commerce, for example, transformed many people formerly classified as private traders into employees of the state commercial network. Their work was roughly identical but only in the latter case were they included among the number of workers and employees. The figures for the production departments were somewhat less subject to this influence largely because they excluded commercial employees except in 1958, when many handicraft organizations were turned into small- and medium-scale industrial enterprises. The other advantage of production department data is that they more clearly reflect the degree of control over employment of labor in industrial and construction firms. This is clearly brought out by the fact that, during each of the three

[16] Hsing Yu-hung, "Make a Good Job of Labor Allocation for 1957," *Lao-tung,* June 3, 1957, translated in *ECMM,* no. 94, pp. 23–24; Wage Office, Labor Wage Bureau, Ministry of Commerce, "Draw Up the 1957 Labor Plan for Commercial Organizations on 'Increasing Production without Increasing Men' Principle," *Lao-tung,* April 3, 1957, translated in *ECMM,* no. 86, pp. 29–30; and the directive cited in note 10.

[17] This relation between the tightness or laxity of financial policy and compliance with plan targets was discussed at length in the preceding chapter.

TABLE 12. Nonagricultural employment, year-end data (1000 persons)

Type of employment	1949	1950	1951	1952	1953	1954	1955	1956	1957	1958
Number of "workers and employees,"[a]	8,004	10,239	12,815	15,804	18,256	18,809	19,076	24,230	24,606	45,323[d]
Handicrafts (excluding "workers and employees")[b]				7,364	7,789	8,910	8,202	6,583	6,540[c]	870[d]
Commerce (excluding "workers and employees")[e]		5,653	6,233	5,851	5,313	4,027	3,586	2,325		
Total[f]				29,019	31,358	31,746	30,864	33,138		
Production departments ("workers and employees," excluding handicrafts)[g]	5,203	6,237	8,176	10,446	12,359	12,922	13,067	17,494	17,938	38,570
industry (excluding handicrafts)	3,060[h]			5,260[h]	6,009+[i]	6,158+[i]	5,861+[i]		7,907[i]	23,734[k]
basic construction	200[h]			1,050[h]			1,190[l]	2,950[h]	1,910[i]	5,336[k]
transport and communications	640[h]			1,130[h]			1,120[l]	1,560[h]		
Nonproduction departments ("workers and employees")[g]	2,801	4,003	4,639	5,358	5,897	5,887	6,009	6,736	6,668	6,753

[a] SSB, Ten Great Years, p. 180. "Workers and employees" excludes all personnel who work for themselves or in a cooperative organization.

[b] The 1952–1956 figures are from SSB, Ten Great Years, p. 36.

[c] In 1957, 90 per cent of all handicraft workers, or 5,890,000 men, were in cooperatives; see SSB, "Report on the First Five Year Plan to Develop the National Economy (1953–1957)" (April 13, 1959), HHPYK, April 25, 1959, p. 48.

[d] This figure is for May 1959. During the latter half of 1958 and early part of 1959, handicraft cooperatives were turned into local state factories, cooperative factories, and commune factories. By May 1959 only 13.3 per cent of those formerly in cooperatives remained so. If one assumes that the number of handicraft personnel was the same in 1958 as 1957, one can derive the above estimate; see Chien-kuo shih-nien, 1949–1959 (Ten years of national construction; Hong Kong, 1959), I, 225.

[e] The figures for 1950–1955 are derived by subtracting the number of workers and employees in private commerce from the total number of people engaged in private trade (Yin and Yin, Economic Statistics of Mainland China, p. 79). These data may be somewhat too high, since the number of workers and employees in private commerce given in this source (917,000) is much less than that (2,320,000) given in the First Five Year Plan for Development of the National Economy of the People's Republic of China in 1953–57, p. 190. In 1956 the number of handicraftsmen, small tradesmen, and other such persons converted to the status of workers and employees was 2,880,000 persons (TCKTTH data office, "The 1956 Labor Wage Situation," HHPYK, May 25, 1957, p. 116). If one makes the crude assumption that these were all from the handicraft and commercial sectors and that total employment in these sectors was changed only by the above-mentioned change in status, one arrives at the figure 2,325,000 which is roughly equal to that given for transformed private commerce (TCKTTH, August 14, 1956, p. 6), but it is not clear whether this includes former workers and employees.

[f] This total does not include fishermen, certain services, or various persons employed in transport using other than modern conveyances.

[g] Derived from totals and percentage breakdown, SSB, Ten Great Years, pp. 180, 185. Production departments include industry, construction, transport and communications, and agricultural extension, water conservation, and forestry; see SSB, "Report on the 1958 National Economic Development Situation" (April 14, 1959), HHPYK, April 25, 1959, p. 54. It must also include other categories, since the above four items do not add up to the total unless part of handicrafts is included. Nonproduction departments include government organs, commerce, and so forth.

[h] Yin and Yin, p. 68.

[i] These figures are derived by adding employment in private and joint public-private industry (ibid., pp. 69–70) to socialist industry employment figures; the latter are derived from percentage increases (HHPYK, January 25, 1957, p. 58) and "The Great Leap Forward in Basic Construction Work," TCYC, September 23, 1958, pp. 5, 10.

[j] TCYC data office, "The Flying Leap in Our Industrial Construction," and "The Great Leap Forward in Basic Construction Work," TCYC, September 23, 1958, pp. 5, 10.

[k] J. P. Emerson, "Chinese Communist Party Views on Labor Utilization before and after 1958," Current Scene, vol. I, no. 30 (April 20, 1962), p. 5.

[l] Given in or derived from data in TCKTTH data office, "The Breakdown and Organization of the Number of Workers and Employees in Our Country in 1955," HHPYK, January 25, 1957, p. 89. These data are as of September 30, 1955, and thus differ slightly from the true year-end figures.

years (1953, 1956, and 1958) when the rate of investment was sharply accelerated, employment in production departments showed an equally sharp rise. The widest fluctuations, of course, were in employment in basic construction, which was most directly affected by investment. Industrial employment also varied, but the variation was in the rate of increase, the decrease in 1955 probably mainly resulting from the bad harvest of 1954, although tight financial controls in that year may also have played a part. Increases in various production departments during the three years mentioned were, at least in the latter two cases, far greater than called for under the plan. In 1956 the actual increase in total number of workers and employees was 2.2 times the planned increase.[18] In 1958 the plan only called for an increase of 419,000 men over 1957, a figure that was exceeded many times before the year had ended.[19] Relaxation of financial control was not solely responsible for these unplanned increases. As in the case of various other secondary plan targets and regulations, the anticonservative spirit of the times was also of importance.[20] Therefore, whereas in the Soviet Union lax financial controls led to wage inflation, in China, owing to differences in the two countries' labor markets, it led to large increases in employment in urban areas.

The data in Table 12 also bring out another aspect of the technique used by the Chinese Communist regime to limit increases in urban employment. This took the form of tight control over the number of personnel in what the Communists termed "nonproductive" employment, which included such categories as government, commerce, education, and health. It also included all personnel in production departments who were not directly engaged in production. The number of people in government work was more or less frozen at the level of the early 1950's, and those in commerce were reduced (although the number of "workers and employees" in commerce was increased). Within production de-

[18] *TCKTTH* data office, "The 1956 Labor Wage Situation," *HHPYK,* May 25, 1957, p. 116.

[19] Po I-po, "Draft Plan for the Development of the National Economy in 1958" (February 3, 1958), *NCNA,* February 13, 1958, translated in *CB,* no. 494.

[20] See the discussion in Chapter VI.

partments the regime had somewhat less success largely because it was apparently one area where it was easiest for individual enterprises to expand the number of their employees. As a result, when controls have been relaxed, the proportion of "nonproductive" labor has tended to increase.[21]

There also were a number of measures undertaken that were peculiar to the control of either unskilled or skilled workers. Although most rural people were probably attracted by prospects of steadier employment and greater opportunity to get ahead rather than by immediately higher wages, the regime's minimum-wage policy prior to 1958 tended to aggravate the problem. These wages were generally much higher than those received by farmers doing comparable work, and this was accentuated by the 1956 wage reform, which raised wages of the lowest grade by 8 per cent.[22] The regime somewhat belatedly recognized the problem with passage of regulations in February 1958 calling on enterprises to lower the bottom-grade wage to that of rural people in areas where the majority of workers came from (with a certain cost of living differential).[23]

Special problems involved in controlling the supply of skilled workers depended on the level of skills involved. There was a serious shortage of highly trained personnel, and they were so few in number that they could be and were allocated by centralized direct means. There were, for example, only 31,940 engineers in China in 1955 and 654 people who were considered capable of undertaking some fairly rudimentary form of scientific research,[24]

[21] "Some Problems Concerning the Increase in Employees and Workers in Shanghai Industrial Enterprises in 1956," *TCKT*, no. 15, August 14, 1957, p. 29; Chang Chih-hua, "Try Hard to Lower the Proportion of Nondirectly Productive Personnel in Enterprises," *Lao-tung*, May 18, 1962, translated in *ECMM*, no. 322, pp. 1–4.

[22] Ma Wen-jui, speech in *Chung-hua Jen-min Kung-ho-kuo Ti-i-chieh Ch'uan-kuo Jen-min Tai-piao Ta-hui ti-san-tz'u hui-i hui-k'an* (The third meeting of the First National People's Congress of the People's Republic of China; Peking, 1956), pp. 733–743.

[23] SC, "Provisional Regulations Governing the Wages for Ordinary and Miscellaneous Workers in Enterprises, Business Units, and Government Agencies," NCNA, February 10, 1958, translated in *CB*, no. 497, pp. 2–3.

[24] *TCKTTH* data office, "The Breakdown and Organization of the Number of Workers and Employees in Our Country in 1955," *HHPYK*, January 25, 1957, p. 88; L. A. Orleans, *Professional Manpower and Education in Communist China* (Washington, 1961).

although this number has increased substantially since. With lower levels of skills the situation was not markedly different from that of unskilled labor. The supply from schools and factory training schools and apprenticeships has greatly outstripped available jobs in urban areas, with the result that recent school graduates have been encouraged to return to rural areas, where their skills in such things as accounting could be of considerable help to communes and large production teams. As in the case of unskilled laborers, the problem was accentuated by labor reforms in early years that pushed wages of apprentices and workers in the process of training well above what they would have been willing to accept.[25]

From the above discussion it should be apparent that wages have played only a very minor role in allocation of the urban labor force. The problem of allocating unskilled laborers among various enterprises does not exist because there have always been far more workers than jobs to fill, whereas with the highly skilled, the small number has made direct physical allocation a relatively simple matter. The major objective in labor allocation, therefore, has been to keep the excessive supply of workers in rural areas, where they would minimize the strain on urban areas. This increased strain has expressed itself in the form of higher costs for housing, sanitation, and the like, and in a greatly increased urban wage bill, which, as we will see, has considerably complicated the problem of maintaining efficient distribution in the urban consumers' goods market.[26] On the whole the regime has achieved considerable success in this sphere largely by various direct controls over the rural urban flow of people, but the degree of success has been reduced considerably during periods of financial laxity and the ideologically and politically motivated "anticonservative" drives of various rectification campaigns. Wage policy has also contributed to Communist success or lack of it in this area, but only in a marginal way. The appeal of urban living depends on far more than the differential between rural incomes and the bottom rung of the urban wage scale, so that a lowering

[25] Ishikawa, *Chugoku ni okeru shihon chikuseki kiko,* p. 58.
[26] See the discussion in Chapters VIII and IX.

of the latter has probably discouraged very few from leaving the cities.

Wage Policy

Wage rates and the average level of wages, therefore, have not been determined primarily on the basis of their effect on labor allocation. Instead, the two major considerations have been the effect on incentives and size of the total wage bill. If China were a completely free-enterprise country, the effect of excessive migration of labor to the cities on the size of the wage bill would be at least partially offset by a tendency for wages to fall toward the subsistence level. But the wage system in China is not determined by free-market forces so much as by central government policy decrees. As a result the tendency of the wage bill to increase rapidly has been slightly accelerated rather than damped.

The essential feature of the Chinese wage and salary system is that it is based on a fixed set of grades into which each employee in some way is fitted. The number of grades varies depending on whether the personnel are ordinary laborers or executive and technical personnel. The basic wage system for laborers in industry, for example, contains eight grades, although there are others.[27] The difference between various grades is a fairly constant percentage, usually about 20 per cent. The top grade is somewhat over three times the lowest grade, with the money value of each grade varying slightly between industries and firms.[28] This system was not established overnight and it appears that a substantial degree of unity throughout the country was not achieved until after the major reforms of 1956. In the first

[27] E.g., Eckstein, *The National Income of Communist China*, p. 128, refers to an eleven-grade system in a private machine and iron casting plant, and *Hsin Chung-kuo kung-shang-yeh-chia-te tao-lu* (New China's road to industrialization and the development of commerce; Hong Kong, 1950), pp. 174–175, gives two seven-grade systems.

[28] This discussion is based on the few published wage tables available. These appear in Ishikawa, p. 126; K. C. Chao, *Economic Planning and Organization in Communist China*, II, 71–72; and Wu Yuan-li, *An Economic Survey of Communist China*, p. 443. Some idea of the variation in the money value of each grade can be seen from eleven of the factories and mines visited by Edgar Snow in Manchuria (*The Other Side of the River*, pp. 203–206).

few years two other systems also were used that were outgrowths of inflation and revolution. Various government employees, for example, rather than being paid completely in the form of wages, were issued, free of charge, such items as housing and electricity, a practice that was ended by decree on August 31, 1955.[29] More important was the procedure whereby workers were paid in work points, each work point being worth a certain quantity of several major consumers' goods.[30] This system protected workers from inflation, but it also made inflationary control more difficult, since it effectively removed wage policy from the sphere of anti-inflationary devices. Under the circumstances, however, this was not too serious and only constituted recognition that the source of inflation was serious imbalances in the government budget. This wage-point system was gradually abolished, once inflation had been brought under control.[31]

The economic purpose of wage differentials was to provide incentives for workers to acquire additional skills and to put out greater effort. There is no real way of knowing, given the available data, whether differentials of this magnitude were required in order to achieve these aims. One cannot use private industrial wage scales as a standard for comparison because these were even more subject to union (and thus government) pressure to provide increases, with the result that wages in private industry were commonly higher than those in the public sector.[32] There was some indication that state enterprises themselves did not

[29] Tu Shao-po and Wang I-cheng, "Why the Changeover from the Supply System to the Wage System," *Shih-shih shou-ts'e,* September 25, 1955, translated in *ECMM,* no. 19, pp. 27–29.

[30] For a discussion of this wage-point system, see Wu Yuan-li, pp. 442–448.

[31] In the 1960's and perhaps earlier, however, another kind of cost of living index was built into the wage system. Under this system, wages were adjusted on a regional basis to take account of the fact that the cost of living in some areas was higher than in others. Wages, however, were not adjusted for price changes over time, as in the wage-point system (Ezra Vogel, unpublished manuscript).

[32] *JMJP* editorial, "Reform the New Joint Public–Private Enterprises' Wage System," *HHPYK,* November 21, 1956, p. 107. Nor does the amount of data available make readily possible any thorough Sino–Soviet or Sino–U.S. comparisons comparable to the Soviet–U.S. comparisons made by Abram Bergson, *The Structure of Soviet Wages* (Cambridge, Mass., 1944).

feel need for so many wage differentials, although this could have been as much from ignorance as from lack of competitive pressure. Whatever the reason, there were complaints by the central government that promotions were not being made where individuals were clearly eligible for them.[33] Proper grading of personnel, therefore, was made an element of the 1956 wage reform, with the result that promotions in that year were excessive[34] and contributed materially to inflationary pressures in urban areas. After 1956, however, grading of personnel again tended to become frozen, a tendency that had a deleterious effect on incentives but was undoubtedly necessary, given the sharp drop in available consumers' goods after 1959. The next major reform in personnel grading did not take place until 1963, when most employees were promoted one grade, a promotion that did not always carry with it an increase in salary, however.[35]

Promotions were not the only method by which the average wage was increased. The general wage level in China was set in principle on the basis of changes in labor productivity and the availability of consumers' goods.[36] One of the reasons for the 1956 wage reform, for example, was the fact that, during 1954 through 1955, increases in the average wage lagged well behind increases in average productivity of labor (see Table 13). But the average productivity of labor as defined in China was of doubtful relevance to the problem of wage determination. In the first place, the figure was usually obtained by dividing gross value of industrial production by the number of workers. Therefore, any increase in output, whether due to increased labor efficiency, higher-quality raw materials, or greater capital, increased labor productivity. This would not have been greatly changed if net-value product were used rather than gross, as some writers

[33] Ma Wen-jui, speech, *Ti-i-chieh Ch'uan-kuo Jen-min Tai-piao Ta-hui ti-san-tz'u hui-i hui-k'an,* p. 733.

[34] *TCKTTH* data office, "The 1956 Labor Wage Situation," *HHPYK,* May 25, 1957, p. 116.

[35] Ezra Vogel, unpublished manuscript.

[36] Hsiao Kung-ju, "The Principle Underlying Wage Increase," *Hsueh-hsi,* August 3, 1957, translated in *ECMM,* no. 106, pp. 12–14; "How to Analyze Worker and Employee Wage Problems," *TCKT,* April 14, 1957, pp. 8–11.

TABLE 13.   Percentage increases in labor productivity and in money wages

Year	Labor productivity	Money wages
1950–1952	33.3	57.7
1953	13.0	5.0
1954	15.0	2.6
1955	10.0	0.6
1956	15.4	14.5

Source: Yuan Feng, "The Ratio of Increases between Labor Productivity and Wages," *Hsin chien-she*, December 3, 1956, translated in *ECMM*, no. 71, pp. 11–12.

recommended.[37] Of more significance was that the relevant concept for wage determination, at least from the standpoint of allocative efficiency, is marginal rather than average labor productivity. There is little doubt that in China marginal productivity of unskilled and semiskilled laborers was well below their average productivity and, while the average increased each year, it is doubtful that there was any rise in marginal productivity at all, owing to the constant excess availability of unskilled workers. Thus the average wage in China was higher than necessary from the point of view of allocative efficiency. This was partially and somewhat indirectly recognized by the reduction in lower-grade wages in 1958. Effects of the use of average productivity were somewhat tempered by the regime's attempt to keep wage increases in line with availability of consumers' goods in urban areas, but this latter figure itself was to some extent determined by the expected size and increases in the wage bill.

The degree of control over the wage bill and the efficiency of that control were also affected by difficulties involved in administration of piecework wages. The advantage of piece wages lay in their incentive effect on workers, but the regime met with a considerable number of problems in establishing realistic work norms. The major difficulty was that improvements in technology and organization occurred so rapidly that norms could not keep up,

[37] E.g., Niu Chung-huang, "Computation of Labor Productivity and the Fixing of the Wage Scale," *Hsueh-hsi*, May 3, 1957, translated in *ECMM*, no. 91, pp. 8–11.

particularly during the "great leap forward." [38] As a result, piece-workers had only risen from 34.5 per cent of the work force in 1952 to 41.9 per cent in 1956, and then fell off again, especially in 1958.[39] It is not clear, however, how much of the elimination of pieceworkers in many factories was a result of a realistic appraisal of the disadvantages and how much was a part of the egalitarian spirit of the communes and the "great leap forward." [40] Whatever the case, mistakes in administration of piecework norms certainly provided an additional source of undesirable wage increases that contributed to inflationary pressure in 1956.[41]

Bonuses apparently also tended to increase more rapidly than was anticipated during the 1956 reform. Rewards of various types in 1956 rose to 10.4 per cent of total wages from 8.2 per cent in 1955.[42] There is no evidence, however, to suggest that this was more than a temporary problem peculiar to the 1956 reforms. Together these various factors raised the average wage level by 76 yuan (see Table 14).

To argue that the principles upon which wage differentials, the average wage level, piecework wages, and bonuses were determined in 1956 led to wage increases greater than would have occurred under a free market system is not, of course, to argue that the resulting wage system was necessarily irrational. It is possible that the nature of labor organization under the Communists tended to damp incentives in ways that could only be offset by greater material rewards. This, however, seems unlikely. Furthermore, the regime had a wide variety of nonmaterial incentives that it exploited fully. Emulation drives, dragon awards, red flags, various honorific titles for workers, and many other

[38] Peter Schran, "The Structure of Income in Communist China," unpub. diss., University of California, 1961, pp. 300, 332.

[39] Sun Shang-ch'ing, "On the Nature and Destiny of Our Current Piece Rate Wage System," *CCYC,* April 17, 1959, translated in *ECMM,* no. 180, p. 38.

[40] There seem to be elements of both aspects in Chang Ch'un-ch'iao, "Break Away From the Idea of the Bourgeois Right," *JMJP,* October 13, 1958; Shih Ching, "Don't Let Money Assume Command," *JMJP,* October 16, 1958; and "Many Enterprises in Peking Do Away with the Piece Wage System," NCNA, October 21, 1958. All three are translated in *CB,* no. 537, pp. 1–5, 5–8, 22–24.

[41] See note 36.

[42] "How to Analyze Worker and Employee Wage Problems," *TCKT,* April 14, 1957, p. 10.

TABLE 14.   The urban wage bill

Year	Average wage (yuan)	Average number of workers and staff (1000 persons)	Total wages (million yuan)
1952	446	15,110	6,700
1953	496	17,800	8,800
1954	519	18,530	9,610
1955	534	18,730	10,000
1956	610	22,310	13,600
1957	637	23,973	15,250
1958	564	32,000	18,050

Source: The average wage for 1952–1957 is given in SSB, *Ten Great Years*, p. 216. The average number of employees and the total wage bill is given in Peter Schran, "The Structure of Income in Communist China," unpub. diss., University of California, 1961, p. 277.

For 1958, the approximate average number of employees is given in *Ten Great Years*, p. 180. The total wage bill is obtained from figures for total purchasing power, rural purchasing power (see Appendix E), and an estimate of the purchasing power of collective units and miscellaneous, leaving the wage bill as the residual. It is assumed that the purchasing power of collective units and the portion not accounted for were equal to the figure for 1957. In the 1958 plan this figure was to be reduced by 300 million yuan, according to Po I-po, "Draft Plan for the Development of the National Economy in 1958" (February 3, 1958), NCNA, February 13, 1958, translated in *CB*, no. 494, p. 19, but this may have been offset by increases in miscellaneous purchasing power under the pressure of the "great leap forward."

awards would, if anything, have reduced the need for material incentives.[43] In addition, many nonwage benefits, such as choice housing assignments, use of automobiles, and vacations at resorts, were given in such a way as to enhance rather than offset incentive differentials in incomes. It seems more likely, therefore, that if, in the years prior to 1958, material incentives were used to a greater extent than they would have been under a free enterprise system, this was due to Chinese adaptation of Russian wage policies with only relatively minor variations, and not to under-

[43] For a more detailed discussion, see Charles Hoffman, "Work Incentive Policy in Communist China," *The China Quarterly*, no. 17 (January–March 1964), pp. 92–110.

lying conditions peculiar to the Chinese Communist economy.[44] It may also have served various political purposes, such as attachment of the loyalty of the proletariat to the regime. In any case, the relative stagnation of wages since 1958, a situation only modestly altered by the 1963 reform, together with the shortage of food and clothing during 1960–1962, have undoubtedly made it necessary for the regime to take whatever steps it could to raise incentives. If the system was somewhat economically irrational prior to 1958, therefore, it is doubtful that such has been the case since that time.

This limited degree of economic irrationality in the Chinese Communist wage determination prior to 1958, if in fact it existed at all, should not be exaggerated. Within the limited role set down for them, wages seem to have performed fairly effectively. They have had little effect on labor allocation, but this has been the result of the nature of the labor market and the high degree of direct control over it and not of the ineffectiveness of wages. These direct controls over labor have been used, on the one hand, because the market has not been able to stop undesired flows of workers from rural areas, and, on the other, because planned allocation of highly skilled labor better fits the needs of a planned industrial sector.

In the realm of incentives, wages have played an important and positive role, although the precise effects are impossible to measure. Irrationality in the sense of too-wide wage differentials, far from hurting, could only have enhanced these positive incentive effects. Only in the realm of control over inflationary pressures on the urban consumers' goods market could it be said that wage policy has had undesirable effects, and even here, the major problem has not been with wage policy so much as it has been with laxity in financial controls over industry and industrial hiring policies. The inefficiencies that these inflationary pressures have caused, however, are the subject of the next two chapters.

[44] For a discussion of the relation between wage policies of China and Russia, see Peter Schran, "Unity and Diversity of Russian and Chinese Industrial Wage Policies," *Journal of Asian Studies*, XXIII (February 1964), 245–251.

CHAPTER VIII

Price Stability on the Consumers' Goods Market *

Controlling inflation on the consumers' goods market of any underdeveloped economy where the emphasis is on rapid economic growth is never easy. Policies for controlling price increases almost invariably affect a country's rate of growth — a fact no less true for Communist China than for any other developing country. One alternative is to allow inflation to occur, but this too is not without cost. It is true that in a socialist planned economy with a variable sales tax there is little danger that retail-price inflation will lead to a major misallocation of investment resources. There is no real probability, therefore, that planners' sovereignty will be replaced by consumers' sovereignty. On the other hand, inflation on the consumers' goods market is fraught with political danger, particularly in Communist China. It also has implications for the equity of distribution and the effectiveness of wage and price incentives.

Until 1958 or 1959 the regime in China had managed not only to achieve a high rate of growth, but to keep price increases at a moderate level. They accomplished this in the face of a development strategy that gave overwhelming priority to the industrial producers' goods sector and the previously described technique of planning that relied on overfull utilization of resources, not to mention pressures generated by the Korean War. Under similar, but probably less severe, handicaps the Soviet Union in the 1930's found it necessary to allow a substantial inflation in prices.

Inflation on the consumers' goods market can be suppressed

* This chapter is based largely on my article "Price Stability and Development in Mainland China (1951–1963)," *The Journal of Political Economy*, August 1964, pp. 360–375, copyright, 1964, by the University of Chicago.

by government directives freezing prices. When industrial whole-sale prices are frozen, the effect is not of first importance in the case of China because most important raw materials and pro-ducers' goods were centrally planned and allocated. Retail prices, however, cannot be held down for any length of time without concurrent control of the sources of inflationary pressure, or the result will be widespread rationing, a black market, or both.

This chapter deals with Chinese attempts to control the sources of inflationary pressure and the extent to which the measures taken made it unnecessary to resort to price freezing by govern-ment fiat. Chapter IX gives a commodity by commodity analysis of why market distribution of consumers' goods was rejected in favor of rationing and the degree to which this was a result of the regime's inability to control general inflationary pressures, considerations of equity, or an ideological predilection toward nonmarket controls.

The present chapter deals first with whether the absence of increases in official price indexes is meaningful, or simply the result of statistical inadequacies or arbitrary price freezes. This is followed by a discussion of the degree to which this stability has been achieved by direct controls over flows of purchasing power onto the consumers' goods market and of the methods used to close the inflationary gap where such direct controls have proved inadequate. Finally, an attempt is made to appraise whether, given the Chinese Communists' goals, selection of al-ternative anti-inflationary measures has been made in the most efficient manner. The analysis is confined to the period since 1951. Measures taken by the Communists to stop the hyperinfla-tion of the 1940's are interesting, but are of little relevance to an analysis of the role of the market in a centrally planned econ-omy.

The Extent of Inflation since 1951 and Its Significance

The major sources of information on price increases are the official retail price indexes published by the Communists (see Table 15). These show an average annual rate of increase since 1951 of barely 1 per cent, with the largest rises being only 3

TABLE 15.   Retail price indexes of consumers' goods in China
(1952 = 100)

Year	All-China	Rural	Industrial products, rural areas	Eight large cities	Urban[a]
1951	100.1	—	100.5	101.0	—
1952	100.0	100.0	100.0	100.0	—
1953	103.2	100.9	98.5	104.9	—
1954	105.5	104.5	100.2	106.9	—
1955	106.3	105.7	101.4	107.9	—
1956	106.3	105.3	100.4	107.8	—
1957	108.6	107.7	101.6	109.1	100.0[b]
1958	108.3	107.1[c]	101.0	108.2	99.1[b]
1959	—	—	—	—	99.1[d]

Source: See Appendix B.
[a] Forty-one main consumers' items in 30 large and medium cities.
[b] December only.
[c] First half year only.
[d] June only.

and 2 per cent in 1953 and 1957 respectively. Although the last
date for which official price indexes were published was June
1959, refugee and other first-hand evidence indicates that official
prices did not rise significantly through 1962 and perhaps 1963.[1]

These indexes, however, do not completely reflect the true
extent of price increases during periods of greatest inflationary
pressure, 1953, 1956, and 1960–1962. This was a result of the
inability of the regime to collect adequate nationwide price data
for any but a few dozen major consumer items — commodities
that were either formally rationed or at least had their prices
held below what they would have been on a completely free
market. The remaining commodities, the ones that were not
generally included in the indexes, not only were not subject to
such rigid price control, but had, in addition, to soak up excess
purchasing power that normally would have been soaked up by

[1] A number of official prices were raised in 1963, but not enough data are
available to ascertain whether these increases had a significant effect on the
indexes.

major commodities. These excluded commodities made up approximately 30 per cent of all retail sales[2] and were sold mostly on the free markets.

Evidence to support the belief that official price indexes tended to have a downward bias can be found for all three periods of particularly severe inflationary pressures. For example, in 1953 the official prices of grain hardly rose at all (the cotton-cloth price actually fell), but some grain was being sold on the free market at 20 to 30 per cent above the official price. Urban vegetable prices (many of which did not enter the official indexes) were about 30 per cent above their 1952 level. In the second half of 1957, vegetable prices in the eight largest cities had risen by 17.9 per cent over what they had been in the first half of 1956.[3] This was a rise which might of itself have caused an additional 1 per cent increase in the retail price index, if all, instead of just a few, vegetable prices had not been excluded from the official indexes.[4] Finally, refugee evidence indicates that between 1960 and 1962 free- and black-market prices (it was not easy to distinguish between free and black markets at this time) were many times the official prices.[5] Under the assumption that all nonincluded prices fluctuated as much as vegetable prices, the bias in the official indexes would be 9 per cent in 1953, 5 per cent in 1957, and considerably more in 1960–1962.[6] Vegetable

[2] *TCKTTH* data office, "The 1956 Domestic Market Price Situation," *HHPYK,* May 25, 1957, p. 115.

[3] These price data are taken from Young Po, "Planned Purchase and Planned Supply," *CCYC,* February 17, 1956, p. 37; and Peking *TKP,* September 24, 1957.

[4] Vegetables made up approximately 7 per cent of the total expenditure of the average urban worker, according to data in "On the Question of Industrial and Agricultural Standards of Living," *TCKT,* July 14, 1957, p. 4; and Peking *TKP,* September 24, 1957.

[5] This is based on refugee interviews made by the author and others in Hong Kong in 1961 and 1962.

[6] The situation is least clear for 1958 and early 1959. Both production and purchasing power rose sharply. Prices fell, but this appears to have been the result of government directives to lower prices. Vegetable prices in 1958, for example, were directed to be returned to the 1955 level in spite of the fact that the demand for vegetables exceeded supply. Sun Chien and Tung Chia-chen, "On Prices of Vegetables in 1958," *CCYC,* March 17, 1959, translated in *ECMM,* no. 171, p. 35; CCPCC and SC, "Directive on Strengthening Leadership over Vegetable Production and Supply Work so as to Have a Timely

prices, however, tended to be erratic for reasons only partly connected with general inflationary pressures so that this is probably an extreme assumption. It is more likely that the bias was seldom more than 3 or 4 per cent, except perhaps during 1960–1962. During periods of retrenchment such as 1954 and 1957, official indexes may even have overstated the rise because official prices tended to be as inflexible downward as upward. The combination of retrenchment and better harvests has also caused free-market prices in 1963 to fall from their crisis levels, though not yet all the way back to the official prices at which the same goods could be bought with ration coupons.[7] None of these qualifications, therefore, negates the basic contention that price increases in Communist China have in fact been quite modest.

One may question whether these relatively modest price increases, including increases on the free market, adequately reflect the extent of inflationary pressure on China's consumers' goods market. Certainly rationing was widespread and became progressively more so. Formal rationing of a sort began as early as November 1953 in conjunction with the introduction of compulsory farm delivery quotas. It gradually spread to urban areas and to an increasing number of commodities.[8] In addition, during periods of tight supply there has been considerable queuing up to purchase commodities not subject to formal rationing. Even taking the existence of widespread rationing into account, however, one can still support the contention that the unfilled inflationary gap was relatively small. With the exception of short periods during 1955–56 and 1958–59, a free market has existed in Communist China onto which most of the excess purchasing power has flowed. As a result, inflationary pressures have generally manifested themselves in the form of price increases rather than through the accumulation of idle cash balances. The actual price level (including free-market prices), therefore, has been

and Well Handled Fall Vegetable Sowing Season" (July 17, 1958), *FKHP*, VIII, 238–239.

[7] "Food Supply Improved," *Far Eastern Economic Review*, XL (April 11, 1963), 55; "Back to Normal," *Far Eastern Economic Review*, XLI (August 15, 1963), 370; "Press Communique of National People's Congress," *Peking Review*, no. 49 (December 6, 1963), p. 7.

[8] For a complete discussion of rationing, see Chapter IX.

a meaningful indicator of the true degree of inflationary pressures, even though these pressures have not been fully reflected in the official indexes. Furthermore, controlling this inflationary pressure has had a considerable effect on the efficiency of distribution on the consumers' goods market. When control has been tight, only a few major commodities have been rationed, but when it has been loose, the extent of formal and *de facto* rationing has expanded rapidly.

Controls over the Sources of Purchasing Power

The Chinese Communists have had two basic means at their disposal for maintaining a balance between aggregate supply and demand on the consumers' goods market. First, unlike their free-enterprise counterparts, they had a number of direct controls over the sources of purchasing power entering the consumers' goods market that could be manipulated in order to maintain a balance. Second, they had several devices that could be used to fill any inflationary gap that did appear. To understand how the first of these alternatives worked, it is necessary to look more closely into the exact nature of mainland China's consumers' goods market.

The main characteristic of the consumers' goods market was that it was not one but two distinct markets, urban and rural. Rural-money purchasing power was derived primarily from the sale of farm and handicraft products and between 70 and 75 per cent of it was spent on industrial products.[9] Urban-money purchasing power, on the other hand, came mainly from the wages of urban employees and was expended on both agricultural and industrial products, the former accounting for approximately 70 per cent of the commodity outlay of the average worker.[10] Therefore, stability of the urban consumers' goods market depended primarily on conditions of food supply in the cities, whereas that of the rural market relied instead on distribution of industrial products in rural areas.

---

[9] This is derived from data in Table 16 and in *TCKT* data office, "Price Gaps between Industrial Products and Farm Products," *ECMM*, no. 104, p. 23.

[10] "On the Question of Industrial and Agricultural Standards of Living," *TCKT*, July 14, 1957, p. 4.

The extent to which activities on one market influenced those on the other was limited. State control of commerce, when combined with turnover and profits taxes, made it possible to determine urban sales prices of major agricultural products independently of their purchase prices. These taxes and controls prevented an increase in inflationary pressure in urban areas from automatically spilling over onto the rural market. The only loopholes were urban free markets and black markets, where peasants sold their produce directly. Price increases on these markets, therefore, led to commensurate increases in peasant incomes and purchasing power. Control of the general level of purchasing power and prices in one market, therefore, was not necessarily the same as control in the other.

The two principal sources of purchasing power over which the authorities exercised control were the urban wage bill and state and cooperative purchases of farm products. Unlike market economies, where wages are usually influenced only through manipulation of general monetary and fiscal controls and occasional interference in the process of collective bargaining, in China control was exercised directly through the planning apparatus. Both the number of workers an individual enterprise could hire and the total amount of wages that it could pay out were determined by the central planning authorities in Peking. The precise nature of these controls was discussed in some detail in the previous chapter. It was pointed out there that, whereas in theory the regime had all the control it needed over urban purchasing power, in fact these controls were often evaded.

Evasion in China meant large unplanned increases in unskilled labor hired by industrial and construction firms in contrast to the situation in the Soviet Union, where a tight labor market made increases in the urban work force difficult so that funds were used instead to bid up wage rates. The result in both cases, however, was large unplanned additions to the wage bill (in 1953, 1956, and 1958 in China) and inflationary pressures on the urban consumers' goods market. Limits on the authority of the regime to adjust wage rates in a way to offset inflationary pressure were also described in the previous chapter. Thus, although the Chinese Communists had the legal authority to adjust the wage bill and hence urban purchasing power at will, the best they could do in practice was to slow down its rate of increase (see Table 16). Even this amount of restraint was im-

TABLE 16. Sources of purchasing power entering the consumers' goods market (million yuan)

Year	Total purchasing power[a] (1)	Total urban wage bill (2)	Rural purchasing power[b] (3)	Total sales of agricultural and subsidiary products[c] (4)	State and cooperative purchases of farm products (5)	Purchasing power of collective units (6)
1950	17,660	—	9,500	8,000	780	—
1951	22,080	—	—	10,500	2,500	—
1952	27,600	6,700	16,500	12,970	5,630	—
1953	33,120	8,800	—	15,320	8,170	—
1954	37,670	9,610	—	17,360	12,070	—
1955	40,240	10,000	—	17,800	—	—
1956	46,500	13,600	24,500	18,400	13,330	7,440
1957	47,000	15,250	25,000	20,280	15,620	6,400
1958	54,800	—	30,000	22,760	19,680	—
1959	—	—	—	29,180	—	—

Source: For sources and a discussion of the reliability of the data used in this table see Appendix E and Table 14.
[a] Equals the sum of columns 2, 3, and 6.
[b] Equals column 4 plus other rural income.
[c] Equals column 5 plus free-market purchases.

possible during periods when political pressures made tight financial control anathema. The need to expand the urban labor force and to keep worker incentives at a peak so as to maintain the rapid pace of industrial development made any greater restraint undesirable.

The regime's hypothetical authority to determine the level of rural purchasing power through control of funds spent by the state on the purchase of agricultural and subsidiary products was as great as in the case of wages, but in reality this authority was even more circumscribed. The need for rapidly increasing farm purchases in order to feed the growing urban population, to export to the Soviet bloc and elsewhere to pay for imports of vital industrial goods, and to provide consumers' goods industry with the bulk of its raw materials meant that purchases had to be increased as much as peasant welfare and the need to maintain peasant incentives could bear. Nor could purchase prices be freely adjusted, since the regime used relative price changes to alter the emphasis placed on the different crops. In addition, an across the board price fall would have seriously affected peasant incentives and increased their resistance to the marketing of their produce. As a result, Communist policy, as shown in Chapters III and IV, was to freeze all purchase prices subject to state control and raise them only when it was desirable to encourage production of a particular crop. As it was, purchase-price increases for the purpose of increasing production alone brought about a 10 per cent increase in the over-all purchase price index between 1954 and 1958. One should not be left with the impression, however, that state agricultural purchase policies contributed nothing to controlling inflation. Resale of these commodities on domestic retail markets soaked up several billion dollars of urban and rural purchasing power more than their original purchase had created, because turnover and profits taxes raised retail prices well above the prices at which the same goods were purchased without any comparable increase in commercial wages or costs. Reduction of state farm purchases, conversely, caused a net increase in inflationary pressure. Thus during the agricultural crisis from 1960 through the early part of 1962, the need to reduce state purchases increased inflationary pressure by a considerable extent and led to great increases in free- and black-market prices.

One possibility that might have introduced more flexibility into the control of inflationary pressures arising out of fluctuations in farm output and purchases would have been a compensatory agricultural tax. A progressive tax, however, would have had the maximum impact when it was needed least, and a regressive tax would have been an unbearable hardship and would certainly have tended to slow the development of agriculture. In actual practice, the regime went to great lengths to ensure that the agricultural tax would be as close to a fixed lump-sum tax as possible so that production would not be adversely affected.[11]

The remaining sources of purchasing power were far less significant but more easily manipulated. The regime, for example, was able to control expenditure on the urban consumers' goods market by collective units. In 1957 the authorities reduced these groups' purchasing power by 17 per cent for the stated purpose of controlling inflationary pressures then extant.[12] Unfortunately not much is known about the nature of this source of purchasing power. It apparently includes funds of army units, welfare institutions, schools, and the like. There is probably some minimum level below which expenditure in this area cannot be reduced, and it is possible that that minimum was nearly reached in 1957.

State agricultural credit could also be fairly easily manipulated in order to restrain rural inflationary pressures. The bulk of agricultural investment came from the savings of cooperatives and communes and not from the outside. State-supplied credit, therefore, could be cut back without seriously impairing rural investment programs. The level of such credit in 1953 and 1954 was too small to make cutbacks of any great use, but by 1957 the amounts involved were substantial enough to make reductions in rural credit an important element in the anti-inflationary policies of that year.[13] Similar but probably even greater reductions in farm credit and direct budget allocations to the communes apparently were undertaken in 1960.[14]

Adjustments in the level of advance purchases of farm crops, a form of credit, were of little help in combating long-run inflationary pressure, since the government had to pay for the

[11] See Chapter III.
[12] Huang K'o, "How We May Settle the Disequilibrium beween Social Purchasing Power and the Supply Volume of Goods in 1958," CHCC, November 9, 1957, translated in ECMM, no. 119, pp. 30–36.
[13] State-issued agricultural credit was 666 and 783 million yuan in 1953 and 1954 as compared to 3029 million yuan in 1956. Young Pei-hsin, "The Road to Raising the Agricultural Development Fund," CCYC, January 17, 1958, pp. 22–37.
[14] Agricultural credit in 1958 and 1959, which had gotten somewhat out of hand, totaled 9 billion yuan, and there were also large direct allocations of funds to the communes on a grant basis. "Credit Work's Role in the Promotion of Production," JPRS, no. 3869, September 13, 1960, p. 2.

crops when it actually received delivery, at the very latest, but
they could be used as a device for shifting pressure to a period
when the state was better able to handle the inflation by other
techniques. Thus in 1957 these payments were reduced by 160
million yuan,[15] a move that probably shifted some pressure off
the tight conditions of early 1957 and onto the latter half of the
year (when most purchases were actually made), by which time
the inflationary pressure had subsided. Except for 1960, when
the potential for cutbacks in agricultural credit and allocations
was so great, the largest reduction in purchasing power that
could be culled from these various minor sources was less than
2 billion yuan, equivalent to only a 10 per cent increase in farm
purchase prices or quotas, or a 10 to 15 per cent increase in the
wage bill.

The situation faced by the authorities until 1960, therefore,
was one of substantial and largely unavoidable increases in both
urban- and rural-money purchasing power. The importance of
wages and farm purchase prices in maintaining worker and peasant incentives and determining agricultural cropping patterns
transcended their role in controlling inflation. Compounding the
difficulties facing the regime was the erratic way in which these
increases occurred. Periodic wage reforms and changes in farm
purchasing regulations and in the nature of the harvest made
predictions of trends in purchasing power even for a year ahead
of little use. Other sources of purchasing power, such as that of
collective units, farm credit, and the like, were more readily ad-
justable, but too small to offset fluctuations in the major components.

The problem for the authorities, as a result, was how to ensure that consumers' goods production not only kept pace with
the increase in purchasing power but grew at more or less the
same rate as well. A rapidly increasing proportion of consumers'
purchasing power, however, came from wages in the producers'
goods sector, which were only indirectly related to consumers'
goods production. In addition, fluctuations in agricultural production were often not felt on the consumers' goods market until

[15] *TCYC* data office, "The Domestic Market Commodity Circulation Situation in 1957," *TCYC,* April 23, 1958, p. 24.

several months or a year later. Hence there were occasions when the supply and demand for consumers' goods were certain to be out of balance. The resulting gap had to be filled by means other than direct controls over the sources of purchasing power.

Closing the Inflationary Gap

To retrieve this balance the authorities had either to find some means of soaking up the excess purchasing power or allow prices to rise, at least temporarily. Chinese Communist resistance to the latter alternative was great, largely for political reasons. The Kuomintang hyperinflation of the 1940's had been a major factor in the alienation of the people and in the demoralization of the regime itself. The Communists, of course, exploited these feelings to the full and later pointed with pride to the speed with which they had ended the rapid price rise. They oversold this point, not only to the general populace, but, more importantly, to lower-level party cadres as well. It was this latter group that was charged with responsibility for seeing to the proper functioning of the free markets and rural trade fairs. Because of their dislike of price increases, they commonly looked on their duties in this area as the curtailment of capitalist tendencies, that is, as the freezing of prices and the limiting of the scope of the market itself.[16] The penchant for price freezing and suspiciousness of free markets in general carried to some degree even up to the highest level of authority. Price rises were seldom consciously allowed for the purpose of bringing supply and demand on the consumers' goods market into balance except where a price increase might stimulate the increased production of some particularly scarce commodity.[17] Since the turnover and profits taxes kept price increases from affecting industrial consumers' goods production, the only area where such price changes could have any influence was in agriculture. Therefore, the only prices that were adjusted with any degree of regularity at all were those of crops and major subsidiary farm products.

[16] For a fuller discussion see Chapter IV.

[17] One of several exceptions to this rule was the 29 per cent increase in the price of woolens in 1957, which was made to end queuing up on the market and reduce domestic demand so as to increase exports — not to stimulate production (Shanghai Price Book, p. 435).

It was not uncommon, as a result, for the regime to be faced with the task of closing an inflationary gap by some means other than allowing prices to rise. When the problem was minor or short-run, the most obvious possibility was to allow commodity stockpiles to take up the slack. There were, in fact, considerable fluctuations in these stocks, but on the whole the stocks were much too small to make a significant difference. Chou En-lai and others called for a substantial increase in these reserves so as to ease the amount of disruption caused by temporary runs,[18] but the more common approach of those in power was to look on substantial reserves as evidence of waste and excess conservatism. In addition, there was the prevailing optimistic attitude that production on all fronts was bound to be much higher next year or the year after, and so why make people tighten their belts further now. Optimism about future development prevailed in 1956, when the cotton-cloth ration was first raised and then, after cotton output had not come up to expectations and reserves had been depleted, had to be cut in half.[19] The good harvest of 1958 was probably also to a large degree consumed immediately rather than set aside against future disasters.[20]

The most important measure for closing the gap, at least over the long run, was consumer taxes. As in the Soviet Union, by far the most important of these taxes were those that could be classified under the general heading of sales taxes. In the case of China, this would include the industrial and commercial taxes and tax on the profits of state enterprises.[21]

The importance of sales and profit taxes is readily apparent from the data in Table 17. The decision to put so much weight on taxes of this type was a clear case of development considera-

[18] Chou En-lai, "Report on the Proposals for the Second Five Year Plan for Development of the National Economy," *Eighth National Congress,* I, 277.

[19] Ministry of Commerce, "Report on the 1957 Supply of Cotton Cloth," *JMJP,* April 20, 1957, translated in *URS,* vol. VII, no. 17, pp. 220–224.

[20] This statement is somewhat speculative. The lack of good data, particularly for agriculture in 1958 and 1959, makes it necessary to rely on a few scattered refugee reports.

[21] For a discussion of the role of taxes in industrial production, see Chapters V and VI.

TABLE 17. Revenue data and the burden of taxation (million yuan)

Year	Total revenue[a]	Sales and profit taxes	Budget surplus or deficit	Revenue from credits and insurance	Burden of money taxes on consumers	Burden on consumers as percentage of their money income
1950	5,340	3,260	−1,470	330	2,943	16.7
1951	9,160	7,980	−1,050	570	6,620	30.0
1952	17,370	11,880	580	190	10,390	37.6
1953	21,270	15,920	−220	490	12,753	38.5
1954	24,440	18,930	−190	1,790	15,370	40.8
1955	24,840	19,920	−2,080	2,360	14,266	35.5
1956	28,020	23,520	−2,560	720	15,748	33.9
1957	30,320	25,720	1,300	700	16,670	35.5
1958	41,060	36,200	100	800	21,315	38.9
1959	54,160	49,060	1,390	0	—	—
1960[b]	70,020	64,750	0	0	—	—

Source: The sources for the first four columns are given in Appendix C. All figures except the total revenue for 1950 and 1951 are official. The 1950 and 1951 figures are derived from percentage increases in revenue published by Chinese Communist official sources.

I estimated the burden of taxation on the basis of scattered data in Communist sources. For the procedures used see Dwight H. Perkins, "Chinese Communist Taxation" (mimeograph). Other estimates of the burden of taxation, using somewhat different procedures, have been made by Ecklund, Taxation in Communist China; and Ma Feng-hwa, "The Financing of Public Investment in Communist China," Journal of Asian Studies, XX (November 1961), 33–48.

[a] Excluding revenue from credits and insurance.
[b] Plan figures.

tions taking priority over price stability. The high rate of investment, the emphasis on producers' goods, and the lack of foreign aid in any great quantity all meant that the tax burden on the consumer had to be extremely heavy. Considering the low level of per capita income in China, it was crucial that this heavy burden not damp incentives and thus slow development any more than was absolutely necessary. Other taxes might make possible a more flexible short-run response to fluctuations in inflationary pressure, but a sales tax could more easily disguise the true size of this development burden.

Sales taxes, however, could not stop an initial rise in prices; they could only prevent excess demand from increasing retained profits and eventually spilling onto the labor market, thus creating further inflationary pressures. The regime still had the problem of how to close short-run inflationary gaps if it wanted to prevent prices from rising in the first place. One possibility still within the realm of taxation would have been to introduce an income tax. Unlike the Soviet Union, Communist China had no income tax at all, unless one includes the above-mentioned agricultural tax. During the first few years of Communist rule there were substantial levies on the income of capitalists, which had as one of their goals control of inflationary pressures resulting from the Korean War. The main reason for these levies, however, was to help squeeze the capitalists out of existence, a task largely completed by 1955 or 1956. A progressive tax on urban wages and salaries would have been administratively feasible, but the authorities undoubtedly felt that they could accomplish most of the same results by controlling wages and salaries directly, and with a far smaller effect on incentives. Under the circumstances, maintenance of incentives was the more important goal, particularly since the income tax would have had to have been large or sharply progressive to have much of a stabilizing effect.

To control short-run changes in inflationary pressure on the urban consumers' goods market, therefore, the regime had to rely on two other devices, namely, savings deposits and bond sales. The two together accounted for over 1 billion yuan in purchasing power in 1954–1957 and 1959, and 2 billion yuan in 1958 — about 10 per cent of the total wage bill in each year.

According to the regulations, savings deposits and bond purchases were to be voluntary, but in practice Communist cadres were able to bring considerable pressure to bear. Pressure, however, was not the only technique used. Interest was paid on deposits, and the regime even resorted to holding raffles based on savings deposits. That such efforts probably met with some, although limited, success may be shown by the fact that current deposits increased from 19.1 per cent of individual deposits to 29.8 per cent in 1956 after awards for such deposits were introduced, although the rise in income as a result of the 1956 wage reform was undoubtedly also a factor.[22] Nevertheless, it remains a fact that two of the largest increases in deposits, those of 1956 and from April 1959 to July 1960, took place after issuance of major state-council directives calling on cadres to make greater efforts to "educate" the masses to make larger deposits.[23]

The role of bond sales was somewhat different. Their original function had been to aid in soaking up the surplus funds of private capitalists. As industry and commerce were socialized, the state had to turn to other sources. In June 1958 the decision was made not to issue any further national economic construction bonds starting in 1959, and local authorities were empowered to issue a limited amount of short-term bonds at a reduced rate of interest. The official reason given for this change was that the decentralization measures of 1958 made it necessary to increase sources of revenue available to the local authorities,[24] but since most local governments in 1959 apparently decided not to issue any such bonds, there probably is a different explanation.[25] It may be that the element of coercion in such bond sales to workers and peasants was so great that it took on the nature of a tax. Bank deposits could at least be redeemed if the individual was willing to go to the necessary trouble; hence their disincentive effects were undoubtedly less.

[22] "A Survey of the Work of Savings during the First Five Year Plan Period," *Chung-kuo chin-yun,* March 7, 1958, translated in *URS,* vol. XI, no. 3, p. 34.

[23] The first was issued on November 5, 1955 (SC, "Notification of the People's Bank of China's Report on Progress in Developing the People's Deposits," *FKHP,* II, 547–548), and the second on June 5, 1959 (SC, "Directive on Strengthening Leadership over Bank Deposit Work and Positively Developing People's Deposit Work," *FKHP,* IX, 137–140). The lack of complete voluntariness has been verified by interviews of refugees by the author and others; see for example, Suzanne Labin, *The Anthill* (London, 1960).

[24] *JMJP* editorial, "Why Do We Want to Issue Local Economic Construction Bonds," *HHPYK,* June 25, 1958, pp. 91–92.

[25] Not all local authorities decided not to issue bonds, however. Bonds were issued in Heilungkiang, for example (Ezra Vogel, unpublished manuscript).

Year	Urban deposits in People's Bank[a]	Net annual change	Urban bond sales[b]	Rural deposits[c]	Rural bond sales[b]	Sales of producers' goods to agriculture[d]
1950	—	—	242	—	18	730
1951	—	—	—	—	—	1,030
1952	740	—	—	121	—	1,410
1953	1,090	350	—	259	—	1,920
1954	1,290	200	696	362	140	2,500
1955	1,570	280	484	—	135	2,820
1956	2,230	660	469	779	138	3,700
1957	2,790	560	433	1,800	217	3,260
1958	4,000	1,210	470	—	320	6,680
1959	5,123[e]	1,123	0	—	0	8,100
1960	5,749[f]	—	—	—	—	—

[a] Year-end data. The years 1952 through 1956 are reported in Peking *TKP*, August 9, 1957. From 1957 on, urban deposits and total deposits in the People's Bank were used interchangeably. The sources of the latter data are Peking *TKP*, September 26, 1959, translated in *CB*, no. 606, p. 11; SC, "Directive on Strengthening Leadership over Bank Deposit Work and Positively Developing People's Deposit Work" (June 5, 1959), *FKHP*, IX, 137–138; "People Enthusiastic in Making Savings," *JMJP*, January 12, 1960, translated in *SCMP*, no. 2180, p. 3; and "Bank Deposits Increase in China," NCNA, August 1, 1960, translated in *SCMP*, no. 2312, p. 14.

[b] For sources see Ecklund, *Taxation in Communist China*, p. 41.

[c] The years 1952 and 1956 are reported in *JMJP*, May 5, 1957. The data for 1953 and 1954 are in T'an Chen-lin, "A First Step in Research on Farm Income and Standard of Living," *HHPYK*, June 10, 1957, pp. 105–111, quoted in C. M. Li, *The Economic Development of Communist China* (Berkeley and Los Angeles, 1959), p. 155. The 1957 figure is from NCNA, January 9, 1958, quoted in Carin, *China Land Problem Series*, II, 547.

[d] The figures for 1950–1958 are in SSB, *Ten Great Years*, p. 170; those for 1959 and 1960 are in Li Fu-chun, "Report on the Draft 1960 National Economic Plan," *Second Session of the Second National People's Congress*, p. 35.

[e] The figure for April was 3800 million yuan.

[f] July figure.

Control of short-run inflationary pressures in rural areas also depended to some extent on the ability of cadres to increase savings deposits and bond sales (see Table 18), but the relative poverty of the rural population, combined with natural rural suspicion of such things as banks and bonds, made these methods less useful than in urban areas. More important was the state's ability to influence the rate of savings and investment in rural areas through its control over agricultural cooperative and commune cadres. It was through these cadres that most funds from the sale of farm produce were channeled after 1955. This may partly explain the substantial increase in rural deposits that took place after 1956, although both the size and nature of these deposits is difficult to determine.[26] The most significant result of the shift in control over funds to the cadres was the enhanced importance of the supply of producers' goods to agriculture. Since few of these commodities depended on agricultural raw materials, their production was comparatively easy to expand and the party could see to it that there was no lack of sufficient demand. The fact that the state was reducing the prices of these items fairly regularly also increased their potential role as short-run anti-inflationary devices. If the state felt that rural purchasing power was excessive at any particular time it could postpone these price reductions, thus soaking up additional purchasing power. Whether or not these prices were actually controlled for this purpose is difficult to say. What is certain is that the greatly increased delivery of producers' goods to agriculture was probably the main factor preventing excessive demand for consumers' goods in rural areas. Even the increase in rural deposits, in fact, did not affect the total amount of purchasing power entering the market as much as it affected the shift in direction of that purchasing power from consumers' to producers' goods.[27]

[26] K. C. Chao, *Agrarian Policy of the Chinese Communist Party,* p. 211, quotes the Peking *TKP,* January 1, 1958, as saying that cash deposits in rural areas were 4.14 billion yuan in 1958, 60 per cent above 1957. It is not clear how this figure differs in coverage from that given in Table 18. On p. 208, Chao states that deposits increased by 10 billion yuan in credit cooperatives between January 1958 and June 1959, but this figure is difficult to believe.

[27] Deposits in credit cooperatives were the main basis upon which loans were issued to peasants and cooperatives for productive purposes.

Summary and Appraisal

The Chinese Communists were able to maintain a high degree of price stability in the face of rapidly increasing purchasing power and somewhat unstable production conditions, particularly in agriculture. Although some of this stability was bought at the cost of formal and *de facto* rationing, as will be shown in the next chapter, the lack of price increases in the main represented a degree of success in preventing the appearance of excess demand on the consumers' goods market. The absence of inflation was brought about by a combination of efforts designed to restrain increases in purchasing power and to fill any gaps that did appear.

The regime's emphasis on producers' goods industry and a high rate of investment created a large discrepancy between total purchasing power and the value of available consumers' goods when priced at factor cost. This long-run problem was solved primarily by the intrduction of the sales tax — a device chosen because it tended to obscure the true tax burden. Increases in the gap between purchasing power and available goods were also prevented by maintaining as tight a rein as possible on the growth of the wage bill and on rises in agricultural purchase prices. Incentive and other developmental considerations, however, made some increases in wages and prices necessary. In addition, the inflexibility of the sales tax and the erratic rates of increase in purchasing power meant that short-run inflationary gaps were continually reappearing. For political reasons, these gaps could not be closed by temporary price increases. As a result, they had to be filled by such makeshift measures as bond sales and savings-deposit drives.

Two questions may be raised concerning these developments. First of all, if it was in fact necessary to hold prices down as rigidly as was the case in Communist China, did the regime go about controlling suppressed inflationary pressures in the most efficient manner? Second, was it really desirable to exercise such tight price control, or were the costs of the required measures greater than the benefits derived?

As to the first question, it is difficult to escape the conclusion that the situation, except perhaps during the "great leap forward," was handled about as well as it was reasonable to expect in light of the basic goals of the regime. Given the emphasis on rapid industrialization in the producers' goods sector and the erratic pace of development likely to occur in any ambitious country so inexperienced in planning and so dependent on agriculture, there were bound to be times when the amount of purchasing power entering the consumers' goods market did not match the supply of commodities available. The only real question, therefore, is whether, once inflationary pressure appeared, it was dealt with quickly and effectively. On the negative side there were few measures that could be classified as "automatic stabilizers," as that term is presently used in the United States. Only an agricultural crisis, because it led to reductions in purchases of agricultural products and eventually in urban employment, thus partially offsetting inflationary pressure deriving from the drop in supply of farm products, tended to adjust purchasing power automatically to meet the smaller amount of goods available on the market. As already explained, however, a reduction in purchases still had a substantial net inflationary effect, and offsetting reductions in urban employment were far from fully automatic. Individual enterprises could and often did keep on unnecessary workers long after their output had been curtailed. The graduated income tax, the most important single automatic stabilizer in the United States, would have been impossible in the rural areas and would have had too great an effect on incentives in the cities. Even savings deposits and bond sales in China did not primarily respond to changes in the level of income.

As a result, the central authorities had to rely mainly on timely administrative action in the form of direct adjustments of the sources of purchasing power or intensified savings-deposit drives. With the possible exception of savings deposits, however, these various measures also played important roles in promoting economic development, roles that usually had a higher priority than the control of inflation on the consumers' goods market.

The lack of automaticity also meant that the regime had to recognize the existence of difficulties and then to take action. In

theory there should have been no difficulty in recognizing inflationary pressure, because the state directly controlled most of
the relevant elements and determined them according to the
needs of the national plan, but the crude state in which planning
still operated made recognition in reality a complicated task. In
1953 and 1956 the regime was aware fairly promptly of the inflationary pressure, since price increases on the free market and
runs on commodity stores were difficult to ignore. In late 1958
and early 1959 the authorities also seem to have realized that
some pressure existed, but tight price control and the spirit of
the period eschewed frankness on the part of lower-level cadres,
which may well have delayed the regime's recognition of the
true situation.

Once the existence of pressure was recognized, there were
further unavoidable lags before the required policies could be
decided and acted upon. The Chinese Communists may not have
had to worry about what a recalcitrant Congress might say,
but the measures available to them could not be manipulated
rapidly at will without seriously impairing production and development. Even bank deposits could not be too speedily pushed
unless the regime were willing to eliminate all pretense of voluntariness — in which case they might as well have had an income tax. That the lag involved can be substantial is evidenced
by the fact that the top leadership was uniformly aware of the
inflationary pressures of 1956–57 by the time of the Eighth Party
Congress in September 1956 and had already called for action
to be taken, but the pressure did not subside until late 1957,
reaching a peak in early 1957 — six months after the congress.
This lag was partly due to the fact that budget cutbacks had
to await the introduction of the new budget if they were to
be accomplished systematically, and partly due to the fact that
many of the policies affected consumer purchasing power only
indirectly.[28] The corresponding lag during the 1958–59 "great leap
forward" was, if anything, longer than in 1956–57, if for no

[28] For instance, cutbacks in investment only affected the consumers' goods
market when they actually resulted in the termination of employment of
workers employed on the various projects. Increases in bank deposits may
often have merely been temporarily substituted for other methods of holding
the idle cash.

other reason than that the greater the inflationary gap in the first place the longer it is likely to take to eliminate it. One can argue for the 1958–59 case that the regime had it in its power to control pressure on the consumers' market more efficiently by planning as well as it was able in the first place, but careful planning, whether for better or worse, would have interfered with the basic idea of the "great leap," which was to decentralize virtually all authority to the lowest-level industrial and agricultural units. If one accepts the Chinese Communists' basic goals, therefore, they were about as efficient as possible in handling inflationary pressure, under the circumstances. Certainly their performance was more impressive than that of the Soviet Union in the 1930's, although part of the credit for this must go to the differences between the two countries' labor markets.

As for the second question — whether or not such rigid price control was desirable — it can be stated first that insofar as control was exercised indirectly rather than by administratively freezing prices, it was undoubtedly a good thing. Inflationary financing of government investment in industry would have made no sense, since all funds that could feasibly be taken from the population could be secured from the turnover and profits taxes. The people were probably far less aware of the true extent to which they were paying these taxes, and hence their incentives were affected less, than if a substantial part of the investment funds had been provided by simply printing the necessary amounts of money. The experience with hyperinflation of the 1940's ensured that the Chinese people's incentives would be adversely affected to a significant degree at the first sign of a recurrence of inflation. Furthermore, the nature of managerial personnel in government enterprises was such that they tended to ignore financial considerations, and often planning in general, except when funds were tight. In theory it was, of course, possible to divorce tight financial control over industry from inflation controls on the consumers' goods market, but in practice, as shown in Chapter VI, the former was necessary in order for the latter to be effective. Of all the control measures available to the Chinese Communists, only the savings-deposits drives and bond sales could conceivably be said to have had enough of a negative effect on incentives to outweigh their usefulness in controlling inflation or in accomplishing other objectives. The authorities themselves apparently came to this conclusion about bond sales, whereas savings-deposit drives could be justified on the grounds that they were the only device available, except for allowing prices to rise, that could offset temporary imbalances on the market.

The more important question, however, is whether it was desirable to adopt such a policy of inflexible opposition to almost all price increases, even when this involved direct as well as indirect price controls, particularly since direct controls often made widespread formal and *de facto* rationing unavoidable. The reasons behind the introduction of rationing, however, were complex and involved factors other than the Communists' penchant for freezing prices. A final appraisal of whether benefits from rigid price control were greater than the costs must therefore await a commodity by commodity analysis in the next chapter.

CHAPTER IX

Retail Price Policy and Rationing

Rejection of market distribution of consumers' goods in favor of formal or *de facto* rationed distribution, where such rejection occurred, was made in response to essentially pragramtic economic and political considerations. Ideology was a dominant element only during certain periods, and then only with respect to a small number of commodities.

Of the two types of rationing, formal rationing is the more interesting both because its effects on the efficiency of the consumers' goods market were greater than those of *de facto* rationing and because the history of the introduction of formal measures provides more information on why the Chinese Communists preferred or rejected market controls. Formal rationing as used here refers to distribution by means of specially issued coupons and similar devices that had to be presented (along with money) at the time of purchase. With *de facto* rationing a consumer could buy all he could pay for when a good was available, but goods available were less than demand for them, resulting in queuing up and distribution on the basis of first come, first served.

The analysis begins with a discussion of why formal rationing was introduced for a number of key commodities such as grain and cotton textiles, first in rural and subsequently in urban areas. This is followed by a section dealing with the extent of *de facto* rationing in areas where retail prices are supposed to be the main means of distribution. Finally, an attempt is made to appraise the over-all efficiency of the consumers' goods market and whether the cost of rationing was greater than the benefits derived from it.

Formal Rationing in Rural Areas

Formal rationing began first in rural areas as a result of the introduction of compulsory purchase quotas for certain major agricultural crops. The reasons behind the introduction of compulsory quotas have been dealt with elsewhere.[1] Since quotas took a greater portion of these crops than peasants would have voluntarily sold on a free market at existing prices, some method other than the market had to be devised for distributing the portion not taken out of the rural sector.

For areas classified as "self-sufficient" or "surplus" with respect to a particular food crop, the process was comparatively simple. It was mainly a question of seeing that individuals, co-operatives, or communes, as the case may have been, met their purchase quotas and that they did not use their excess purchasing power to subvert successful completion of the purchase plan in other areas. This was accomplished by prohibiting peasants from selling these crops to anyone other than authorized state or cooperative commercial organizations. Reopening of the free market, for example, did interfere with the meeting of state purchase quotas until a special directive was passed listing commodities that could and could not enter the free market.[2] When the situation was particularly tight, the state also had to take action to prevent farmers from going to cities and making purchases of key foodstuffs on the urban market.[3] The fact that market prices of grain in rural areas in October 1953 — just prior to the introduction of compulsory grain quotas — were 20 to 30 per cent above the official prices gives some indication of

[1] See Chapter III.

[2] For the text of the directive, see SC, "Regulation on State Planned and Unified Purchase of Agricultural Products and Other Commodities Not Allowed to Enter the Free Market" (August 17, 1957), *FKHP*, VI, 366–369.

[3] In the summer of 1955 a number of directives were passed prohibiting peasants from buying grain in urban areas and bringing it back to the rural areas. This prohibition was also one of the elements in the decision to introduce urban grain rationing. I am indebted to Mr. Reiitsu Kojima for this observation; his sources included the *Tsingtao jih-pao*, June 19, 1955, the *Chekiang jih-pao*, July 8, 1955, and others.

the strength of unsatisfied demand for these commodities in rural areas.[4]

Somewhat more complicated was the problem of supply of foodstuffs to the large number of farmers who produced industrial crops such as cotton and then exchanged these crops for their food requirements. As demonstrated in Chapter III, relative prices of such commodities as cotton and grain materially affected the production of these crops. If the central government had continued to distribute as much grain and other food crops subject to compulsory quotas as the growers of industrial crops desired, this would in effect have been discrimination in favor of these peasants, with the result that everyone would have wanted to concentrate on industrial crops. The alternatives were to lower the purchase prices of industrial crops to a point where the attractiveness of concentrating on these crops was eliminated or to introduce rationing of grain and other major foodstuffs, which would have served the same purpose. The regime chose the latter course, probably because it was somewhat more equitable. The former course would have made it possible for the more prosperous of those peasants producing industrial crops to obtain more than their share of these basic items.[5]

With the advent of cooperatives and later communes, the method of distribution within a village or group of villages was changed, but not as much as the method of determining individual incomes. The greatest single change was the introduction of communal mess halls in 1958 for reasons of ideology and a misguided belief that these mess halls would free labor for the fields, thereby raising over-all efficiency. Mess halls, however, soon were made voluntary, and the major method of distribution within the village gradually returned to a combination of direct allocation by cadres, informal adjustments by commune members, and the free market.

This analysis of formal rationing in rural areas is not exhaustive, but it does cover the main points. Additional consider-

[4] See Chapter VIII, note 3.

[5] The introduction of grain rationing may also have made it necessary to raise the purchase prices of industrial crops more than would have otherwise been required.

ations specifically related to individual commodities are sub-sumed under the discussion of urban areas.

Formal Rationing in Urban Areas

The most important single commodity in the urban consumers' budget was grain. Grain made up nearly 30 per cent of a typical Shanghai worker's food expenditure and over 15 per cent of his total consumption in 1956.[6] Some of the relevant data pertaining to urban grain supply are presented in Table 19.

TABLE 19.   China's grain market (million catties of husked grain)

Year	Total purchases of husked grain	Draw-backs to rural areas	Taken out of rural areas	Sales	Exports	Imports	Urban population[a] (thousand persons)
1950	66,850	—	—	55,510	—	—	—
1950–51	—	—	—	—	—	—	61,690
1951–52	—	—	—	—	—	—	66,320
1952	—	—	—	63,060	—	—	—
1952–53	61,000	—	—	—	—	—	71,630
1953–54	83,000	34,230	48,770	66,640	1,760	—	77,670
1954–55	90,270	46,360	43,910	80,900	2,290	—	81,550
1955–56	85,990	36,350	49,640	70,200	2,295	—	82,850
1956–57	83,430	46,000	37,430	83,300	2,590	—	89,150
1957–58	92,910	—	—	—	—	—	—
1958	—	—	—	89,950	2,570	—	—
1958–59	111,500	47,430	64,070	—	—	—	—
1959	—	—	—	95,800	3,160	—	—
1961	—	—	—	—	—	11,840	—
1962	—	—	—	—	—	7,000	—
1963	—	—	—	—	—	10,600+	—

Source: See Appendix D. The years 1950–51, 1951–52, and so on are grain years, not calendar years.

[a] Figures are given for the end of the calendar year (for instance, 1952), which is the midpoint of the grain year (for instance, 1952–53).

[6] "Changes in the Standard of Living of Shanghai Workers during the Past 27 Years," *TCKT*, July 14, 1957, p. 6.

To understand conditions in the market for any particular commodity it is necessary to know not only the rate of increase in supply, but the demand situation as well. Urban demand for grain was a function of the rate of urban population growth, changes in the per capita level of urban incomes together with the income elasticity of demand for grain, and the sales price of grain.

Of these, the last was the least important. Although it cannot be demonstrated statistically because of lack of sufficient data, demand for grain by China's urban population is undoubtedly price inelastic. This results from the lack of adequate substitutes for grain as the main staple in the average Chinese worker's diet, a phenomenon prevalent in all countries with low per capita incomes and accounted for by the relative expensiveness of the principal grain substitutes.

Chinese Communist data on income elasticity of demand for grain are also lacking, but certain basic conclusions can be arrived at by investigation of several different types of data. This investigation would not be necessary if per capita urban income had not increased significantly during the period under review, but such was not the case, as is readily shown by the 28 per cent rise in real wages between 1952 and 1956 and the 19 per cent rise in per capita consumption.[7] Professor Ishikawa has used both Chinese and non-Chinese data in an attempt to estimate income elasticity of demand for grain.[8] His principal conclusion is illustrated by the accompanying chart, which is reproduced from his book.[9] There are, of course, always dangers involved in making international comparisons, but the primary reason for divergence between behavior of Communist and non-Communist countries

[7] Wage statistics from Yin and Yin, *Economic Statistics of Mainland China*, p. 82, and consumption statistics derived from *TCKT*, July 14, 1957, p. 24.

[8] Ishikawa, *Chugoku ni okeru shihon chikuseki kiko*, pp. 139–185. He primarily uses United Nations data supplemented by various Mainland Chinese sources and Western studies of Eastern Europe.

[9] Ishikawa, p. 172, supplemented by the graph data on p. 156. The procedure used was to measure the per capita net national product against the per capita calorie consumption for food in general and grain and potatoes in particular for about 35 non-Communist countries. The curve for Communist countries was then superimposed, having been derived primarily from United Nations data on Eastern Europe plus various Mainland Chinese sources.

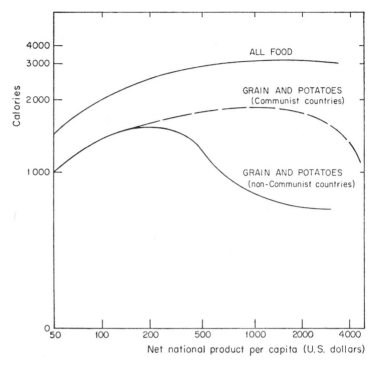

Chart 1.   Income and demand for grain

lies not here but in the fact that it is disposable income, not net national product, that mainly determines behavior of consumers.[10] It is not possible to determine precisely where the typical Chinese urban consumer should be placed on this graph due to lack of a meaningful exchange rate for the *jen min pi,* but probably his income per capita was somewhere near the hundred-dollar mark.[11] Therefore, if Chinese consumer behavior was not markedly different from that of the rest of the world, the Chinese

[10] Professor Ishikawa uses net national product because it is his objective to analyze the relation between economic growth and the demand for grain, and not the behavior of consumers per se.

[11] China's per capita urban consumption was around the 200 yuan mark (*TCKT,* July 14, 1958, p. 24), which, at the current official rate of exchange, was over U.S. $80. Adjustments for the difference between net national product and consumption from disposable income bring it to about U.S. $100.

urban dweller had an income elasticity of demand for grain which was less than 0.2.

This low elasticity estimate is supported by data from Taiwan that give the income elasticity of demand for rice, the principal grain in the Taiwan diet, as .06.[12] The relevance of the Taiwan situation to that on the mainland lies not only in that its inhabitants are Chinese, but that per capita income on Taiwan is approximately the same as that in urban areas of the mainland.[13] A similar picture is given by the experience of Japan in the forty to fifty years prior to 1930. During that time per capita consumption of rice rose by only 25 per cent, part of which increase was not an increase in calories but only substitution for barley, while real per capita national income increased by four and a half times.[14] From this accumulation of evidence it is not possible to arrive at a precise estimate of the income elasticity of demand for grain in the cities of Mainland China, but there is little doubt that that elasticity probably was not great. The principal determinant of increases in urban grain demand, therefore, was the rise in urban population.

Keeping this in mind, it is useful at this point to turn to a direct analysis of conditions on China's urban grain market. Several salient features are immediately in evidence. The first is that the grain market became tight and uncontrolled grain prices rose sharply immediately prior to the introduction of compulsory quotas for all grains in November 1953. Second, rationing of grain in cities was instituted following the issuing of a directive ordering it on August 25, 1955.[15] Finally, in 1960, and especially in 1961 and 1962, the rationing of grain in cities be-

[12] S. C. Hsieh and T. H. Lee, *The Role of Demand Projection in Agricultural Planning in Taiwan* (Taiwan, n.d.), p. 8. The year for which the estimates were made was 1958. The significance of Taiwan data may be reduced somewhat by the increasing substitution of wheat flour for rice.

[13] Average per capita income on Taiwan at current prices in 1958 was NT $3064, which is about U.S. $75 at the current rate of exchange.

[14] Rice consumption and population figures are taken from W. W. Lockwood, *The Economic Development of Japan* (Princeton, 1954), p. 146 and p. 86; real national income statistics are taken from Kazushi Ohkawa, *The Growth Rate of the Japanese Economy since 1878* (Tokyo, 1957), pp. 248–249.

[15] For text of directive, see SC, "Temporary Methods of Handling Urban Fixed Grain Supply," *HHYP*, September 28, 1955, pp. 163–164.

came increasingly severe, but was relaxed in late 1962 and 1963. What is far less obvious is why rationing was introduced in late 1955 and to what extent rationing actually existed between that time and 1960, when the farm crisis clearly necessitated a reduction in rations along with a large importation of grain. An understanding of these points is crucial, however, to understanding the strength (or lack of it) of the Chinese desire to avoid use of rationing on the consumers' goods market.

Timing of the institution of planned purchasing of grain was determined mainly by the beginning of the forced-pace industrial development of the first five-year plan. Under this pressure, as already mentioned, the demand for grain was such that grain prices in many markets were 20 to 30 per cent above the official price, and the general grain-price index in October 1952 was 10 per cent above that of December 1952.[16] Since the central government was undoubtedly planning to institute forced state grain purchases in the not very distant future anyway, this was obviously a logical time to do so. That the results were immediate is clear from statistics that show an increase in grain purchases of 35 per cent over the previous grain year.[17] The effect of this on urban grain supplies was equally rapid, and the rise in price of grain was brought to a halt.[18] From the end of 1953 to the end of 1955 neither the nonagricultural work force, urban population, nor wages increased by very much (wages rose by 6 per cent, while the urban population rose by about the same amount).[19] Since, during this span of two years purchases of grain reached a high level, exports were not greatly increased, grain prices did not rise, and there is evidence that central government grain

[16] Young Po, "Planned Purchase and Planned Supply," *CCYC*, February 17, 1956, p. 37. For the general grain-price index, see grain prices in Appendix B. Further evidence of pressure on the grain market is indicated by the fact that between September and December of 1953 the state grain-purchase plans were only completed on the average of 54.5 per cent, whereas with the sales plan it was 133.3 per cent (Shanghai Price Book, p. 410).

[17] See Table 19. November 1953 was itself 38 per cent above November 1952 (Young Po, p. 38).

[18] See Appendix B, Tables 22 and 24.

[19] For urban population, see Table 19. For real wages, see Yin and Yin, *Economic Statistics of Mainland China*, p. 82.

stores were increased,[20] it does not appear likely that rationing was introduced in response to an already-existing crisis in the grain market.[21] To understand the probable reason for the adoption of rationing it is necessary to look ahead to the policies contemplated after rationing of grain had been instituted. The most important such policy was the establishment of cooperatives in agriculture, which was carried out that winter. There was, in addition, the beginning of a rapid push along the industrialization front combined with a wage reform that led to a substantial increase in the urban work force and a large rise in the average wage.

The significance of the decision to push cooperatives in agriculture for the grain market lay primarily in the grain-purchase policy that was carried out in conjunction with those cooperatives. Two principal features of this policy were a planned reduction in the amount of purchases and a statement that there would be no change in levies and purchases for three years. The stated reason for reduction in purchases was that it was to correct the mistake of purchasing too much the previous year. This may have been the case, but in light of the substantial increases from 1957 on, it seems likely that the mistake was more a matter of timing than any permanent desire to reduce purchases and part of a policy to make cooperatives palatable. Seen from this point of view, it appears likely that the institution of rationing resulted at least in part from this desire to reduce purchases temporarily. It may also be that the central authorities anticipated some trouble in connection with cooperatives that might have resulted in further reductions in grain deliveries and wanted to eliminate the need for precipitous action later on.

[20] The belief that central government reserve grain stores were built up in this period is based on the belief that, because of the run on these stores in 1953, they could not have been very large by the end of the year. By the middle of 1957, however, these stores were at a level of 20 billion catties (Ma Yin-ch'u, "A New Principle of Population," *JMJP*, July 5, 1957, translated in *URS*, vol. VIII, no. 6, p. 93). It is probable that these stores were primarily increased before the big increase in urban population in 1956 and the cutback in grain purchases. The differences between the purchase and sales figures also suggest this.

[21] For the principal exception to this statement, see note 3.

Further complications that could have been and probably were anticipated were the above-mentioned substantial increases in per capita purchasing power in 1956 brought on by the wage reform, and, more important, from the standpoint of demand for grain, the rise in urban population accompanying the accelerated pace of development in early 1956. These various factors were enough to cause any prudent planner to take anticipatory action. The choice was essentially between adoption of grain rationing, planned or *de facto,* and a rise in the price of grain. There were probably several reasons for preference for rationing, one of which was the political undesirability of any rise at all in such a basic price.[22] Another was that, since demand for grain in China was price inelastic, the resulting rise in grain prices would have had to have been very large to accomplish its purpose.

Events of 1956 appear to have justified the caution of late 1955, although one cause of the reduction in purchases turned out to be unanticipated natural disasters, which were particularly severe that year. Per capita grain consumption in cities was reduced even though wages increased. It is undoubtedly true that it was the institution of rationing that made this possible without accompanying sharp price rises. Available evidence suggests that there were no increases at all in urban sales prices of grain in 1956.[23]

The picture for 1957 through 1959 is less clear. From Table 19 it can be seen that grain purchases and sales both rose significantly, particularly in 1958 and 1959. Grain taken out of rural areas also increased substantially.[24] Part of this increase went to rebuilding grain stores, which had been depleted in 1956–57, and a large part went to feeding the increased urban population. What remained, however, appears to have been enough to make possible an increase in urban per capita consumption.

There is some evidence that rations were increased as early as the grain year 1956–57, that is, less than one year after the

---

[22] Substantial increases in sales prices of basic staples usually have a significant political impact in most underdeveloped countries.

[23] See Appendix B, Tables 22 and 24.

[24] State and cooperative stores rose 24 per cent ("Effectiveness of the First Half Year of the 1958 National Economic Plan," *HHPYK,* August 25, 1958, p. 69).

institution of rationing. Supplies to urban areas were reported to have increased by 5900 million catties and the average monthly grain ration per capita raised from 25.72 to 27.6 catties.[25] Per capita urban consumption of food grains in 1958 is given as 40 per cent above 1952, which would imply a further increase in 1958 over 1957.[26] In the first half of 1959 the urban population was higher by 7.7 per cent than during the first half of 1958, whereas the urban grain supply had increased by 34.21 per cent, making for a 24.62 per cent increase in per capita supply.[27] The magnitude of these increases in relation to the rise in urban per capita income combined with low income elasticity of demand for grain would seem to indicate that pressures during this period in the urban grain market were not great and that rationing, at least of lower-quality grains, was not severe, if it existed in any meaningful sense at all.[28]

Cotton cloth was second only to grain as the most important commodity entering the consumers' goods market both in urban and rural areas. Fortunately there is also a comparative wealth of information available on the supply of this commodity and to a lesser degree on the demand for it.

As early as January 4, 1951, the Financial and Economic Committee had ordered the unified purchase of cotton yarn. In September 1954 the order instituting the planned purchase and supply (rationing) of cotton cloth was issued.[29] The necessity for this move and its timing are not difficult to discover. Cotton-cloth sales reached a peak in 1953 and then fluctuated around that level for the next five years (see Table 20) while per capita income in urban areas was rising rapidly, as was purchasing power in rural areas. Available evidence suggests that the income elasticity of demand for cotton cloth was high. One source states that it was the first commodity upon which increases in consumer

[25] Chu Ching-chih, "A Review of Urban Food Rationing and Some Suggestions for Improvement of the System," *Liang-shih,* August 25, 1957, translated in *ECMM,* no. 110, p. 29.

[26] *HHPYK,* October 27, 1959, p. 52.

[27] Chou Po-p'ing, "This Year's Condition of Food Supply in China," *Chung-kuo hsin-wen,* October 3, 1959, translated in *URS,* vol. XVII, no. 6, pp. 80–81.

[28] This may account for why refugees usually date the beginning of formal rationing not from 1955, but from 1959 or 1960.

[29] Shanghai Price Book, p. 414.

TABLE 20. Nationwide state, cooperative, and private retail sales

Item	1950	1951	1952	1953	1954	1955	1956	1957	1958	1959
Index of purchasing power	100	125	156	188	213	228	263	266	310	—
Index of wage bill	—	—	100	131	143	149	203	228	—	—
Cotton cloth (millon meters)	1,668	2,256	2,813	3,899	3,791	3,849	5,101	4,150	4,860	5,200
Index	100	135.2	165.1	226.6	222.2	223.7	296.4	196.6	220.0	235.4
Edible oils (1000 tons)	540	—	778	—	—	1,060	1,230	1,050	1,065	1,140
Index	100	—	144.1	—	—	196.3	227.8	194.4	197.2	211.1
Pork (1000 tons)	1,710	—	2,396	—	—	2,420	2,350	1,454	1,764	—
Index	100	—	140.1	—	—	141.5	137.4	85.0	103.2	—
Salt (1000 tons)	2,061	2,930	2,978	—	—	4,000	3,800	3,900	4,000	—
Index	100	142.2	144.5	—	—	194.1	184.4	189.2	194.1	—
Sugar (1000 tons)	243	—	471	—	—	640	—	880	981	1,079
Index	100	—	193.8	—	—	263.4	—	362.1	403.7	440.0
Cigarettes (1000 crates)	1,720	1,930	2,465	—	—	3,590	3,701	4,324	—	—
Index	100	112.2	143.3	—	—	208.7	215.2	257.2	—	—
Coal (1000 tons)	17,596	20,380	25,422	—	—	41,500	52,298	64,570	—	—
Index	100	115.2	144.5	—	—	235.8	297.2	367.0	—	—
Rubber shoes (1000 pairs)	41,927	—	59,770	—	—	66,350	100,857	108,780	178,190	—
Index	100	—	149.4	—	—	158.2	252.1	259.9	425.0	—
Bicycles (1000)	140	—	365	—	—	510	729	—	—	—
Index	100	—	260.8	—	—	364.3	520.7	—	—	—
Paper (1000 tons)	140	—	218	—	—	—	275	335	519	—
Index	100	—	155.7	—	—	—	196.4	239.3	370.7	—

Sources: For sources and a discussion of the statistical reliability of the above data, see Appendix D, Table 32, except for indexes of purchasing power and the wage bill, which are derived from data in Tables 14 and 16, respectively.

income were spent.[30] Behavior of the market in 1956, when loosening of control led to a run on cotton cloth in both urban and rural areas necessitating a subsequent large cut in the ration, is further evidence of the disparity between demand and supply at that time.[31] This rapid increase in expenditure on cotton cloth in both urban and rural China[32] took place, even though prices of cloth were relatively very high. The retail price of white cotton cloth in Tientsin and Shanghai, for example, was over four times the prewar average in 1934–1936, whereas the price of grain had only risen about 2.5 times. Another indication of the relative level of the price of cloth was that it was about three times cost, whereas the markup above cost of the price of grains in urban areas was less than 20 per cent.[33] The relatively high level of cotton-cloth prices may have been one factor discouraging the use of further increases as a means of restricting demand, although a more important factor undoubtedly was that the required price rise would have had to have been very large if it were to accomplish its aim. The objections to this on political grounds, if no other, would have been substantial. Instead of raising prices the authorities accompanied the institution of rationing with a slight price reduction throughout the country.[34]

Difficulties in the cotton-cloth market were, of course, primarily due to difficulties in increasing raw-cotton production. They were aggravated, however, by the state's desire to expand textile exports, which were increased by nearly 400 per cent between 1952 and 1956 [35] and were continued at a high level during the crisis years 1960–1962. Another problem facing those in charge of cloth

[30] "How to Conduct Surveys on Commodity Supply and on the Purchasing Power of Social Commodities," *Chi-hua yu tung-chi*, August 23, 1959, translated in *JPRS*, no. 1023D, p. 5.

[31] For a discussion of this cutback, see Ministry of Commerce, "Report on the 1957 Supply of Cotton Cloth," *JMJP*, April 20, 1957, translated in *URS*, vol. VII, no. 17, pp. 220–224.

[32] *WKKT*, p. 185.

[33] See Table 10.

[34] See Appendix B. This price reduction may have been similar in intent, though opposite in direction, to the rises in the prices of edible oils and pork, since it was made in conjunction with a reduction in the purchase price of cotton. There is, however, no statement by the central authorities to this effect (see discussion of pork and edible-oil prices below).

[35] *WKKT*, p. 173.

distribution was the conflict between urban and rural demands. Since most cloth was produced by urban industries, these same industries had to supply both markets.[36] Introduction of rationing in one market without also introducing it in the other would have been possible, but of doubtful political desirability, since it would have been difficult to justify except on grounds of preference for one group over the other.[37] In any case, the supply of cloth was so limited that it probably would have required cutting supplies in one market to the bone in order to obviate the necessity of rationing on the other.

Rationing of edible oils and pork in urban markets was instituted for reasons similar to those for cotton cloth but with emphasis on production difficulties more than on high income elasticity of demand. The drop in pork sales resulting from these production difficulties was particularly severe. Pork rationing began in late 1956 and that of edible oils in November 1953.[38] Neither has been lifted since. The most distinctive feature of the rationing of these two commodities was the fact that it was accompanied by substantial increases in the sales prices of the two goods. The purpose of those price increases was not primarily to reduce demand. Rather, the rise in sales prices almost exactly matched the rise in purchase prices, which, as already mentioned, were undertaken in order to stimulate production. The purpose of this action appears to have been an attempt to ensure that these increases in purchase price did not affect the existing balance between consumption and accumulation by increasing purchasing power in one area without subsequently reducing it in another.[39]

[36] *WKKT*, p. 186. Statistics in this book give production figures of locally produced or handicraft cloth for 1954–1956, which are only about 10 per cent of total cotton-cloth production.

[37] There would, of course, also have been serious enforcement problems if rationing were introduced in one market but not the other. Unlike grain needs, a family's annual cloth needs could be met by a single trip to the unrationed market.

[38] Shanghai Price Book, p. 412.

[39] This is the principal reason given in SC, "Directive on Raising the Sales Prices of Vegetable Oil, Sesame Oil, Tea Oil, Tung Oil, Wood Oil, Tallow Oil, and Northeast and Inner Mongolian Bean Oil" (March 22, 1957), *FKHP*, V, 185–186, and the directive ordering the pork retail price rise on February 15, 1957 (text in Shanghai Price Book, p. 596), as well as in articles explaining the

Other commodities that were formally rationed in one way or another were coal and a few items such as bicycles and radios. Rationing of the latter two items took the form of requiring the purchaser to put his name on a waiting list for several months before receiving delivery.[40] The reason why this was necessary was certainly not the slow increase in the production or sales of these goods. Production and sales of industrial consumers' goods that did not depend on agriculture for their raw materials increased very rapidly. Sales of radios, for example, increased by 59 per cent in 1956 and by 160 per cent in 1958.[41] In 1959 the sales of clocks and watches, washing machines, radios, bicycles, and household utensils were from 12 to 35 per cent above 1958, whereas sales of most products depending on agriculture only increased from 2 to 9 per cent.[42] These examples could easily be multiplied.[43] The necessity for rationing in these cases, when such a necessity existed, undoubtedly arose from the fact that the absolute level of their production was low and that they were luxury items par excellence for higher-grade industrial workers and cadres and hence had very high income elasticities of demand by the urban population. The alternative of price rises was not used, probably because of price inelasticity in the demand for these goods plus the fact that rationing was fairly simple to administer because of the limited quantities involved.[44]

The rationing of coal consumption by individuals also was not due to a slow rate of growth in production, but rather to higher-priority, competing demands of industry. The supply of kerosene

----

directives ("Why Were the Prices of These Commodities Raised?" *HHPYK*, May 25, 1957, pp. 110–111; SC spokesman, "Discussion of the Market Price Problem with an NCNA Reporter," *ibid.*, pp. 109–110).

[40] This information is based on a number of interviews with recent mainland residents. It applies to both urban and rural areas.

[41] SSB, "Report on the Results of the 1956 National Economic Plan," *HHPYK*, September 10, 1957, p. 204; SSB, "Report on the 1958 National Economic Development Situation" (April 14, 1959), *HHPYK*, April 25, 1959, p. 53.

[42] *Chi-hua yu t'ung-chi*, February 1960, p. 44.

[43] See Table 20 above and production figures in SSB, *Ten Great Years*, pp. 99–100.

[44] For example, the total number of bicycles produced in 1958 was just over 1 million (SSB, *Ten Great Years*, pp. 99–100).

to consumers was limited for similar reasons.[45] The shortage of coal did not lead to rationing until 1957.[46] Prior to that time the state had relied on maintenance of the sales price of coal at a very high level. Urban sales prices in Shanghai and Tientsin were two or three times the cost of production.[47] The promotion of small-scale coal mining was in part a move to solve the problem of rapid increase in consumer demand.

Formal rationing, therefore, was introduced into China on pragmatic grounds. Foremost among these was the desire to prevent substantial price increases in basic commodities, increases that would have had undesirable political side effects. On the positive side, rationing also placed considerable power over individuals in the hands of the state, particularly in urban areas. Individual movements were restricted, for example, by the inability of an individual to obtain food coupons unless his move had been approved by the cadres involved.

Considerations of equity were also important. The slow pace of agricultural development, when combined with the relatively rapid growth in wages, meant that higher-income groups could bid away key commodities from those with lower incomes. In a relatively wealthy society this would not cause any serious hardship. People at the lower end of the income scale would still have plenty of those commodities basic to health and survival, but such was not the case in China. It was pointed out in Chapter

[45] Chang Hsuan-wen, "Do a Good Job of the Oils Supply for 1957," *Shang-yeh kung-tso,* February 14, 1957, translated in *ECMM,* no. 79, pp. 14–15.

[46] For the text of the principal directive, see SC, "Report on the Organization of the Coal Market for 1957" (March 18, 1957), translated in K. C. Chao, *Economic Planning and Organization in Mainland China,* II, 41–43, and for further discussion, see Keng Tsun-san, "A Brief Discussion on the Existing Price of Coal," *CCYC,* March 17, 1959, translated in *ECMM,* no. 171, pp. 36–39.

[47] The average cost of producing coal varied between 7 and 13 yuan per ton, depending on the mine (*JMJP,* March 15, 1958, in "Coal Mines," *China News Analysis,* no. 266, February 27, 1959, p. 2; *TCKT,* March 14, 1958, p. 21), whereas the sales price in Tientsin varied mainly between 20 and 30 yuan (Tientsin TKP). Some of the difference is determined by transport costs, but even in the case of Shanghai this is probably less than 10 yuan per ton; see Ministry of Communications, *Shui-yun yun-chia hui-pien* (Compendium of water transport prices; Peking, 1956).

III that, although the average Chinese peasant's income was near the subsistence level, he did have some surplus with which to work. Nevertheless, that surplus was small and in constant danger of being wiped out by either natural or man-made disasters. Most Chinese Communist agricultural policy was directed toward raising production so that this marketed surplus could be increased, but all efforts in this direction failed. The small increases in the marketed surplus that did occur were wiped out, so far as their effect on per capita consumption was concerned, by population increase and the need to expand agricultural exports.

Per capita incomes in urban areas were higher than in rural areas, but the food situation was no better. Increased food deliveries to the cities were matched by peasant migration to those cities. Both in urban and rural areas, therefore, the ability of higher-income groups to bid away food might have caused those with lower incomes severe hardship even in relatively good times (after a good harvest). During the 1960–1962 agricultural crisis, the ability of the state to distribute key products equitably throughout the country was the only thing preventing widespread starvation and all it would have implied. One alternative would have been to equalize wages, but this would have destroyed the system that was so vital to rapid industrialization. Rationing of many basic food items, therefore, is likely to remain necessary until the Chinese Communists are able to solve their agricultural difficulties.

Only in the distribution of such items as housing (and the communal mess halls) can one argue that ideological considerations were important in the decision to reject the market. Rents were set at levels that were meaningless in terms of supply and demand.[48] Even here, however, the ideological bias against rent was only one element in the decision. Direct allocation of housing, automobiles, paid vacations in desirable spots, etc. gave the state great powers for reward and punishment particularly for

[48] As an indication of how low rents were, rent made up less than 2 per cent of the total consumption expenditure of the average Shanghai worker ("Changes in the Standard of Living of Shanghai Workers during the past 27 Years," *TCKT*, July 14, 1957, p. 6).

higher level cadres.[49] Communal mess halls may also have been established in order to tighten rations in a way not as readily apparent to consumers, but this was not a major factor.[50]

Retail Price Policy and De Facto Rationing

Commodities not formally rationed made up over half of all consumers' expenditures.[51] Throughout its rule, the regime has attempted to use the price mechanism to distribute certain categories of consumers' goods. Although the free market was reopened in 1956, primarily in order to stimulate production, it was also a way of freeing retail prices from the excessive control of the previous two or three years. Up to the middle of 1958 prices of small and diverse commodities, commodities that, because of their great number, could not be satisfactorily controlled, were allowed to fluctuate with conditions on the market. Goods that had to be kept fresh or alive were distributed in a similar manner. In many cases the regime had to allow substantial price increases in order to maintain an orderly market, but it apparently preferred this to the disorder that would have resulted from rigid administrative price determination. Where prices were determined by administrative authorities without constant semiautomatic reference to market conditions, it was often for commodities whose supply was steadier and hence more predictable. For these commodities, prices could be held rigid for some time and the market could still be cleared without frequent queuing up. When a shortage appeared, the regime would then raise its price. The price of woolens in 1957, for example, was raised in response

[49] This is based on refugee interviews.

[50] For a similar interpretation of the role of this factor in the establishment of urban communes, see H. J. Lethbridge, *China's Urban Communes* (Hong Kong, 1961), chap. iv.

[51] The percentage for urban consumers can be derived from various already-mentioned budget studies of workers in cities by adding up the percentage of goods subject to rationing and subtracting from total expenditures (that is, 100 per cent). It is not possible to arrive at a precise estimate in this manner because the reported categories are not sufficiently broken down, but a crude impression can be obtained. A rough idea of the proportion for rural consumers can be obtained from the fact that a high percentage of the commodities marketed in rural areas were industrial goods, most of which, except for textiles, were not formally rationed.

to a desire to eliminate queuing, which had occurred for several months prior to the price increase. To do this the regime had to tolerate a price increase for woolens of 29 per cent.[52] The price of sugar was lowered in 1953 and then raised again when supply proved to be insufficient.[53] Vegetable prices between April 1956 and April 1957 rose in some cases as much as 100 per cent, and eggs as much as 25 per cent.[54] Similar examples can be found for hundreds of commodities.

The extent of consumers' goods distribution through the price system, however, should not be exaggerated. Before 1954 and 1955 much of the fluctuation in prices was allowed because the state still felt it needed the services of capitalist commerce, particularly retail traders. When the regime decided that the power of private commerce and industry was too great, they proved in the "five-anti" campaign that they were quite willing to sacrifice the needs of market equilibrium, with the result that the market was temporarily glutted, owing to tax and price policies that made its orderly operation impossible.

Even during periods when inflationary pressures were weak and the free market was at its freest, the regime was reluctant to allow sufficient price flexibility to clear the market.[55] Retail price policy was at its most flexible between the time of reopening of the free market in 1956 to its closing in mid-1958 (except for the first two or three years of the regime's existence). Rural trade fairs kept a semblance of a free market for a few commodities open in rural areas after mid-1959, but free markets initially were only intermittently extended to cities, and in both areas price flexibility was severely limited. When the agricultural crisis of 1960–1962 brought heavy inflationary pressure, *de facto* rationing became universal for all commodities sold at official prices. Pressure was so heavy, in fact, that state marketing pro-

[52] Shanghai Price Book, p. 435. Another factor in the increase in woolen prices was a desire to cut off domestic demand so as to increase woolen exports ("Why Were the Prices of These Commodities Raised?" *HHPYK*, May 25, 1957, p. 111).

[53] Shanghai Price Book, p. 413.

[54] *Tsingtao jih-pao*, July 26, 1957.

[55] There are, for example, numerous articles discussing the problem of distributing nonrationed goods in a rational manner without raising prices. Street committees are often called on to help shops over such temporary crises.

cedures often were circumvented in favor of black marketing. As a result there were two prices for most commodities, the black-market price being several times the official price. In the Soviet Union these two sets of prices became legally institutionalized in the collective-farm markets at an early stage. In China, however, it was not until 1962 that the regime formally sanctioned the widespread use of such an arrangement (except for a few major agricultural products for which the relevant date is 1961). During the 1960–1962 crisis the Chinese Communists also instituted general-purpose ration coupons (in effect, a second currency) that could be used to purchase a wide variety of items. With the advent of better crops in late 1962 and 1963, much semiformalized rationing disappeared and free- and black-market prices fell, but not all the way down to the level of officially set prices.[56]

The Chinese Communists have never tried to justify their penchant for price freezing and *de facto* rationing except as a device for preventing politically undesirable price increases for their own sake, and secondarily as means of suppressing latent "capitalist" tendencies.[57] *De facto* rationing gave the state little added measure of political control, since rations were not distributed by means of cadre-issued coupons. Nor could a system that gave priority to those who could stand in line the longest be considered more equitable. These points should not be overemphasized, however. The regime did take fairly elaborate, though informal, steps to reduce inequities resulting from *de facto* rationing.[58] These same measures undoubtedly also enhanced cadres' political control to at least some degree.

---

[56] This information on the 1960–1963 period is based primarily on refugee information obtained by the author or from Vogel, unpublished manuscript. Some of this information is available in published sources as well: see, "What Do People Eat?" *China News Analysis,* no. 364 (March 17, 1961), p. 2; "Back to Normal," *Far Eastern Economic Review,* XLI (August 15, 1963), 370.

[57] The Soviet system of keeping retail prices below the level needed to just clear the market is justified on grounds that it brings home to workers the insufficiency of consumers' goods and hence the need for continued hard work. Morris Bornstein, "The Soviet Price System," *American Economic Review,* LII (March 1962), 92.

[58] Ezra Vogel, unpublished manuscript.

The Chinese Communists, therefore, paid a fairly heavy price in terms of market efficiency for their penchant for rigid retail price controls. With formal rationing they received additional benefits in the form of greater political control and some increased equity, but no comparable benefits were obtained from *de facto* rationing.

To improve market efficiency, the regime would have had either to give up tight price controls and take the political consequences of some price increases or devise more effective means of controlling the sources of inflationary pressure. It was argued in the previous chapter, however, that anti-inflationary devices were used about as effectively as possible given China's development strategy. A third alternative would have been to emphasize development of consumers' goods, particularly in agriculture, but this would have flown against basic principles of the regime. Shifts toward greater investment in agriculture since 1961 have been made in order to ensure some minimum standard of living and level of exports, not to increase efficiency of distribution on the consumers' goods market.

CHAPTER X

Conclusion

Attempts to direct the development of Mainland China's economy, at least in part through the market mechanism, have been numerous, but not always successful. The analysis in previous chapters has dealt with the questions of where market controls have been used, and, more important, why they have been used, or rejected, as the case may be. There also has been an attempt to ascertain, wherever it was possible to do so, with what degree of economic efficiency these controls were utilized.

Scope of Market Controls

The question of where the market played a significant role can be handled most easily. In the case of industrial production and construction, prices played only a marginal role, their functions being circumscribed by centrally determined physical plan targets and rationed allocation of most key inputs. However, as time passed, the regime took several important steps, even in the industrial sector, to enhance the market's function, primarily by attempting to raise the importance of the profits target in the eyes of factory managers. These steps, however, were largely negated by lax control of enterprise finances and an attitude of opposition to all constraints on factory managers' behavior, particularly during the "great leap forward" of 1958–59.

In agriculture the market's function was of much greater significance. During the early years of the Communist regime, 1949–1953, farm purchase prices were the only means for controlling agricultural production then at the disposal of the central authorities. To make purchase prices a more effective tool, they had to devise means of eliminating many of the uncertainties connected with such prices — uncertainties that arose out of the instability of rural markets and the ease with which they were manipulated by middlemen for their own ends. Elimination of these uncertainties was accomplished by a system of state-guaranteed purchase prices, with advance purchase contracts to back them up.

By late 1953, however, compulsory quotas for major crops began what was to become a substantial encroachment on the role of the market in rural areas. With the establishment of cooperatives in agriculture in the winter of 1955–56 this encroachment was carried a step further, not because use of compulsory quotas was extended, but because rural cadres tended to ignore price and income incentives. Nevertheless, a free market was still the major determinant of a wide range of subsidiary products, and the state continued to try to influence major crop output through manipulation of purchase prices. Communes in late 1958 and early 1959 briefly eliminated private plots and the free market, but these were gradually restored beginning in the latter half of 1959. The market, therefore, continued to be a major determinant of perhaps half of all agricultural produce.

The two sectors of the economy of the Soviet Union where market forces play their largest role are the labor and consumers' goods retail markets. The labor market has not been as important in Communist China. A continuing surplus of unskilled and semiskilled labor has made recruitment a comparatively simple task. The major problem, in fact, has been to prevent migration of such labor to the cities, where their upkeep was more expensive — a migration that is not very responsive to wage-rate variations. Highly skilled technical personnel, on the other hand, have been few enough in number to allow centrally planned physical allocation of such personnel. This high degree of physical control over the labor market has existed almost from the beginning of the Communist regime, the only variations over time being in the degree of enforcement of relevant state regulations.

Unlike its role in other sectors, the market generally has been dominant in the distribution of consumers' goods. Even in this sector, however, nonmarket allocation of commodities has been important. Rationed distribution of a few key consumers' goods began in rural areas at the same time as the introduction of compulsory purchase quotas. In urban areas, grain, cloth, and a few other major items were subjected to rationing, beginning at various times between 1954 and 1957. It was only during the agricultural crisis of 1960–1962, that rationed distribution (including *de facto* rationing in the form of long queues) could be said to have become the main form of allocation of consumers' goods. With recovery in farm output in late 1962 and in 1963–1964, the market once again began to reassert its predominance.

The market, therefore, has continued to play an important role in directing the Chinese economy, but a role subordinate to that of centrally determined physical controls. Generally speaking, the importance of market forces declined steadily between 1949 and 1956 as the Chinese Communists gradually attained the power necessary to establish other forms of control. After 1956, however, the role of the market as opposed to that of physical controls, instead of continuing to decline, fluctuated with basic changes in Communist economic policies and with underlying political conditions. Thus during 1956 and 1957, market forces reasserted themselves in agriculture and consumers' goods distribution, and even to a slight extent in the industrial sector. During the commune movement and "great leap forward" in 1958 and 1959, however, market constraints, and in fact all constraints on the actions of lower-level cadres, went by the board. Tightening of financial discipline from 1960 on, reopening of the free market, and re-establishment of central direction in general tended to enhance the role of all types of control, including that of the market. On the other hand, the importance of the market in certain areas was further undermined by the agricultural crisis, which made market allocation of consumers' goods nearly impossible. Restoration of farm output since late 1962 has considerably alleviated this difficulty. In addition, a number of measures introduced in 1957 and 1958 that would have enhanced the role of the market at the time if financial discipline had not been so lax, were still in force in 1962 through 1964, and presumably had some effect. The role of the market in 1962–1964, therefore, may have been roughly comparable to what it was in 1956 or 1957, with, of course, some not altogether minor differences.

Reasons for Using or Rejecting the Market

Of far greater interest than the sectors where market controls were utilized by the Chinese Communists are the reasons why the market was or was not used. As with almost all economic decisions, historical accident has played a part. The particular level at which producers' goods prices were frozen in 1953 and 1954, for example, was greatly influenced by the level where these prices happened to be when the decision to freeze them was taken. In Communist China, however, chance occurrences are only a small part of the explanation for most economic actions. Unlike the governments of most underdeveloped countries, the Peking regime has the necessary political power to chart its own course. To be sure, this course has to be determined according to the policies of the regime and the underlying nature of the economy with which it has to deal. The authorities, therefore, cannot act arbitrarily without paying a heavy price for the privilege. On the other hand, they have seldom been under pressure to reject an action because they lacked the power to carry it out. Much of the particular interest of the Chinese case stems from this fact, and is further enhanced by the Chinese Communist penchant for experimentation, experimentation that has often involved the trial of policies long advocated by non-Communist economists but never thought practical because of insufficient political strength in the non-Communist underdeveloped world to carry them out.

China's Underdeveloped Economy

The key economic fact with which policy makers have had to deal in deciding whether or not to use market controls is the underdeveloped nature of the Mainland Chinese economy and the dominance of agriculture in that economy. In several respects, this fact has made the decision to reject the market in favor of centralized physical controls easier. Because China is underdeveloped, its industrial sector has produced fewer commodities and central planning is easier the smaller the number of items with which planners have to deal. In 1956 in China, only

235 products were centrally planned and allocated, as compared to over 1500 in the Soviet Union in the 1950's. Even the consumer diet in China is simple enough to allow for rationed allocation of a few major consumers' goods, goods that make up a substantial portion of total consumer expenditure.

Not only are the total number of commodities produced less than in a developed country, but interdependence in the production and allocation of these commodities is less complex. In Chapter II an attempt was made to show how the Chinese Communists have been able to isolate major sectors such as agriculture, industry, and the urban consumers' goods market from each other. This has been done by a combination of variable sales taxes and state control of commerce. Isolation would not have been as easy in a developed economy. The separation of urban and rural areas, in particular, would be almost impossible in a highly developed economy, but is virtually complete in some respects in China. Highly mechanized agriculture, for example, requires the purchase of large quantities of producers' goods and even processed consumers' goods from the industrial sector. If industrial production decisions are made without regard for the needs of agriculture in such circumstances, agricultural production will suffer.

Interdependence within the industrial sector of an underdeveloped country is also more limited and allocation on the labor market is simpler. Only China's small number of highly skilled technical and professional personnel and the comparatively few firms in which they can be used makes possible their efficient allocation by direct means. China's large surplus of unskilled labor, also a product of the underdeveloped nature of the economy, makes control through the market unnecessary, for the only problem is how to prevent excess labor from flooding into cities.

Finally, central planning by physical means has been made easier by China's ability to borrow technology from more highly developed nations. If China had to develop this technology herself, powerful arguments for decentralizing control to the factory level and below would present themselves. The most important technology borrowed, moreover, is not manufacturing technique, but methods of planning and knowledge of the economic development process, knowledge that can be gained only by others' having successfully gone through that process.

None of these considerations provide arguments favoring the position that centralized controls are superior to those of the market. All they prove is that centralized direction may be easier to implement in an underdeveloped than in a developed economy. The economic arguments why the market actually may be inferior in an underdeveloped economy are based on the belief that market imperfections are so extreme that prices lead to major misallocations of resources. Market imperfections, however, are not why the Chinese Communists favor centralized controls. Many of these imperfections, particularly those in argiculture, in fact, were eliminated by the regime during the early years, when there was no choice but to rely on the market. The real reasons why the regime rejected the market were connected with political considerations and economic policies, which were only indirectly related to the underdeveloped nature of the Chinese economy, the one major exception being Peking's desire to achieve rapid structural changes in the Chinese economy, changes that might have been slowed considerably if not centrally controlled.

China's backward economy, in fact, has also provided powerful arguments favoring decentralized market controls, arguments that bring into serious question whether the above-described advantages of centralization, or more properly the ease with which centralization could be carried out, have not been more than offset by certain disadvantages. Foremost among these disadvantages is the lack of accurate and timely data. China's totalitarian controls provide the regime with the political power necessary to acquire whatever data it needs, but this is not sufficient. As will be argued below, political-power considerations also often interfere with collection of reliable statistics. China, therefore, is not much better off than any other underdeveloped country in this respect.

Another problem is China's lack of sufficient numbers of trained managerial personnel in agriculture and industry. For industry one can make out a case that centralization, although increasing the need for highly skilled personnel at the top, reduces the quality of managerial personnel required at the plant level. In agriculture, however, centralization of control in the hands of cooperative and commune cadres has created a demand for complex organizational skills that are largely unnecessary in a free peasant economy.

China's size also increases the problems of centralization, particularly when such centralization is carried all the way to Peking. There may not be so many commodities produced, but there are over 100,000 industrial firms and 120 million peasant households producing them. The Chinese consumers' diet may be simple, but there are 700 million consumers to whom rationed commodities have to be distributed.

Even borrowing of technology is not an unmixed blessing. The West and the Soviet Union's highly capital-intensive technology is hardly ideal, given China's shortage of capital and surplus of labor. It was to make better use of China's factor endowment that the Communists in 1958 and 1959 introduced a variety of small-scale, decentralized industries, the best known but least successful of which were the back-yard iron and steel furnaces. Direct application of Soviet development strategy to China was also of dubious value. If copying of the Soviet pattern was to be rejected in favor of a strategy better adapted to the Chinese scene, however, it was at least as probable that personnel at operational levels in the economy were better able to make the necessary adaptations than a few planners in Peking.

Finally, the most important single fact about the Chinese economy that militates against the use of centralized controls is the nature of agriculture. First of all, low per capita farm output has forced the Chinese Communists to utilize an agricultural policy designed to raise agricultural output, not simply the marketed surplus, as in the Soviet Union. But given the number and diversity of Chinese farms and the labor-intensive nature of cultivation, raising output is a task that, as Chinese Communist policies have demonstrated, cannot readily be centralized, even in the hands of the head of a single village, let alone all the way up to Peking.

Inability to centralize control over agriculture, and hence inability to control or even predict wide fluctuations in agricultural output, make centralization in nonagricultural sectors difficult as well. A drop in cotton output, for example, means that the textile industry operates well below capacity and that exports might have to be cut back. If exports are not cut back because of a desire to maintain imports of key producers' goods, the amount of cloth issued to Chinese consumers has to be reduced, with resulting increases in demand pressure on other commodities. If, on the other hand, cotton imports replace domestic production, imports of other producers' goods might have to be reduced for this reason as well. These difficulties are more serious the more general the fall in agricultural production. Flexibility at all levels is required, and central plans, enforced by centralized targets and rationed allocation of key inputs, tend to be inflexible.

In one area, however, agricultural output's lack of predictability made centralized controls more rather than less desirable. If key consumers' goods had been distributed by the market during the 1960–1962 agricultural crisis, inequalities in incomes and in the ability to wait in line to make purchases may well have caused starvation or serious malnutrition for the less fortunate minority. Rationed allocation assured that no one got more than the minimum necessary until all had been supplied, although inefficiencies in the system did cause certain areas, particularly rural ones, to suffer more than the average.

Emphasis on Producers' Goods Industry

Another key factor in determining the relative weight to be given to centralized versus market controls are the economic objectives of the Chinese Communists. Many of these objectives have been taken from the pattern established by the Soviet Union. In part, as argued above, this is a result of the underdeveloped nature of China's economy, which has forced the Chinese regime to copy other countries' policies because of lack of sufficient skill to develop its own policies. This explanation, however, is at best a partial one.

The most important objective of Soviet economic policy adopted by the Chinese Communists is emphasis on producers' goods industry. This emphasis has been adopted by Peking not only because the Russians stress this sector, but because Peking has also wanted to build up its military power as rapidly as possible and wanted to be economically independent of the rest of the world, including the Soviet Union.

Whereas the underdeveloped nature of China's economy contains many elements encouraging the use of decentralized market controls, emphasis on producers' goods industry primarily encourages use of centralized controls. In the first place, use of centrally determined plan targets is easier because demand in the producers' goods sector does not depend on unpredictable consumer preferences. Instead, these goods are produced in relatively few large firms and according to technique adopted from the Soviet Union, and hence demand for them is readily predictable. To the extent that producers' goods come from small-scale enterprises using labor-intensive technique, this argument does not hold true, but the movement toward small-scale enterprises has proved least successful in the producers' goods sector.

This overwhelming emphasis on producing machines in order to produce more machines has also made the use of market control in other sectors of the economy more difficult, particularly in agriculture. Since most investment has been channeled into producers' goods industry and supporting sectors, there is little left for agriculture. As a result, the regime has had to find a method of increasing agricultural output other than raising state investment. The method the authorities have chosen, and not solely for the above-stated economic reasons, was first to set up cooperatives and later communes in agriculture. It was hoped that, by centralizing control over agricultural production in the hands of cooperative and commune cadres, underemployed labor in rural areas could be mobilized for capital formation through digging irrigation ditches, building roads, and other such construction. Cadres could also order the introduction of new technique where extension workers earlier had to persuade farms to try something new voluntarily, a process taking more time and more extension workers than were available. The establishment of cooperatives also made possible pooling of land, elimination of many boundaries, and raising the rate of rural self-investment. Comparable changes could have been brought about in a market economy through concentration of resources in the hands of the better and richer farmers, but such an alternative was not acceptable on political or ideological grounds.

In practice, however, centralized control in agriculture has not worked out as anticipated. As already pointed out, China's underderdeveloped economy lacks sufficient numbers of qualified managerial personnel to handle these rural tasks efficiently. Individual incentives have been harmed by partial removal of effort from reward. Furthermore, areas where the market was still supposed to play a role, as in the choice of major crops to be planted, have no longer in fact been directed by the market, but by slogans calling for rapid increases in cotton and grain output. These results have caused the failure, in terms of economic performance, of centralization through cooperatives and communes. This failure in turn forced the regime to abandon its exclusive emphasis on producers' goods industry. Inability to find an adequate substitute for the market, in this area at least, has thus caused a major modification in one of the Chinese Communists' most fundamental economic goals.

Emphasis on producers' goods industry has also encouraged rejection of the market and resort to rationed distribution in the allocation of consumers' goods. This emphasis has caused wages to outstrip greatly the available output of consumers' goods. To bring supply and demand into line required heavy taxes. In order that these taxes not appear too heavy a burden on the population, the regime has done its best to disguise the true burden with a variety of sales taxes rather than an income tax. Sales taxes, however, have not provided the regime with a flexible enough tool for dealing with inevitable uncoordinated fluctuations in purchasing power and consumers' goods production. As a result, the regime either has had to allow prices to fluctuate or introduce some form of rationing. Generally it has chosen the latter.

Lack of investment in agriculture has also helped to account for rationing on the consumers' goods market. The pace of development of basic foods and clothing has been so slow compared to the rise in money income, particularly in urban areas, that pressure on the prices of these commodities has been quite heavy. If these prices had been allowed to rise, however, those at the lower end of the income scale would have suffered. Equity considerations, therefore, have also dictated a certain amount of rationing.

Closely connected to the problem of rationing is that of maintaining income incentives for urban and rural workers. The greater the extent of rationing on the consumers' goods market, the less meaningful income differentials have been, since the added income could not be used to purchase commodities most desired. Widening income differentials and introduction of piece-rate wages could partially have offset the influence of rationing, but they in turn have caused increased inflationary pressure and further aggravated equity problems, thus encouraging the introduction of even more rationing.

Communist China's most fundamental economic objective, that of concentrating resources on development of producers' goods industry, therefore, has tended to encourage and often require the rejection of the market in favor of centralized controls on economic grounds alone. The underdeveloped nature of the Chinese economy and particularly its reliance on agriculture encourages the use of decentralized controls, on the other hand. Decentralization does not necessarily imply market control, but some constraints on cadre behavior are necessary, as experience with communes and the "great leap forward" have demonstrated. Market controls are decentralized controls that tend to encourage plant managers and rural cadres to operate in an economically efficient manner. Administrative measures could conceivably be devised to accomplish the same ends, but the Chinese Communists to date have not been successful in this endeavor. A conflict therefore exists between an objective calling for a high degree of centralization and an economy that could only be efficiently directed with the use, to a considerable degree, of market controls.

This dilemma came to a head over agriculture. As already mentioned, failure of centralized attempts to raise farm output brought about a partial shift in investment resources to agriculture. There also have been modest increases in the role of the market as in the opening of rural trade fairs. These moves, however, have not been carried very far. Emphasis on producers' goods industry has not been abandoned but only modified; and centralized controls have been, if anything, increased, but at the expense of nonmarket decentralization, not at the expense of the market.

This conflict between means best suited for carrying out Communist goals and those best suited to the nature of the economy, it should be pointed out, is not necessarily fatal to China's prospects for economic development. Centralized controls are not completely unsuitable or unworkable. They are only less efficient in economic terms than the market. Economic inefficiency, however, usually can be offset by raising the rate of investment. The one area where increased investment may not be able to wholly overcome inefficiency from overcentralization is agriculture, and even this remains to be proved. The real conflict, therefore, is between emphasis on producers' goods industry and the key importance of agriculture to the whole economy and, in turn, the key importance of particular types of organization and control to agricultural performance.

Ideology and the Market

Failure of the Chinese Communists to modify their system of centralized controls in favor of the market, in a major way, is probably due only partly to a failure to recognize the extent to which overcentralization has caused many of their problems. More important are Marxist ideological and political-power considerations that offset many economic disadvantages of particular organizational forms. These considerations, in fact, have undoubtedly colored even economic appraisals of the effect of various types of controls.

As between ideology and politics, the effects of ideology are most difficult to appraise mainly because it often is impossible to draw the line between ideology sincerely held and that used as an excuse for taking action, whose true explanation is hidden for reasons of political power. Nevertheless, some conclusions can be drawn.

First of all, Marxist ideology sets certain limits on the kinds of policies that can be pursued. Given a choice between two means of control, both of which accomplish the same purpose, the one that is more socialist, that is, the one that rejects market or similar "capitalist" elements, is the one chosen. The problem is that very few such choices are between true equivalents.

Ideology has also helped to determine basic long-run Chinese policies. Socialization of the economy has been a measure toward which the regime would have worked, whatever its economic and political-power advantages or drawbacks. Marx favored planning and was against the anarchy of the market, and, although these feelings have little specific content, they have influenced the attitudes of the Chinese Communist leadership. Many organizational forms undertaken by the Soviet Union on pragmatic economic and political grounds have acquired an ideological sanctity for other Communist states that have followed.

Ideology, however, has not been a major determinant of either the timing of most basic policies or the detailed form they took. For example, Marxist ideology may have caused the Peking regime to favor cooperatives some day, but it was not a major element in the decision to pick the winter of 1955–56 to set them up. Nor did it dictate the particular form that lower and higher level cooperatives took with regard to such elements as labor organization and leadership structure. Ideology probably had some influence on the fact that private land ownership was abolished, but even here political-power considerations were paramount. Socialization of industry was not so much an ideological step as a step thought necessary for instituting planning, and planning in turn was considered to be a fundamental prerequisite to rapid economic growth.

Belief that central planning brings about more rapid economic growth was, to be sure, a belief that was more strongly held because of the ideological underpinnings of party personnel. Ideology in this sense also influenced the timing of cooperatives, because Mao and others believed that peasants really would work harder and better under a socialist form of organization. These beliefs, however, were not so strongly held that they were not modified when experience proved them partially or wholly wrong.

The one situation where ideology was anything but a secondary factor in economic decision making was during the decentralization and rectification campaigns of the "great leap forward." The essence of this period was a transfer of decision-making authority to lower-level, ideologically oriented cadres. The rectification campaign (in this case in late 1957 and early 1958) was introduced to ensure the necessary ideological purity. Resulting from this were greater egalitarianism in agriculture and industry, abolition of free markets and private farm plots, and a distaste for all types of monetary control — all measures that could be justified primarily only on ideological grounds. Whether these lower-level cadres really believed in these steps or advocated them only to protect themselves from political oblivion is impossible to tell. There is evidence that the top leadership in this period felt that such extreme measures were not always desirable, but tolerated them rather than damping the enthusiasm and initiative of lower-level personnel. The reason for the "great leap" was to raise output quickly, not necessarily to move rapidly toward a true communist society, but the result was less output and more communism. Similar but less extreme situations have occurred following other rectification campaigns. In 1956, it was partly for ideological reasons that cooperatives and other forms of centralization were carried farther than was desirable on economic grounds.

Marxist ideology, therefore, has at times reduced the role of the market. In part this has resulted from prejudice against the use of market controls, as in the rejection of free-market distribution of subsidiary agricultural products. More commonly, however, it has resulted in weakening of measures necessary to the proper functioning of the market rather than direct rejection of the market itself. Included in the latter category were the ignoring of profits targets by factory managers, lax control of enterprise funds, abolition of private plots, and the like.

Political-Power Considerations

Of far greater importance to the choice between market and centralized controls, and an importance not confined to a few selected periods, are a number of fundamental political-power considerations. These considerations are related both to the problem of maintaining political control over the nation, in the sense of having the power necessary to enforce the regime's desires, and to the related problem of gaining popular support from the people as a whole or from various large groups within the populace.

Of these two considerations, the latter is the less important. In Communist China's totalitarian society, popular support is neither fundamental to maintenance of political control nor to enforcement of various economic policies. On the other hand, active popular opposition or even sullen acquiescence would make the regime's tasks more difficult and perhaps impossible. There are limits, therefore, below which standards of living cannot be lowered, limits that are well above minimum subsistence. Some investment resources have to be channeled into agriculture and consumers' goods industry for this reason, if no other. Since emphasis on producers' goods industry has tended to increase the need for centralized controls, these reverse pressures have tended to reduce that need.

The regime's anti-inflationary policy on the consumers' goods market has also been heavily influenced by political considerations of this type. Price freezes were instituted because of the political impact that price increases had come to have as a result of the Kuomintang inflation. Disguising the heavy burden of taxation through sales taxes, a burden made necessary by the desire not to tax through inflation, was done not only to maintain worker economic incentives, but to gain their political support or acquiescence as well. Similarly, high urban wages had a political as well as economic aspect. As shown in Chapter VIII, these measures all tended to reduce the role of the market.

Of far greater importance to the Chinese Communists, is the need to maintain the apparatus of political control. This control requires that all power possible be vested in the main control mechanism, the Communist party. The Communist party, however, is not an abstraction, but an organization of men deeply imbued with a particular set of principles, and a loyalty to those principles and their superiors in the organization. Loyalty to principles is, in fact, a major way of ensuring loyalty to superiors, whatever the value of the principles in and of themselves. In this respect, the Communist control system is not unlike that of Confucian China, but is quite unlike the feudal loyalties of medieval Europe or Japan.

The most important results of this system for market control arose from the need to place loyal party personnel at the head of most factories and cooperatives (or communes). This policy ensured the regime's power, but it also placed in control of economic activities men who only incidentally knew much about economics or technology. In dealing with market forces, they not only lacked training but were actively hostile to the proper functioning of this mechanism. One alternative would have been for the regime to give party personnel more technical training, but this step, although it might not have jeopardized Communist power, would certainly have changed the nature of the Communist system, as has already happened in the Soviet Union. From the Chinese Communist point of view, such a development had to be fought with vigor.

The regime has paid a high price for this control. Poor performance of cash crops other than grain and cotton, production of large quantities of output in industry without proper regard for what the output was to be used for, disorganization in all aspects of the economy during certain periods, and reduced incentives for the working population, are only some of the costs of party-cadre control. The demands of political power are not the sole cause of this situation, as other factors mentioned above indicate, but they are extremely important.

Political control also was one reason for the introduction of rationing on the consumers' goods market and the placing of certain restrictions on labor migration. An individual, theoretically at least, was not allowed to stay over in a place other than his home for even one night without permission from local cadres. If he did stay longer without permission, one of many sanctions against him was not issuing him any ration coupons. Not surprisingly this control system often broke down, but undoubtedly had a material effect on labor allocation.

Thus the politics of power, Marxist ideology, and emphasis on producers' goods industry have all encouraged the use of centralized controls, not the market. Only the underdeveloped nature of China's economy and its vast size have encouraged the use of market control, and even here the case is somewhat ambivalent. The one area where centralized control has been least suitable on economic grounds, however, is agriculture, and this is the same area where it is most necessary, for political reasons. Decentralization by nonmarket means of certain types of control to ideologically safe commune cadres in 1958 and 1959 was an even worse solution than overcentralization, from an economic point of view, although that was not the intent. Because of the key importance of agriculture to the Chinese economy, this conflict between political and economic objectives, particularly in recent years (since 1959), has been the key problem for Chinese policy makers.

APPENDIX A

Reliability of Chinese Statistics

A widespread feeling that Chinese statistics are not reliable is based on the fact that China's economy is both underdeveloped and Communist. This feeling has been reinforced in recent years by Chinese Communist admission that agricultural production figures for 1958 were exaggerated and the obvious fact that 1959 data bear little relation to reality. This belief in the unreliability of all Chinese statistics, including those prior to 1958, has an element of truth in it. This is particularly true if one compares these data with comparable figures for the United States or Western Europe. But the real issue is whether Chinese statistics are sufficiently reliable to be used to answer various important questions about China's economy.

Just as in the case of Soviet statistics, one must from the outset distinguish between the question of deliberate falsification in the sense of "free invention and double bookkeeping" by the central statistical authorities and inaccuracies due to deficiencies in collection, compilation, and publication of data.[1] It is desirable to deal first with the issue of deliberate falsification, since its widespread existence would make study of the Chinese economy today nearly impossible.

There is little doubt that the top leadership of the Chinese Communist Party recognizes the need for accurate and timely statistics on progress of the economy. Planning, particularly planning that emphasizes physical production targets and rationed allocation of major raw materials, would be impossible unless planners knew such things as how much of each commodity was be-

---

[1] For a discussion of the significance of this distinction for Soviet statistics, see Abram Bergson, "Reliability and Usability of Soviet Statistics: A Summary Appraisal," *The American Statistician,* vol. VII, no. 3 (June–July 1953), pp. 13–16.

ing produced and the technology used in that production. The real question with respect to statistical falsification, therefore, is not whether the Chinese regime has made an attempt to collect useful statistics, but whether they have found it desirable also to compile a second set of data for publication.

If deliberate falsification were practiced, it would presumably be done for propaganda purposes directed either toward the Chinese or the outside world. Considerations that might discourage compilation of a second set of books for propaganda purposes might be ineffectiveness of certain types of false data as propaganda, difficulties in compiling a convincing second set of statistics, and the danger that economic decisions, particularly at the lower levels, might be adversely affected by publication of false data. If propaganda is to be effective, those being propagandized must have some degree of faith in the truthfulness of materials presented to them. In the case of China, there is little doubt that those whom the regime is most interested in propagandizing are the Chinese in China, not experts and others in the outside world. Most data available to Western analysts do not come from publications directed at foreigners, such as the *Peking Review,* but from journals and newspapers meant primarily for domestic consumption. Even when data appear in foreign-language publications, they have almost invariably appeared first in documents primarily intended for a Mainland Chinese audience. Furthermore, the data are often repeated (without adjustment) in dozens of provincial newspapers, which cannot legally even be taken out of China, but which have, nevertheless, made their way to Hong Kong on occasion. Thus statistics, to be convincing, must convince those who are often best in a position to check the data on the basis of personal experience.

Deliberate falsification of many types of disaggregated data, therefore, would appear highly improbable. If prices and tax rates of individual products, wage scales, the size of cooperatives, and so on are falsified, the falsification would be discovered immediately — thus serving no purpose and, in addition, tending to discredit all other materials published by the regime. The more aggregated data become, the less likely this is to be true. An individual peasant does not know what nationwide grain production was the previous year. On the other hand, if reports he reads in the newspapers about total output of grain or other crops consistently diverge from his personal experience, he is likely to be suspicious. Falsification of such aggregates as national income is even easier, since fairly sophisticated readers often do not fully understand the concept and problems involved in measuring it.

Falsification of aggregated as well as disaggregated data is made more difficult, however, because it is usually the percentage increase, not the absolute amount, that one wants to falsify. Percentage increases have a cumulative effect. A growth rate reported as 10 per cent that is actually 3 per cent leads in a few years to an absolute level of reported output that is double the true figure. A discrepancy of this magnitude would be difficult to hide, even from foreign observers, since China is not completely cut off from the outside world. A few non-Communist travelers do get in, and many refugees get out.

Finally, as mentioned above, publication of falsified data may have a harmful effect on many types of economic decisions. The Chinese Communists rely on newspapers and journals to promulgate information, laws, and directives to lower-echelon cadres. These materials often contain statistics to help illustrate what it is the regime wants done. Falsified data may on occasion encourage cadres to do what the state desires, but, to the extent that decisions are best when based on "objective reality," the opposite would seem more normally to be the case. Falsification of grain production data in 1958, for example, may have made it very difficult for state purchasing organs to do an effective job.[2] If the state attempted to direct the heads of over 700,000 cooperatives or production brigades through secret channels, relying on open publication for propaganda purposes alone, the economic effects would undoubtedly be highly disruptive. Furthermore, it would be extremely difficult to keep the general population from finding it out if secret orders included material contradicting what was appearing in newspapers. Use of confidential channels for information becomes more practicable the smaller the number of people who must be reached. Thus, it is possible that the regime might compile two sets of books for heavy industries under cen-

[2] C. M. Li, *The Statistical System of Communist China*, pp. 95, 97.

tral government control, but it is sectors such as this where actual performance has been impressive enough to make a propaganda boost unnecessary.

Lack of falsification has not meant that the Chinese Communists have not published statistical data in ways that have been deliberately misleading. As with Soviet statistics, however, a policy of withholding unfavorable information would "appear to be more an alternative than a complement to a policy of falsification." [3] The almost complete lack of national production statistics for 1960–1963, when the Chinese economy suffered a severe severe setback, is a case in point. Nor does this conclusion appear to be refuted by the experience of 1958 and 1959. As Professor Li has shown, falsification during this period was primarily at lower levels and a result of heavy pressure on rural cadres to achieve impossible goals rather than a deliberate policy of the central government or party.[4] When falsification was discovered, an attempt was made at considerable cost in propaganda to correct the figures publicly.[5] The fact that the corrections were undoubtedly inadequate and that the 1959 data were, if anything, worse was due not to a change in policy but to the fact that the underlying conditions that had caused falsification in the first place were basically uncorrected.[6]

In the period of 1950–1957, the Chinese would appear to have had a more open publication policy (as related to the amount of data available to them) than did the Soviet Union in the 1930's and 1940's. This may in part have been due to a relative lack of conspicuous failures during this period, in contrast to Soviet experience with collectivization and the drop in real wages during

[3] Bergson, "Realiability and Usability of Soviet Statistics," p. 16.

[4] C. M. Li, *The Statistical System of Communist China*, pt. 2. Also of crucial importance was the decentralization of the State Statistical Bureau and putting "politics in command" over statistical work.

[5] Chou En-lai, *Report on Adjusting the Major Targets of the 1959 National Economic Plan and Further Developing the Campaign for Increasing Production and Practicing Economy* (Peking, 1959). *Time,* for example, used the statistical revision to play up the "great leap," as the "big fumble" ("Red China: The Mechanical Man," October 12, 1959, p. 30).

[6] Professor Li (*The Statistical System of Communist China*, pt. 3) implies that the situation was beginning to improve in 1959. If so, it certainly does not show up in the published data.

the early 1930's, but does not appear to be the entire explanation. There were substantial declines in retail sales of a number of major commodities[7] and in the production of a number of important agricultural products[8] in 1956 and 1957 in China. The Chinese Communists, however, have seldom published their data in a form that would make these declines readily apparent. Where 1957 statistics are below those of 1956, for example, the usual procedure is to compare 1957 with either 1950 or 1952 which, given wartime disruptions, were almost invariably very low. More complete series can be reconstructed from similar earlier comparisons of 1955 and 1956 with either 1950 or 1952, which were published separately. The explanation of why these difficulties were not sufficiently disguised seems to lie, first of all, in the relatively free attitude toward publication and discussion during 1955–1957 and, second, in the eagerness of authorities to advertise their accomplishments by statistics. Once the 1955 data were out, the choice was either to progressively restrict publication of later data or publish it all in the manner described above and hope that few would refer back to earlier materials.

The Chinese regime also has consciously attempted to mislead through publication of statistics that purport to represent something that they actually do not. From 1950 through 1955, it was not uncommon to see articles on the rising standard of living of the Chinese people backed up by statistics showing huge increases in retail sales by state-run commercial establishments when in fact these data mainly represented the increasing socialization of commerce.[9] To take another example, the near doubling of the number of "employees" between the end of 1957 and 1958 was in part due to a reorganization of handicraft personnel into state factories,[10] and not solely to the rapid increase in industrial development during the initial year of the "great leap." Problems of definition such as these require constant care in the use of the

[7] See Chapter IX, Table 20.
[8] See Chapter IV, Table 5.
[9] See, for example, Yao Yi-lin, "Development of Domestic Commerce during the Past Three Years," *JMJP*, October 3, 1952, translated in *CB*, no. 219, p. 34; and SSB, "Report on the Results of the 1954 Economic Development and State Planning," *HHYP*, October 28, 1955, p. 169.
[10] See Table 12, note d.

statistics, but the Chinese normally label their data, and the correct definition can usually, though not always, be found.

A third major consideration that has influenced my belief that Chinese Communist statistics are not falsified deliberately is based on the high degree of internal consistency between widely diverse data (several internal-consistency checks appear in subsequent appendixes). These checks show a considerable degree of consistency between raw price data and various price indexes, between data of grain purchases and sales in both calendar and grain years, between total purchasing power and its components, and, finally, between price data, tax rates, tax revenue, and industrial production statistics. Studies by others have shown a close relation between output of various industrial products and their technological coefficients and factor inputs[11] and between total purchases of agricultural products by the state and state purchases of individual farm products.[12] The degree of consistency varies between the different checks, but this is not surprising, given the number of assumptions that must be made in order even to begin to reconstruct any particular series from raw data. Internal consistency, of course, does not prove that falsification could not exist. The State Statistical Bureau conceivably could compile data in such a way as to ensure its consistency, but this does not seem plausible on two grounds. In the first place, this would have involved a considerable effort on the part of the authorities — particularly in earlier years, when statistics were not unifiedly collected and distributed by the State Statistical Bureau. Second, it has been pointed out that disaggregated data are very difficult to falsify without such falsification being discovered. Since a number of the above checks were attempts to verify consistency between aggregate and disaggregated statistics, a finding of consistency in these cases would appear to have considerable bearing on the reliability of some aggregate data.

Perhaps even more significant is the close correlation between quantitative data and various qualitative indicators. The "hun-

---

[11] Chao Kang, "Testing the Reliability of Industrial Output Data of Communist China," unpublished paper presented to the First Research Conference of the Social Science Research Council on the Economy of China, Berkeley, January 31–February 1, 1963.

[12] Ronald Hsia, *Agricultural Output in Mainland China.*

dred flowers" campaign in 1957 would have made little sense if the establishment of cooperatives in agriculture had not been carried out smoothly a year earlier, with at most minor declines in production. Introduction of rationing for a number of prducts has usually been accompanied by declines in sales or purchases of the commodity or by insufficient increases combined with a high income elasticity of demand for the product.[13] Impressions to the contrary are usually the result of insufficient digging into the true causes and nature of both qualitative and quantitative materials. The major exceptions to this statement are the materials for 1958 and 1959, particularly the latter. Various actions taken by the government in 1960 and 1961 (reorganization of communes, cutbacks in exports, import of grain) would make little sense if production had been anywhere near the reported level. It is worth noting that for these two years, when I made an internal consistency check on price data, tax revenue and rates, and industrial production data, there turned out to be a wide disparity between the calculated and the official figures. If the State Statistical Bureau was manipulating data to make them consistent, it is difficult to explain why it failed to do so in 1958 and 1959.

Finally, although there is no check for China comparable to the classified and unclassified versions of the 1941 Soviet plan, a number of aspects can be checked against first-hand observations. Travelers to China are not too useful in this respect, since they are usually given an even more selective version of the facts than the one that appears in official publications. Refugees, however, are another matter. Whatever their value for gaining a general impression of such things as political discontent, they can be used to verify certain types of statistical data such as rations, individual prices, and price changes. In a dozen different interviews I was not once given a statistic on these items that was not identical with or within a reasonable range of officially published data, where such data existed.[14] The weakness of refugee interviews is not their unreliability, but the fact that few refugees have held

[13] See Chapters III and IV.
[14] Although I feel that there is great potential for properly conducted and utilized refugee interviews, no essential point in this book depends primarily on refugee information.

responsible positions and hence know little of what is going on in China outside their personal experiences. They cannot be used, therefore, to verify or discredit aggregate data.[15] It is worth noting, however, that of all the people who daily go in and out of China, not one has produced evidence of the existence of two sets of books.

As pointed out at the beginning of this discussion, proof of lack of deliberate falsification by the central authorities does not constitute proof that Chinese statistics are accurate. China is an underdeveloped economy, and statistics of underdeveloped economies are not distinguished by their reliability. But China is also a Communist country and one with a centrally planned economy. Therefore, China has both the need for accurate statistics and sufficient authority, with its totalitarian controls, to collect them — providing they set about the task of compilation properly. Fortunately, the task of tracing the history of China's statistical organization and the evaluation of that organization's capabilities has already been completed by Professor C. M. Li in his excellent work *The Statistical System of Communist China*. On the basis of Professor Li's work one can conclude that statistics are more accurate the greater the importance of having the data is to the regime, the fewer the number of units from which data have to be collected, the less backward these units are, and the greater the degree of control the state exercised over them. In addition, the political atmosphere, at least in 1958 and 1959, has had considerable influence on the willingness and ability of lower-level statistical workers to compile reliable data.

Although nothing will be added to Professor Li's work here, it is useful to make more explicit the relation of these considerations to specific types of data,[16] particularly those used in this book. Statistics on tax revenue, purchases and sales of grain and other major crops, production in large-scale state-operated indus-

---

[15] One exception to this is Professor Li's interview with a Chinese statistical worker reported in C. M. Li, "Statistics and Planning at the *Hsien* Level in Communist China," *Current Scene*, vol. I, no. 28 (March 27, 1962), pp. 1–11.

[16] Professor Li quotes a statement by the director of the State Statistical Bureau on the relative quality of various types of data, but the categories cannot always be readily applied to statistics used in this book (*The Statistical System of Communist China*, pp. 63–64).

trial plants, and price indexes of major commodities, where those prices are determined by central or provincial government authorities, would appear to score high on each of the four above-mentioned criteria. At the bottom of the scale one should place such items as handicraft production, rural household output, price trends on the free market, and almost all production statistics since the beginning of 1958 — although those in agriculture are undoubtedly much worse than those in industry. Much more work will have to be done on data in these latter categories before they can be used with any confidence at all.

In between these two extremes fall a number of items over which there is still considerable debate. The data are those for output of agriculture and consumers' goods industries. In the latter case the question is mainly over aggregate figures, whereas with the former it is over both aggregate and disaggregated data. Since disaggregated agricultural-production data for major crops are of some importance to this study, it is desirable to look into these further here — although the discussion must necessarily be brief.

The major question with respect to the validity of statistics for individual agricultural products is over grain output data. As for the other eleven major crops (excluding grain) for which the Communists publish production figures, the fact that most can only be raised in a comparatively limited area and a high proportion of their output is marketed by centrally controlled state commercial organizations would seem to indicate that the state, for these crops, has the means with which to collect valid production statistics. These crops also make up a large percentage of Chinese exports, and hence having accurate data on them is important to the regime. Furthermore, production of these crops (excluding grain) increased between 1952 and 1957 at an annual average rate of only about 3.0 per cent, dropping to 2.0 per cent per year in 1956 and 1957,[17] hardly anything to make propaganda about, especially considering the fact that

[17] The data used in making this computation are taken from T. C. Liu and K. C. Yeh, *The Economy of the Chinese Mainland,* pp. 557–558. They cover soybeans, peanuts, rapeseed, cotton, jute, sugar cane and beets, tobacco, tea, domesticated and wild cocoons.

many of these crops by 1957 admittedly had not even recovered their prewar levels.

As for grain production there appears to be a general belief among Western specialists that these statistics exaggerate the rate of growth in output because they include increases due primarily to improvements in coverage of the reporting system. This may well be true, but the case is far from proven.

Individual farmers did have reasons for attempting to under-report their crops, but their ability to do so is not so obvious. Cadre knowledge of and control over the rural areas did not begin with the cooperatives but with land reform, and cadre incentives were such as to influence them to overestimate production. There are also grounds for believing that the ability of individuals to estimate production increases may have been somewhat greater than their ability to estimate the absolute level of output in their area.[18] Furthermore, it should be kept in mind that, although the number of full-time statistical workers in China in 1957 was double the number in 1954,[19] the latter figure (100,000) was ten times the number in India at the end of the second Indian five-year plan.[20] The quality of statisticians in India may have been higher, but lack of sufficient political control, particularly in rural areas, must have made the task of these workers much more difficult than it was in China, except in 1958 and 1959.[21] In China, even before 1958 and 1959, mistakes in compiling grain-output data undoubtedly were numerous, but the case for a consistent bias has yet to be made.

Grain-production statistics of particular interest for this study are those for 1955–1957.[22] By the 1955 harvest China certainly

[18] If a given small area were affected more or less evenly by weather conditions and other influences on production such as the nature of rural cadres, the problem of picking an unbiased sample for estimating the percentage change in output would be easier than picking one for estimating total grain output in the area. Furthermore, the total acreage estimates do not necessarily have any influence on the former, but they do on the latter.

[19] C. M. Li, *The Statistical System of Communist China*, p. 51.

[20] *Third Five Year Plan* (1961), Government of India, Planning Commission, p. 180.

[21] The power of rural voters in India, for example, is such that the government levies a disproportionately low tax on the agricultural sector.

[22] See Chapter IV.

had enough trained statistical workers to collect reasonably accurate grain-output data.[23] The major question, and one that cannot be answered without more research, is whether or not a desire to demonstrate the benefits of cooperatives influenced cadres to inflate production data for 1956.

Nothing has been said here about a number of questions that have an important bearing on the usability of Chinese Communist statistics. For example, the Chinese price structure, in my opinion, undoubtedly distorts official national income estimates. But this and other similar issues are extremely complex and generally have little bearing on arguments presented in this book. The purpose of the above discussion has not been to demonstrate that all Chinese statistics are valid, but only that data can be utilized meaningfully — provided they are used with care and with full realization of the many pitfalls. This statement, of course, does not apply to 1958 and 1959 data. Whether it will apply to statistics after that date, assuming they are ever published, remains to be seen.[24]

[23] This is the position taken by C. M. Li, *The Statistical System of Communist China*, p. 58.

[24] In 1963 and 1964 the regime began to publish a few percentage increases rather than absolute figures.

APPENDIX B

Official Price Indexes

There are basically four types of prices in Communist China: retail, wholesale, purchase, and ex-factory. The purchase price is that paid to the farmer for his produce, while the ex-factory price is that paid the industrial producer, including the industrial and commercial taxes paid at the factory and profits of the industrial plant. The wholesale price is the purchase or ex-factory price plus the costs, taxes, and profits of wholesale commercial establishments and, where relevant, transport costs. Retail prices include additional taxes, profits, and costs at the retail level. Articles occasionally also refer to "transfer" prices on transactions between state firms in order to differentiate between these and higher prices paid by private plants when buying from the state. It is not clear how these differ from ex-factory or wholesale prices, if at all. In years prior to the socialization of most private commercial establishments there was also a distinction between "official" and "un-official" wholesale and retail prices, the difference being that the former were controlled prices at which goods were sold by state organizations, whereas the latter were those of the private or uncontrolled sector. Finally, there are the "free market" prices, which are essentially retail prices and differ mainly in that they carry only one tax, the tax on retail trade, if that. During certain periods, such as 1957–58, these "free market" prices have only been on goods for which there were no official quotations or state marketing arrangements. During other periods (1956 and 1961–1964), commodities subject to state purchasing could be sold on the free market once purchase quotas had been met. In the latter circumstance, there could be two sets of prices for a single commodity,

TABLE 21. Official price indexes (1952 = 100 except where otherwise stated)

Year	Wholesale		Retail, 8 large cities		All-China retail	Rural retail[a]	Industrial products, rural areas	Urban retail[b] (Dec. 1957 = 100)	Worker cost of living[c]
	Mar. 1950 = 100	1952 = 100	Mar. 1950 = 100	1952 = 100					
1951	92.4	—	94.6	101.0	100.1	—	100.5	—	—
1952	92.6	100	93.7	100	100	100	100	—	100
1953	91.3	98.7	98.3	104.9	103.2	100.9	98.5	—	105.6
1954	91.8	99.1	100.2	106.9	105.5	104.5	100.2	—	106.9
1955	92.4	99.7	101.1	107.9	106.3	105.7	101.4	—	107.3
1956	91.9	99.2	101.0	107.8	106.3	105.3	100.4	—	107.1
1957	92.7	100.1	102.2	109.1	108.6	107.7	101.6	100[e]	109.2
1958	92.7	100.1	101.4	108.2	108.3	107.1[d]	101.0	99.1[e]	—
1959	—	—	—	—	—	—	—	99.1[f]	—

Source: Data are from SSB, *Ten Great Years*, pp. 172–174, except where otherwise noted.
[a] Hong Kong *Wen hui pao*, June 1, 1958.
[b] Forty-one main consumers' items in 30 large and medium cities. *HHPYK*, October 12, 1959, p. 134.
[c] Including noncommodity section in 12 large cities. Yin and Yin, *Economic Statistics of Mainland China*, p. 62.
[d] First half year only.
[e] For December only.
[f] For June only.

just as in the Soviet Union, where many goods were sold both in state stores and on the collective farm markets.

In this appendix we are concerned first with the extent to which official Chinese price indexes (see Table 21) reflect the actual degree of price increase on the consumers' goods market, and second with whether the index of the "scissors differential" between purchase and sales prices in rural areas accurately represents changes in that part of the price structure.

1. Price indexes and price increases. Unfortunately relatively little is known about the method of computation of Chinese Communist price indexes. What is known tends to cast some doubt on the extent to which these indexes reflect actual price increases on the consumers' goods market. The principal problem, arising from the fact that the retail indexes only include about 70 per cent of the commodities that enter the market, and, furthermore, are biased toward commodities subject to a large degree of state control, has been discussed in the text.[1] There are, however, a number of additional problems. The wholesale price index, for example, includes a large number of industrial goods, which do not enter the consumers' goods market. This, combined with the fact that prices of these particular commodities were sharply reduced in 1955 and 1956, means that this index is of little use in any attempt to measure the extent of inflation on the consumers' goods market. The lack of much movement in retail prices of industrial products in rural areas is due partly to a similar inclusion of agricultural producers' goods in the index. Here, however, their inclusion is more meaningful, since these goods do to some extent compete for rural consumers' cash expenditure.[2]

Two other problems in connection with retail price indexes merit further discussion. The first of these arises from the already-mentioned fact that these indexes use official prices, which are not necessarily those actually charged the consumer. It is

---

[1] See Chapter VIII at note 2. The source containing the above information on the nature of the commodities entering the retail price index is *TCKTTH* data office, "The 1956 Domestic Market Price Situation," *HHPYK*, May 25, 1957, p. 115.

[2] See Chapter VIII between notes 25 and 26.

my opinion, however, that the problem is not very serious.[3] In the first place, divergence of official prices from actual prices can only occur where prices are allowed to fluctuate freely. This has not been the case with such major commodities as grain and cotton cloth, at least not since these goods have been rationed.[4] This problem, therefore, is more closely connected with the indexes' lack of comprehensive coverage than it is with the degree of reliability of the indexes as indicators of actual price movements of controlled goods. The issue was probably more serious prior to nationwide unification of retail prices in 1955.[5] Before that time the existence of private commerce and price preferences for supply and marketing cooperatives meant that a large number of commodities were sold at prices different from official quotations. It does not follow, however, that prices prior to 1955 rose faster than the official index would indicate. The true price rise was probably less than the reported one when a lower price policy for cooperatives was instituted and somewhat greater when it was abolished.[6] The effect of private commerce on this type of divergence is more difficult to appraise. Private retail prices were subject to considerable control but may have been slightly higher than those of state commerce.[7] As a result, unification in 1955 may have lowered prices slightly more than is indicated by the index, though probably not enough to offset the

[3] For a somewhat different opinion, see C. M. Li, *The Economic Development of Communist China* (Berkeley and Los Angeles, 1959), p. 26.

[4] Even the decentralization of price-control authority on April 11, 1958, left the determination of most of these prices in the hands of the Central Committee so that they would be subject to unified and centralized control (CCPCC and SC, "Regulation on Spheres of Price Control," *FKHP*, VII, 315–318).

[5] Shanghai Price Book, p. 422.

[6] The order to abolish the price differentials was issued in July 1954, to take effect by February 15, 1955. The differential that was wiped out averaged 3.9 per cent (*JMJP* editorial, "Supply and Marketing Cooperatives Should Adjust Retail Prices," *HHYP*, March 28, 1955, p. 148). The change in the index of rural retail prices, however, would have been considerably less than this, since a large part of rural retailing was still handled by private commerce. The percentage of retail commerce handled by private enterprise was over 26 per cent in 1954, the larger part probably being in rural areas (Yang Chien-pai, *Ching-chi-chung chi-chung chu-yau pi-li kuan-hsi-te pien-hua*, p. 16).

[7] This is based on statements that the retail-wholesale price differential was greater at least for some privately retailed commodities than it was for state-retailed ones (Shanghai Price Book, p. 423).

downward bias in the index created by the change in cooperative price policy.

Not all divergences between the two indexes were due to the institutional pattern. Although most prices fell to the official level during the "five anti" movement in 1952,[8] differences among prices of even major commodities began to appear with the beginning of the industrial development plan.[9] Unification in 1955, combined with the lack of substantial inflationary pressure at that time, probably caused many prices to remain at or near the official level — not diverging again until reopening of the free market and inflationary pressures in 1956–57 led to some divergence among prices of those commodities that entered this market, legally or otherwise. A directive of August 9, 1957, clearly limiting the number of commodities that could enter the free market put an end to many of these differences.

The second and potentially more serious problem is the method used by the Chinese Communists to compile their price indexes. The question is whether or not the Communists have chosen their weights or have selected commodities entering the indexes in such a way as to seriously bias the results. The predominance of controlled commodities in the retail indexes is one element of this, but our concern here is rather with the extent to which the indexes represent what they claim to, namely, the movements of official prices of major consumer commodities. One approach to this problem is to investigate the internal consistency of various price indexes published by the mainland regime for various areas. The consistency of many of these indexes is apparent from a cursory glance at Table 21. Local wholesale and retail price indexes for Shanghai and Tientsin are also very similar to those for the nation as a whole. Another approach is that taken by Mr. Mizoguchi, who first investigated the nature of index number compilation methods advocated by Chinese statisticians and then attempted to determine the weights used in actual practice by analyzing the Shanghai wholesale price index. His conclusion is that, whereas the statisticians advocate the use of the Paasche

[8] Shanghai Price Book, p. 391.

[9] For instance, the actual price of grain in many areas diverged from the official price (Chapter IX, p. 184).

index, the Shanghai index appears to use a Laspeyres index.[10] For purposes of this discussion, what is important is that the index is consistent with an accepted method of index compilation.

Further evidence of the validity of various price indexes, at least within their limited sphere, can be obtained by investigating raw price data of certain major commodities for a number of large cities. The data themselves appear on subsequent pages. Three facts are evident from the data. First, prices of major commodities were at approximately the same level in the various cities for which data were available. There are differences in the absolute level of prices of particular commodities in almost all cases, but these are easily explained by quality differences or differences in transportation costs to the consuming area. The second point is that changes over time in the prices of individual commodities in individual cities have been similar in both direction and magnitude. There are, of course, differences — as in the case of rice and flour prices in Shanghai and Tientsin in 1954 and 1955 — but these differences are comparatively minor and could be due to differences in local conditions. The final point is that these price changes were also roughly commensurate with changes in the nationwide indexes for particular commodities where they exist. These three different types of consistency in data published in different areas at widely different points in time would seem to indicate that at least the raw price data have been accurately recorded and reported.

The relevance of this discussion to the reliability of more general indexes can be demonstrated by a crude attempt to construct a price index for commodities whose prices appear in Tables 24–27, at the end of this appendix. To construct such an index it is necessary to make rough and somewhat arbitrary assumptions with respect to national average changes in certain prices. The result (see Table 22), therefore, is not intended in any way to act as a substitute for the official index. It is only a check of internal consistency, and a very rough one at that. The

[10] Mizoguchi Toshiyuki, "Examination of Price Index Materials in China," in Ishikawa Shigeru, ed., *Chugoku keizai hatten no tokeiteki kenkyu*, I (Research on statistics of Chinese economic development; Tokyo, 1960), chap. ii.

TABLE 22. Reconstructed price index (1952 = 100)

Item	1952	1953	1954	1955	1956	1957	Weights[a] (million yuan)
Reconstructed index	100	102.8	105.5	107.0	107.0	108.9	—
Grain[b]	100	106	106	107	107	107	11,300
Cotton cloth[c]	100	97	95	95	95	95	4,200
Edible oils[d]	100	104	113	122	122	129	1,400
Sugar[e]	100	76	85	94	94	94	900
Salt[f]	100	95	95	95	95	105	900
Pork[g]	100	108	122	122	122	132	3,400
Official retail							
Nationwide	100	103.2	105.5	106.3	106.3	108.6	—
8 large cities	100	104.9	106.9	107.9	107.8	109.1	—
Shanghai wholesale food and clothing[h]	100	96.8	104.8	108.8	109.5	112.4	—

a The quantities of retail sales in 1955 are given in Chapter IX, Tables 19 and 20. The prices used to obtain the value figures for edible oils, sugar, salt, and pork were rounded-off averages of the prices for 1955 given in Tables 24–27. The cotton-cloth price is the national average price for 1957 of 35.7 yuan (Huang K'o, "How We May Settle the Disequilibrium," ECMM, no. 119, p. 33). The price used for grain is 14 yuan per 100 catties and sales are for the 1954–1955 grain year, but these choices, although based on the data in the table, are somewhat arbitrary. The weight for grain, therefore, may contain an error as large as 10 per cent in either direction. These prices and quantities together give a total value of 22.1 billion yuan, which is 56.3 per cent of the total value of retail sales (39.22 billion yuan in SSB, Ten Great Years, p. 166). The principal virtue of choosing 1955 is that it is in the middle of the period, it is a year for which data are available, and it is not subject to particular objections such as 1956, when cotton-textile sales were abnormally high.

b The grain price index is based on the nationwide index figures for 1952 and 1957 combined with the evidence that most of the increase took place in 1953 (except possibly in Shanghai, where there were further increases in 1954) and evidence that there were no increases in 1957.

c The cotton-cloth price is based on the 1952 and 1956 index of yarn and wholsale cloth prices for the whole country plus the knowledge that these prices were not changed from 1954 through 1957 and that the decrease appears to have taken place in 1953.

d The procedure used here was to compute an index of the arithmetic average of three fairly complete series (two for Tientsin and one for Shanghai). The figures thus derived are used for the 1952, 1953, 1954, and 1957 index numbers. The figure for 1956 is derived from the national average increase, and the 1955 figure is based on the evidence that edible oil prices did not change between 1955 and 1956.

e Because of the close similarity in the movement of sugar prices between Shanghai, Tientsin, and Tsingtao, it is assumed that Shanghai prices were representative of all large urban areas, and the index was computed accordingly.

f It is assumed that most of the drop in the nationwide index of salt prices for the years 1951 and 1954 occurred in 1953. (The drop in the Shanghai price index between 1952 and 1953 was 5 per cent. If part of the drop occurred in 1952, then the index is slightly biased downward, but not enough to affect the over-all index significantly.

g Once again, it is the relative uniformity of price movements combined with the knowledge that urban pork prices were centrally controlled that makes it possible to assume that the prices of Shanghai, Tientsin, and Tsingtao are representative of other areas except for 1956 and 1957, where a nationwide average was available. It is assumed there was no movement in average pork prices from 1954 to 1956 although the Shanghai price did change slightly.

h This index was computed from three separate Shanghai wholesale indexes for major foodstuffs, supplementary foodstuffs, and clothing (Shanghai Price Book, pp. 454–459), weighted by the percentage of total Shanghai worker expenditure on these items for 1957 (P. Noirot, "Facts on the Evolution of the Standard of Living," Economie et politique, special issue, nos. 66–67, January–February 1960, pp. 121–145, translated in JPRS, no. 3639, pp. 44–78). Using 1952 percentages would have given similar results although basic foodstuffs would have been weighted somewhat more heavily.

nature of the assumptions makes it clear that even the exact timing of changes in the index is sometimes difficult to pinpoint precisely. It is the author's opinion, however, that the result is still useful for the purpose for which it is intended. The commodities included make up well over half of total retail sales in 1955 (as compared to 70 per cent in the official index).

Wholesale prices are used principally because there are time series of such prices available for a number of areas, whereas the same cannot be said for retail prices. It is my impression that for many, if not all, items appearing in the reconstructed index the sales price is both a wholesale and a retail price, although there may be a small additional markup to cover retailing costs. Since the retail-wholesale price differential is not manipulated to increase state revenue[11] and both prices are tightly controlled by the same authority in the case of the products appearing in the reconstructed index, these prices probably are representative of retail price movements. Commodities have been chosen not only on the basis of data available, but because they are all major items in the consumer budget and are all closely regulated goods of the type that the Communists include in their indexes.

Agreement of the computed results with the official indexes is to some extent due to chance, since official indexes include approximately 20 per cent more commodities. The Shanghai index is included because the computed price index is heavily weighted with Shanghai prices, as can be seen from relevant notes. Although there are a number of discrepancies and the calculations are crude, there is certainly no evidence of deliberate falsification in the compilation of the indexes. The indexes thus appear to be representative of changes in official prices of major commodities.

2. *Indexes of purchase prices and the "scissors differential."* Since half of the "scissors differential" (that is, the relation between prices paid to farmers and those paid by them) is made up of the index of industrial retail prices in rural areas, it is

---

[11] This conclusion can be inferred from discussions in Shanghai Price Book; see for example, page 423.

subject to most of the same criticisms leveled at the general retail price index. The rural industrial price index, however, may be presumed to be somewhat superior to the over-all retail price index because of the greater ease with which industrial prices can be controlled — although this may be somewhat offset by the greater difficulty of controlling prices in rural areas.

There are three other considerations that must be taken into account as well. The first is whether the index of the scissors differential (see Table 23) accurately reflects changes since 1950

TABLE 23. Rural price indexes

Year	Purchase[a] (1950 = 100)	Industrial products[a] (1950 = 100)	"Scissors differential"[b] (1930–1936 avg. = 100)
1950	100	100	131.8
1951	119.6	110.3	124.4
1952	121.6	109.7	121.8
1953	133.9	108.2	109.6
1954	138.4	110.3	109.2
1955	137.7	111.9	113.3
1956	141.8	110.8	107.0
1957	148.8	112.1	103.0[c]
1958	152.1	111.4	—

[a] Figures for 1951–1958 derived from SSB, *Ten Great Years*, pp. 172–173; for 1950, see note b.

[b] *TCKT* data office, "Price Gaps between Industrial Products and Farm Products," *ECMM*, no. 104, p. 20. This index is almost identical with one published for 1952–1957 in *TCYC* data office, "Changes in 1957 Market Prices and Their Influence on the People's Livelihood," *TCYC*, April 23, 1958, p. 25.

[c] Estimate.

in indexes of farm purchase and retail prices. The second is whether the 1950 index number represents the actual extent to which industrial prices rose relative to agricultural purchase prices. The third is the question of the reliability of the purchase price index itself.

The first question is quickly answered by a check of data in

Table 23. The third index is certainly roughly consistent with the first two. A really definitive answer to the second question would require much more material on rural prices in China than is available, but considerable light can be thrown on the issue by available sectoral price indexes for urban areas. Indexes of this type are available covering both the 1930's and the post-1949 period for Shanghai and Tientsin. The Tientsin clothing price index in 1950 relative to that of food was 15.5 per cent above the July 1936–June 1937 level. That of miscellaneous (industrial) commodities relative to food was 28.1 per cent above the same level.[12] In the case of Shanghai the same comparisons for somewhat different years (1948/1936), but ones that other data in the same source indicate were subject to the same influences, yield percentages of 23.8 and 15 per cent respectively.[13] Urban prices, especially right after a civil war, may not reflect changes in the rural price structure faithfully, but the fact that the orders of magnitude are similar to the official scissors-differential index gives us some faith in its reliability. An impression that the differential was much greater (a onetime impression of mine) would, on closer inspection, appear to be due to the much greater increase in prices of such items as steel and petroleum, which are not sold in rural areas.

Owing to a lack of sufficient material, the reliability of the purchase price index itself cannot be dealt with as thoroughly as was the retail price index in the previous section, but its general plausibility can certainly be demonstrated. The major weakness of the index is that it may not include prices of items sold on the free market. Purchase prices were uncontrolled prior to the introduction of compulsory quotas at the end of 1953, and their rapid rise was due to free-market forces and the relatively rapid increase in industrial production and urbanization. After 1953 these prices were frozen at their existing levels and further adjustments were made only when the regime felt a

[12] Nankai University Economic Research Office, *Nankai chih-shu tz'u-liao hui-pien* (Compilation of Nankai index data; Peking, 1958), pp. 40–41.

[13] Shanghai Price Book, pp. 153, 448–449. Price data in this source indicate that by 1950 there may have been a slight decrease in the former and increase in the latter percentage.

TABLE 24. Annual average urban sales prices of grain

Commodity and Area	1949	1950	1951	1952	1953	1954	1955	1956	1957	1958	1959[a]
				(indexes)							
All grains											
Whole country[b]	—	—	—	100	—	—	107.1	—	—	—	—
Whole country[c]	100	76.6	88.29	88.24	96.86	—	—	—	—	—	—
Shanghai[d]	24.57	103.46	95.99	100	103.46	104.37	104.37	104.32	104.32	—	—
				(yuan)							
Rice (100 catties)											
Shanghai[e]	2.84	12.9	10.9	12.0	11.3	11.3	12.1	12.1	12.1	—	—
Shanghai[e]	3.20	14.8	12.9	14.2	13.8	14.0	15.2	15.2	15.2	—	—
Tientsin[f]	3.66	16.5	15.9	16.9	—	—	—	—	—	—	—
Tientsin[f]	—	—	—	—	—	14.1	14.1	14.1	14.1	—	—
Tientsin[f]	—	—	—	—	—	14.7	14.7	14.7	14.7	—	—
Canton[g]	—	—	9.4	—	—	—	—	—	—	—	12.5
Peking	—	—	—	—	—	—	14.8[h]	—	—	—	14.8
Tsingtao[i]	—	—	—	—	—	—	14.0	—	—	—	—
Wheat flour (44-catty sack)											
Shanghai[e]	1.36	7.15	7.81	7.28	8.05	8.1	8.7	8.7	8.7	—	—
Shanghai	—	—	—	—	—	—	—	—	—	—	8.7
Tientsin[f]	2.28	7.35	8.05	8.45	—	—	—	—	—	—	—
Tientsin[f]	—	—	—	—	—	9.24	9.24	—	—	—	—
Tientsin[f]	—	—	—	—	—	8.14	8.14	—	—	—	—
Peking[j]	10.6	8.68	8.85	8.88	9.45	9.45	—	—	—	—	—
Tsingtao	—	—	6.3	—	—	—	8.3	—	—	—	—
Canton[g]	—	—	8.8	—	—	—	—	—	—	—	10.1
Millet (100 catties)											
Tientsin[f]	2.84	11.9	11.4	12.2	—	13.0	13.0	13.0	13.0	—	—
Tientsin	—	—	—	—	—	—	—	—	—	—	13.0
Tsingtao[i]	—	—	—	10.6	—	—	11.1	—	—	—	—
Kaoliang (100 catties)											
Tientsin[f]	1.49	5.87	5.05	6.46	—	7.4	7.4	7.4	7.4	—	—
Corn flour (100 catties)											
Tientsin[f]	2.26	9.3	8.6	9.35	—	—	—	—	—	—	—
Tientsin[f]	—	—	—	—	—	11.2	11.2	—	—	—	—
Tientsin[f]	—	—	—	—	—	10.6	10.6	10.6	10.6	—	—
Tientsin[f]	—	—	—	—	—	9.0	9.0	9.0	9.0	—	—
Tsingtao[i]	—	—	9.0	—	—	—	10.5	—	—	—	—

[a] All 1959 data are from Noirot, "Facts on the Evolution of the Standard of Living."
[b] Tseng Ling, "Does Inflation Exist in China Today?" CCYC, October 17, 1957, p. 37.
[c] "State Grain Purchase and Supply Work Situation in the Past 4 Years," HHYP, April 28, 1954, p. 162. The 1949 figure is for March only; the 1950, 1951, and 1952 figures are for December; the 1953 figure is for October.
[d] Shanghai Price Book, pp. 454–459.
[e] All Shanghai data, except for 1959, are from Shanghai Price Book, pp. 470–563. Where more than one listing for Shanghai is given for a particular commodity, it is because the listings are for different qualities or varieties of that commodity (or because I could not be sure that two different sources were referring to the same variety or quality).
[f] Tientsin prices for 1949, 1950, 1951, and 1952 are computed from monthly average prices given in Nankai University Economic Research Office, Nankai chih-shu tzu-liao hui-pien, 1913–1952. The 1952 prices are only the average of the first four months of the year. The 1954 and 1955 data are taken from the Tientsin Ta kung pao, while the 1956 and 1957 data are from the Tientsin jih-pao. Where more than one listing for Tientsin is given for a particular commodity, it is because the listings are for different qualities or varieties of that commodity (or because I could not be sure that two different sources were referring to the same variety or quality).
[g] Canton prices for 1951 are taken from the Ching-chi chou-pao.
[h] Peking data for 1955 are from T'an Chen-lin, "A First Step in Research on Farm Income and Standard of Living," HHPYK, June 10, 1957, p. 111.
[i] All Tsingtao data are from the Tsingtao jih-pao.
[j] Jen-min jih-pao (Peking), except 1959.

TABLE 25. Annual average urban sales prices of cotton cloth

Commodity and Area	1949	1950	1951	1952	1953	1954	1955	1956	1957	1958	1959[a]
				(indexes)							
Cotton cloth and yarn (index)											
Whole country[b]	—	—	—	100	—	—	—	95.4	—	—	—
Shanghai[c]	20.45	81.11	97.55	100	98.18	97.13	97.13	97.13	97.13	—	—
				(yuan)							
Cotton cloth (bolt)											
Shanghai[c]	5.2	24.1	27.5	28.3	28.1	27.8	27.8	27.8	27.8	—	—
Shanghai[c]	6.0	24.0	28.0	28.4	27.6	27.1	27.1	27.1	27.1	—	—
Shanghai[c]	7.8	36.1	42.1	42.6	41.9	41.0	41.0	41.0	41.0	—	—
Tientsin[d]	6.4	27.6	33.1	34.0	—	33.0	33.0	33.5	33.5	—	—
Tientsin[d]	—	—	—	—	—	34.5	34.5	34.5	34.5	—	—
Tientsin[d]	5.4	24.1	28.6	29.6	—	28.5	28.5	28.5	28.5	—	—
Peking	—	—	—	—	—	—	—	—	—	—	33.0
Peking[e]	—	—	—	—	—	—	28.8	—	—	—	28.2
Tsingtao[f]	—	—	—	28.0	—	—	28.0	28.0	28.0	—	—
Tsingtao[f]	—	—	—	32.5	—	—	32.5	32.5	32.5	—	—
Tsingtao[f]	—	—	—	43.0	—	—	41.0	41.0	41.0	—	—
Canton[g]	—	—	25.1	—	—	—	—	—	—	—	26.7
Socks (dozen)											
Shanghai[c]	1.25	5.58	7.40	7.36	7.33	7.33	7.33	7.33	7.33	—	—
Canton[g]	—	—	6.54	—	—	—	—	—	—	—	4.68
Towels (dozen)											
Shanghai[c]	1.49	7.77	9.40	8.78	8.75	8.71	8.71	8.71	8.71	—	—
Canton[g]	—	—	6.0	—	—	—	—	—	—	—	6.24
Tientsin[d]	—	—	4.0	—	—	—	—	5.28	5.28	—	—

[a] All 1959 data are from Noirot, "Facts on the Evolution of the Standard of Living."

[b] Tseng Ling, "Does Inflation Exist in China Today?" *CCYC*, October 17, 1957, p. 37.

[c] All Shanghai data, except for 1959, are from Shanghai Price Book, pp. 470–563. More than one listing for Shanghai is given for cotton cloth because the listings are for different qualities or varieties of cloth (or because I could not be sure that two different sources were referring to the same variety or quality).

[d] Tientsin prices for 1949, 1950, 1951, and 1952 are computed from monthly average prices given in Nankai University Economic Research Office, *Nankai chih-shu tzu-liao hui-pien, 1913–1952*. The 1952 prices are only the average of the first four months of the year. The 1954 and 1955 data are taken from the Tientsin *Ta kung pao*, while the 1956 and 1957 data are from the *Tientsin jih-pao*. More than one listing for Tientsin is given for cotton cloth because the listings are for different qualities or varieties of cloth (or because I could not be sure that two different sources were referring to the same variety or quality).

[e] Peking data for 1955 are from T'an Chen-lin, "A First Step in Research on Farm Income and Standard of Living," *HHPYK*, June 10, 1957, p. 111. Two listings for Peking are given because they are for different qualities or varieties of cotton cloth.

[f] All Tsingtao data are from the *Tsingtao jih-pao*. Three listings for Tsingtao are given because they are for different qualities or varieties of cotton cloth.

[g] Canton prices for 1951 are taken from the *Ching-chi chou-pao*.

TABLE 26. Annual average urban sales prices of edible oils (yuan except for indexes)

Commodity and Area	1949	1950	1951	1952	1953	1954	1955	1956	1957	1958	1959[a]
All edible oils											
Whole country (index)[b]	—	—	—	—	—	—	—	(100)	(105.9)	—	—
Peanut oil (100 catties)											
Shanghai[c]	11.3	50.4	50.5	46.0	45.7	49.3	61.0	61.0	61.0	—	67.0
Tientsin[d]	7.54	43.1	43.8	54.2	50.0	54.5	60.0	60.0	60.0	—	—
Peking[e]	—	—	—	—	—	—	—	—	—	—	66.0
Tsingtao[f]	—	—	44.0	—	—	57.0	—	—	57.0	—	—
Canton[g]	—	—	59.3	—	—	—	—	—	—	—	86.0
Sesame oil (100 catties)											
Whole country (index)[b]	—	—	—	—	—	—	—	(100)	(118.45)	—	—
Tientsin (retail price)[d]	8.95	55.6	67.9	56.2	57.5	63.0	68.0	68.0	80.0	—	—

[a] All 1959 data are from Noirot, "Facts on the Evolution of the Standard of Living."
[b] SC, "Directive on Raising the Sales Prices of Vegetable Oil," FKHP, V, 186.
[c] All Shanghai data, except for 1959, are from Shanghai Price Book, pp. 470–563.
[d] Tientsin prices for 1949, 1950, 1951, and 1952 are computed from monthly average prices given in Nankai University Economic Research Office, Nankai chih-shu tzu-liao hui-pien, 1913–1952. The 1952 prices are only the average of the first four months of the year. The 1954 and 1955 data are taken from the Tientsin Ta kung pao, while the 1956 and 1957 data are from the Tientsin jih-pao.
[e] Peking data for 1955 are from T'an Chen-lin, "A First Step in Research on Farm Income and Standard of Living," HHPYK, June 10, 1957, p. 111.
[f] All Tsingtao data are from the Tsingtao jih-pao.
[g] Canton prices for 1951 are taken from the Chüng-chi chou-pao.

TABLE 27. Annual average urban sales prices of cigarettes, sugar, salt, and pork (yuan except for indexes)

Commodity and Area	1949	1950	1951	1952	1953	1954	1955	1956	1957	1958	1959a
Cigarettes (box)											
Whole country (index for high-grade)b	—	—	—	—	—	—	100	100.9	—	—	
Shanghaic	0.27	1.52	1.93	1.82	1.91	1.94	2.10	2.10	2.10	—	—
Tientsind	—	—	—	—	—	—	2.30	2.50	2.60	—	—
Tientsind	0.34	1.86	2.88	2.98	—	—	—	—	—	—	—
Sugar (100 catties)											
Shanghaic	11.4	63.0	61.4	65.6	50.0	56.0	62.7	62.7	62.7	—	72.0
Tientsind	—	—	—	—	—	67.0	76.0	76.0	76.0	82.0	—
Tientsind	11.7	61.1	61.6	66.0	—	—	—	—	—	—	—
Tsingtaoe	—	—	—	—	—	73.0	—	—	78.0	—	—
Cantonf	—	—	45.5	—	—	—	—	—	—	—	56.0
Salt (100 catties)											
Whole country (index)b	—	—	—	—	—	—	100	111	—	—	
Shanghaic	2.48	17.11	12.4	11.3	10.9	10.5	10.7	10.7	12.3	—	—
Tientsind	1.84	17.3	13.4	13.5	—	—	—	—	—	—	—
Tientsind	—	—	—	—	—	11.0	11.0	11.0	13.0	—	—
Peking	—	—	—	—	—	—	—	—	—	—	13.0
Tsingtaoe	—	—	—	—	—	—	—	—	11.0	—	
Tsingtaoe	—	—	—	—	—	—	—	—	12.0	—	
Pork (100 catties)											
Whole country (index)b	—	—	—	—	—	—	100	107	—	—	
Shanghaic	11.4	61.3	61.4	50.8	55.1	64.1	65.1	67.0	73.1	—	—
Tientsind	—	—	—	—	69.0	76.5	76.5	76.5	82.0	—	—
Tientsind	7.8	41.5	45.6	44.2	—	—	—	—	—	—	—
Tsingtaoe	—	—	60.0	44.0	—	—	70.0	70.0	72.0	—	—
Peking	—	—	—	—	—	—	—	—	—	—	91.0

a All 1959 data are from Noirot, "Facts on the Evolution of the Standard of Living."

b Ho Yu-chung, "A New Page in the History of China's Machine Building Industry," Ching-chi tao-pao, June 14, 1957, translated in ECMM, no. 92, p. 32.

c All Shanghai data, except for 1959, are from Shanghai Price Book, pp. 470–563.

d Tientsin prices for 1949, 1950, 1951, and 1952 are computed from monthly average prices given in Nankai University Economic Research Office, Nankai chih-shu tzu-liao hui-pien, 1913–1952. The 1952 prices are only the average of the first four months of the year. The 1954 and 1955 data are taken from the Tientsin Ta kung pao, while the 1956 and 1957 data are from the Tientsin jih-pao. Where more than one listing for Tientsin is given for a particular commodity, it is because the listings are for different qualities or varieties of that commodity (or because I could not be sure that two different sources were referring to the same variety or quality).

e All Tsingtao data are from the Tsingtao jih-pao. Two listings are given for salt in 1957 because listings are for different varieties or qualities (or because I could not be sure that two different sources were referring to the same variety or quality).

f Canton prices for 1951 are taken from the Ching-chi chou-pao.

particular crop or product needed special encouragement. The major effort to raise prices of such crops was made after the Eighth Party Congress in September 1956. Given the number of products whose prices were raised and the degree of rise, the jump of 11.1 per cent in the index between 1955 and 1957 appears plausible.[14] In addition, there were less dramatic upward price adjustments, such as the 2.1 per cent increase in the purchase price of grain between the end of 1953 and mid-1959.[15] Unfortunately, urban prices of agricultural products cannot be used to help verify these various movements because state control over these urban prices was very tight at an early stage, and it is impossible to argue that they moved in a manner similar to their rural counterparts. Nevertheless, the above-mentioned considerations seem to lend enough support to the reliability of the index to allow it to be used here.

[14] See Chapter IV, p. 70.
[15] *JMJP*, October 25, 1959.

APPENDIX C

Sources and Reliability of State Revenue Data

Statistics on revenue in the national budget are among the most reliable statistics published by the mainland regime. Since revenue is in the form of money and is collected centrally, there is no difficulty in compiling accurate data. There is no need, therefore, for sample surveys or crude guesses. It does not follow, however, that there are no problems in interpreting Chinese Communist budget data. In the first place, there is the question of comparability of Chinese data with those in other countries and even among different years in China itself. Second, there is the problem of deliberate attempts to falsify and mislead, to the extent that these exist.

The difficulty with respect to the first question is that the regime sometimes reports such things as foreign loans, bond sales, and even the previous year's surplus as sources of revenue. It is not uncommon to see several different revenue figures for the same year. Table 28 presents the relevant data where available. In earlier years, it was common to quote revenue figures that included the previous years' surpluses. From 1953 on, however, the part that was "carried-over surplus" was clearly differentiated, and from 1957 on, the item was dropped from budget reports altogether.[1] Revenue figures are now invariably given exclusive of the previous years' surpluses and inclusive of credits and insurance income. "Credits and insurance" includes domestic bond sales, foreign credits, and sales of various types of insurance. Foreign credits ceased to be of great importance beginning in 1956,[2] and bond sales were ended in 1959.[3]

[1] Li Hsien-nien, "Report on the Final State Accounts for 1957 and the Draft State Budget for 1958" (February 1, 1958), *FKHP*, VII, 117.

[2] This remained true between 1960 and 1963. The main source of such credits was presumably the short-term credits given by the Soviet Union to finance

TABLE 28. Chinese Communist revenue data (million yuan)

Year	Including previous year's surplus	Excluding previous year's surplus	Revenue minus expenditure excluding surplus	Revenue from credits and insurance[a]	Revenue excluding surplus and credits and insurance	Surplus or deficit after excluding surplus and credits and insurance
1950	6,950[b]	6,520	−290	330	6,190	−620
1951	14,200[b]	12,960	1,060	570	12,390	490
1952	18,920[b]	17,560	770	190	17,370	580
1953	25,670[c]	21,760	270	490	21,270	−220
1954	30,740[d]	26,230	1,600	1,790	24,440	−190
1955	30,360[e]	27,200	280	2,360	24,840	−2,080
1956	29,750[f]	28,740	−1,840	720	28,020	−2,560
1957	—	31,020	2,000	700	30,320	1,300
1958	—	41,860	900	800	41,060	100
1959	—	54,160	1,390	0	54,160	1,390
1960[g]	—	70,020	0	0	70,020	0

[a] The 1950–1958 data are given in SSB, *Ten Great Years*, p. 21. The 1959 and 1960 budget data are from Li Hsien-nien, "Report on the Final State Accounts for 1959 and the Draft State Budget for 1960," pp. 50, 58.

[b] Po I-po, "Report on the 1953 State Budget of the People's Republic of China," supplement to *People's China*, March 16, 1953 (quoted in Rostow, *Prospects for Communist China*, p. 246).

[c] *I-chiu-wu-szu-nien kuo-chia yu-suan* (The national budget of 1954; Peking, 1954), p. 12.

[d] Li Hsien-nien, "Report on the Final State Accounts for 1954 and the Draft State Budget for 1955" (July 6, 1955), *FKHP*, II, 490.

[e] Li Hsien-nien, "Report on the Final State Accounts for 1955 and the Draft State Budget for 1956," *Chung-hua Jen-min Kung-ho-kuo Ti-i-chieh Ch'uan-kuo Jen-min Tai-piao Ta-hui ti-szu-ts'u hui-i hui-kan* (The fourth meeting of the First National People's Congress of the People's Republic of China; Peking, 1957), p. 57.

[f] Li Hsien-nien, "Report on the Final State Accounts for 1956 and the Draft State Budget for 1957," *ibid*.

[g] Budget figures.

The problem of deliberate attempts to mislead or falsify is more complicated. It has been stated by several Western authorities that revenue figures for 1950 and 1951 were inflated by transfer of funds from 1952 collections. These funds were believed to be fines collected from private businessmen in the course of the "five anti" campaign in 1952.[4] Whatever the source of the extra funds, it is fairly certain that the 1950 deficit was much larger than statistics show. One source published before the "five anti" campaign states that the deficit in the final accounts for 1950 was 16.7 per cent of total outlay,[5] as compared to 4.3 per cent in later official figures. This would imply that revenue in 1950 was actually 5670 million yuan. This figure is close to one that can be derived from the draft budget figure for 1950 (4361 million yuan)[6] and the percentage increase of actual over budgeted income of 1950 (31.7 per cent).[7] The slight difference probably is due to errors in rounding. It appears safe, therefore, to argue that true revenue income in 1950 was about 5700 million yuan.

There is a similar problem with respect to 1951 data. Official figures show a surplus, but a number of statements made by Chinese Communist officials in 1952 would imply that in reality there was a deficit.[8] This is further supported by data on percentage increases in 1952 revenue and expenditure over actual results in 1951. From these data one can derive estimates of revenue and expenditure in 1951 that probably are closer to the true figures than those officially published (see Table 29).[9]

China's trade deficits with her. Even under the depressed agricultural conditions of 1960–1962, China maintained a surplus with the Soviet Union, but the volume of trade dropped.

[3] *JMJP* editorial, "Why Do We Want to Issue Local Economic Construction Bonds?" *HHPYK,* June 25, 1958, p. 91.

[4] See Wu Yuan-li, *An Economic Survey of Communist China,* p. 101; Hsiao Chi-jung, *Revenue and Disbursement of Communist China,* p. 75.

[5] Jung Tzu-ho, "Summary of the 1950 Financial Work and Policy and Tasks for 1951," *JMJP,* March 28, 1951, translated in *CB,* no. 214, p. 8.

[6] Wang Tzu-ying, "Some Lessons from Compiling and Putting into Effect the 1956 State Budget," *HHPYK,* March 19, 1957, p. 93.

[7] See note 5. The derived figure is 5740 million yuan.

[8] For further discussion of this see the sources cited in note 4.

[9] For the source of 1952 draft budget data, see note 6. Percentage increases of the 1952 draft budget over the actual results of 1951 are given in "Fi-

TABLE 29. Estimated revenue and expenditure, 1950 and 1951 (million yuan)

Year	Revenue	Expenditure	Deficit
1950	5,670	6,810	−1,140
1951	9,730	10,210	−480

It is my belief that, with the above-stated qualifications, budget revenue data are accurate. This belief can be buttressed by a test for internal consistency on figures for revenue from industrial and commercial taxes. This test involves use of official tax rates, commodity prices of goods subject to taxation, and the quantities of such goods produced. With these data, an estimate of tax revenue for each year has been made and compared with official figures. Since the estimates are crude and many statistics are lacking, the estimates naturally tend to differ somewhat from the official data, but I contend that the closeness of results for the years prior to 1958 is strong testimony to the fundamental accuracy of official revenue figures. It also tends to support the probable reliability of much of the industrial production data for those years. Divergence between the estimates and official data in 1958, and on an even greater scale in 1959, further supports the widespread belief that industrial production statistics were seriously falsified during those years. It is possible, of course, that there was also some upward bias in the revenue statistics for those years. Since the main sources of falsification were competition among rural cadres, factories, and so forth, and not manipulation at the top, it appears more likely that the revenue reported was actually collected. It may be that taxes were paid on goods as if they were of high quality when in fact they were of low quality and that there were other similar irregularities, but they probably were paid.

There are numerous reasons why one would expect minor discrepancies between the estimates and official data. In the

nance Minister Po I-po Presents the Budgetary Report at the 16th Meeting of the Central People's Government Council" (August 10, 1952), translated in *CB,* no. 214, p. 12.

first place, production data have been used where sales figures would have been better,[10] but time series for sales figures are not complete, and wholesale and retail statistics do not include goods transferred among state industrial enterprises. In addition, the prices used throughout are only crude estimates. Second, there is the problem of estimating value at current prices and tax rates for commodities lacking individual production and price data. The procedure followed here was to estimate unaccounted for gross value (in the case of light industry) in 1952 and 1957 prices and then to make crude adjustments for price changes. Tax rates were more difficult to reconstruct. In the case of heavy industry no attempt was made to estimate the tax on individual products because of inadequate price series. The procedure followed instead was to use estimates of 1952 and 1957 prices together with production data as weights in computing the average tax rate for each year. This procedure was also followed for computing the light-industry tax rate (except that current prices were used), but it was less valid, since I was only interested in discovering a tax rate for the portion not accounted for. The lack of production data, however, made other techniques unfeasible. If one assumes the error in the estimates in 1956 to equal that in 1957 (450 million yuan), the total discrepancy for 1951–1956 (3360 million yuan) almost exactly equals the income tax on the profits of private enterprises during those years (3400 million yuan).[11]

There also was no attempt to account separately for agricultural products not covered by the gross value of consumers' goods industry. This was due both to a lack of adequate sales data and the difficulty involved in determining what agricultural products were included under light industry, since almost all such commodities go through some processing. This problem, however, was not serious, because taxes on such products were few and low. In addition, fluctuations in their sales were closely related and similar to fluctuations in light-industrial production.

[10] This is because taxes are apparently usually paid when a product leaves the factory.

[11] *Ts'ai-cheng*, September 1959, translated in *JPRS*, no. 5755, p. 5. The income tax was a percentage of the profits of the enterprise and not of total business or sales.

TABLE 30. Industrial and commercial tax revenue: estimated and official (million yuan)

Year	Estimated	Official	Difference
1950	2,803	2,360	443
1951	4,751	4,750	1
1952	6,029	6,150	−121
1953	6,949	8,250	−1,301
1954	7,879	8,970	−1,091
1955	8,213	8,730	−517
1956	9,319	10,100	−781
1957	10,855	11,305	−450
1958	16,437	14,180	2,257
1959	22,634	15,700	6,934
1960[a]	28,338	19,450	8,888

[a] Draft budget figures.

When all these qualifications are made and the somewhat contrived nature of the tax on industrial consumer products is admitted, however, the data show a high degree of internal consistency for 1950–1957.

Only the results of the calculations are presented in Table 30. The detailed calculations themselves and the sources of data used are all available, for those interested, in my dissertation, which is on file in the Harvard University Archives in Widener Library.

APPENDIX D

Sources and Reliability of Purchase and Sales Data

The principal problem in any attempt to compile satisfactory purchase and sales figures for grain is that the definitions used are not always the same. Figures quoted may refer to either the grain year or the calendar year, to husked or unhusked grain, with or without soybeans, to total sales or only state sales (see Table 31). This problem can usually be successfully dealt with by taking care to see that statistics reported have the desired coverage. When only percentage increases are given without further explanation, however, there is no completely satisfactory way of dealing with the problem.

It is, of course, also possible that figures for purchases and sales are either inaccurate or even deliberately falsified. The belief that such is not the case is based first of all on the state's great need for accurate purchase and sales statistics in order to carry out successfully rationed distribution of grain in urban and rural areas and to meet grain-export requirements. Further, since all grain collected passes through the hands of the central government (the Ministry of Grain), the authorities do not have to rely on the honesty of cooperative or commune cadres for their data as they do in the case of grain-production statistics, for example. It would conceivably be possible for lower-level commercial cadres to practice falsification, but it would not be easy. They would have to account for the grain that did not show up in the state warehouses either as increased payments in kind for other purchases such as cotton (in which case they would have to deliver the cotton) or as outlays to disaster areas (which would have been hard to explain in the good harvest year of 1958, though somewhat easier in late 1959). There is also the

TABLE 31. China's grain market (million catties of husked grain except for tax in yuan and index; calendar year 1949 is entered under grain year 1949–50, 1950 under 1950–51, etc.)

Item	1949–50	1950–51	1951–52	1952–53	1953–54	1954–55	1955–56	1956–57	1957–58	1958–59	1959–60	1960–61	1961–62	1962–63	1963–64
Calendar-year collections and purchases[a]	—	66,850	—	—	73,900	93,200	87,600	75,700	—	105,920	—	—	—	—	—
Calendar-year index[b]	—	—	—	—	—	—	—	—	100	117	134	—	—	—	—
Grain-year collection and purchases[c]	—	—	61,000	63,060	83,000	90,270	85,990	83,430	92,910	111,500	—	—	—	—	—
Calendar-year grain sales[d]	—	55,510	—	—	66,640	80,900	70,200	83,300	77,550	89,950	95,800	—	—	—	—
Grain-year sales[e]	—	—	—	—	—	—	—	—	—	—	—	—	—	—	—
Grain-year exports[f]	—	—	—	—	1,760	2,290	1,282	—	—	—	—	—	—	—	—
Calendar-year rice exports[g]	—	—	—	—	—	2,295	2,590	2,085	984	2,571	3,157	—	—	—	—
Calendar-year grain imports[h]	—	—	—	—	—	—	—	—	—	—	—	—	11,840	7,000	10,600+
Urban *unhusked* grain consumption[i]	—	—	—	—	43,320	44,610	45,220	49,430	—	—	—	—	—	—	—
Supplies to cities and armies[i]	—	—	—	—	35,410	37,110	35,850	39,100	—	—	—	—	—	—	—
Grain taken out of rural areas[j]	—	—	—	—	48,770	43,910	49,640	37,430	—	64,070	—	—	—	—	—
Drawbacks to rural areas[k]	—	—	—	—	34,230	46,360	36,330	46,000	—	47,430	—	—	—	—	—
Decrease in output due to natural disasters[l]	—	—	—	—	15,000	17,700	12,700	24,400	—	—	—	—	—	—	—
Agricultural tax															
In fine-grain equivalents[m]	40,600	35,340	43,740	38,800	35,100	38,000	38,000	36,800	36,000	—	—	—	—	—	—
In millions of yuan	—	1,910	2,169	2,704	2,711	3,278	3,054	2,965	2,931	3,260	3,300	—	—	—	—

[a] Excluding soybeans. The 1950 and 1958 data are from SSB, *Ten Great Years*, p. 169. Others are in T'an Chen-lin, "A First Step in Research on Farm Income and Standard of Living," *HHPYK*, June 10, 1957, pp. 105–111.

[b] The percentage increase of 1958 over 1957 is given in SSB, "Report on the 1958 National Economic Development Situation," *HHPYK*, April 25, 1959, p. 54. The increase of 1959 over 1958 is in "Communes Greatly Demonstrated Their Prowess in Last Year's Massive and Rapid Purchase of Farm Products," NCNA, January 26, 1960, translated in *SCMP*, no. 2189, pp. 18–20.

[c] Including soybeans. The figures for 1953–54 are from the source given in note f. The 1952–53 statistic is derived from a reported increase in grain purchases of 22 billion catties (Wu Shuo, "An Inquiry into the Grain Situation during the Transition Period," *Liang-shih*, January 25, 1957, translated in *ECMM*, no. 85, p. 12). The figures for 1956–57 are from the First Five Year Plan. SSB, "Report on the First Five Year Plan," *HHPYK*, April 25, 1959, p. 50, gives total purchases and taxes of husked grain for a five-year period, but it does not specify whether soybeans are included or whether the years reported are calendar or grain years. The most conservative estimate is arrived at by assuming that it includes soybeans and is for the first five grain years rather than calendar years. This also gives the most reasonable figure when the percentage increase for 1958–59 over 1957–58 is applied (Chai Mou, "The Superiority of the People's Commune," *CCYC*, November 17, 1959, p. 37). The 1958–59 estimate, arrived at by applying the percentage increase over 1957–58 to the 1957–58 derived figure, is reasonable in the sense that it does not leave an unduly large residual when the reported figure for grain taken out of the rural areas is subtracted from it. It is also consistent with reported percentage increases for the calendar year. Whatever the exact figure, there is little doubt that purchases were increased substantially during 1957–58. One source (Peking *TKP*, November 10, 1957, quoted in Carin, *China's Land Problem Series*, II, 549) reported that grain already in the granaries as of that date was 12,580 million catties above the previous grain year and that 57.14 per cent of the collection and purchases (the normal percentage for mid-November) had been met.

d The 1950 and 1958 statistics are from SSB, *Ten Great Years*, p. 167. The 1959 figure is calculated on the basis of the 1959 percentage increase (NCNA, January 23, 1960), and the 1957 figure on the percentage increase from 1957 to 1958 (*Peking Review*, April 21, 1959, quoted in Kirby, *Contemporary China*, IV, 188). The 1952 figure is from the percentage increase between 1952 and 1957 (SSB, "Report on the First Five Year Plan, p. 50). There are other statistics given for 1950, 1952, and 1956 in *First Five Year Plan for Development of the National Economy of the People's Republic*, and Yang Chien-pai, *Chung-chi-chung chi-chung chu-yao pi-li kuan-hsi-te pien-hua*, p. 40. The reason for the not insubstantial discrepancies between the various sources is not known, but it probably is due to a difference in what the statistics are supposed to include.

e Hou Chien-chung, "Some Understanding of the 'Make Up Shortage by Plenty' Policy," *Liang-shih*, September 25, 1957, translated in *ECMM*, no. 106, p. 23, gives the sales figures for the grain years 1955–56 and 1956–57, and *CHCC*, 1958, p. 25, gives the percentage changes in retail sales for all four years. Evidence that the two sources are referring to the same data is that the percentage increase of 1956–57 over 1955–56 is 18.6 per cent in both cases.

f Excluding soybeans. *TCKT* data office, "The Basic Situation with Respect to Our Country's Unified Purchase and Sale of Grain," *HHPYK*, November 25, 1957, pp. 171–172. The data are given as a percentage of total output of husked grain (the total output figures are given in the same article). The percentage of grain exports consisting of soybeans is also given. The amount of grain exports excluding soybeans was then derived from these percentages.

g *Far Eastern Economic Review*, XXXXI (January 26, 1961), 178. Rice makes up the bulk of China's non-soybean grain exports. Rice exports continued, but in reduced amounts between 1960 and 1963; the data are not included here.

h *Far Eastern Economic Review, Yearbook, 1962* (Hong Kong, 1962), p. 57; *ibid., 1964* (Hong Kong, 1964), pp. 133–134. The 1963 figure does not include additional purchases from Canada after August 1963.

i For source, see note f.

j For the source of the data for 1953–54 to 1956–57, see note f. This figure is derived by subtracting drawbacks to rural areas from total purchases. The 1958–59 figure is given, in terms of unhusked grain, as 74.5 billion catties (Chou Po-p'ing, "This Year's Condition of Food Supply in China," *UKS*, vol. II, no. 6, p. 81) and has been converted to husked grain using the conversion factor 0.86, the one that is usually used. Since the percentage of unhusked crops in total purchases varies (for example, the wheat percentage decreased, as can be seen by calculating from the percentages of total output purchased in *Liang-shih* commentator, "Certain Basis and Ideas for Wheat Collection and Purchases," *Liang-shih*, May 25, 1957, translated in *ECMM*, no. 89, p. 4), the conversion factor has also varied, but it is unlikely that it varied significantly.

k For the source of the data for 1953–54 to 1956–57, see note f. The 1958–59 figure is obtained by subtracting grain taken out of rural areas from total purchases.

l Chou Po-p'ing, "The Policy of the Unified Purchase and Sale of Grain Shall Not Be Frustrated," *Liang-shih*, July 1957, translated in *ECMM*, no. 101, p. 31.

m K. C. Chao, *Agrarian Policy of the Chinese Communist Party*, p. 301.

n Yin and Yin, *Economic Statistics of Mainland China*, p. 85; Li Hsien-nien's budget reports for 1957–58, 1958–59, and 1959–60.

TABLE 32. Production[a] and retail sales of consumers' goods

Commodity	1950[b]	1951[c]	1952[d]	1953	1954	1955[e]	1956[f]	1957[g]	1958[h]	1959[h]
Total retail sales[a] (million yuan)	17,060	23,430	27,680	34,800	38,110	39,220	46,100	47,420	54,800	63,800
Gross value of consumer industrial products (million yuan)										
1952 prices	13,470	17,850	22,110	28,020	31,980	31,980	38,320	40,450	50,000	—
1957 prices	—	—	—	—	—	—	—	37,400	—	67,000
Cotton cloth (million meters)										
Production	2,520	3,060	3,830	4,690	5,230	4,360	5,770	5,050	5,700	7,500
Sales[l]	1,668[j]	2,256	2,813	3,899	3,791	3,849	5,101	4,150	4,863	5,200
Edible oils (1000 tons)										
Production	607	731	983	1,009	1,060	1,165	1,076	1,100	1,250	1,470
Sales	540	—	778	—	—	1,060	1,230	1,050	1,065	1,140
Salt (1000 tons)										
Production	2,464	4,346	4,945	3,569	4,886	7,535	4,940	8,277	10,400	11,000
Sales	2,061	2,930	2,978	—	—	4,000[k]	3,800	3,900	4,000	—
Sugar (1000 tons)										
Production	242	300	451	638	693	717	807	864	900	1,130
Sales	243	—	471	—	—	640[k]	—	880	981	1,079
Cigarettes (1000 crates)										
Production	1,848	2,002	2,650	3,552	3,728	3,567	3,907	4,456	4,750	5,500
Sales	1,720	1,930	2,465	—	—	3,590	3,701	4,324	—	—
Rubber shoes (1000 pairs)										
Production	45,670	65,060	61,690	76,360	85,840	97,450	103,480	128,850	182,360	—
Sales	41,927	—	59,770	—	—	66,350	100,857	108,780	178,190	—
Bicycles (1000)										
Production	21	44	80	165	298	335	640	806	1,174	—
Sales	140[f]	—	365[f]	—	—	510	729	—	—	—
Coal (1000 tons)										
Production	42,920	53,090	66,490	69,680	83,660	98,300	110,360	130,000	270,000	347,800
Sales	17,596[f]	20,380	25,422[f]	—	—	41,500	52,298	64,570[i]	—	—
Hogs (head)	—	—	89,770	96,131	101,718	87,920	84,026	145,900	160,000	—
Pork (1000 tons)	1,710	—	2,396	—	—	2,420	2,350	1,454	1,764	—
Paper (1000 tons)										
Production	380	492	539	667	842	839	998	1,221	1,630	—
Sales	140	—	218	—	—	—	275	335	519	—
Marine products (1000 tons)										
Production	912	1,332	1,666	1,900	2,293	2,518	2,648	3,120	4,060	—
Sales	721	—	—	—	—	—	—	—	2,470	—

a All production data and the figures for total retail sales are from SSB, *Ten Great Years*, pp. 87, 95–97, 99–100, 166, except for the 1959 data, which are from Li Fu-chun, "Report on the Draft 1960 National Economic Plan," *Second Session of the Second National People's Congress*, pp. 4, 29, 35.

b 1950 and 1958 quantities of retail sales were taken from SSB, *Ten Great Years*, p. 167, except for cigarettes, bicycles, coal, and the 1950 sales of pork.

c The 1951 data are derived from percentage increases over 1959 given by Yao Yi-lin, "Development of Domestic Commerce," *CB*, no. 219, p. 34.

d 1952 quantities of retail sales are taken from *First Five Year Plan for Development of the National Economy of the People's Republic of China (1953–1957)*, pp. 154–155, except for coal and bicycles.

e The 1955 figures are derived from percentage increases given in SSB, "Report on the Results of the 1956 National Economic Plan," *HHPYK*, September 10, 1957, p. 204, except for salt and sugar.

f 1956 quantities of retail sales are taken from Yang Chien-pai, *Ching-chi-chung chi-chung chu-yau pi-li kuan-hsi-te pien-hua*, p. 40, except for sugar. This source gives data for 1950, 1952, and 1956 for the same list of commodities. The 1952 data are the same as those given in the source in note d, except for sugar. The 1950 data are almost the same as data in SSB, *Ten Great Years*. Discrepancies between 1950 data in the two different sources are less than 5 or 10 per cent, except in the case of pork. The pork sales figure in *Ten Great Years* is only 1400 tons, but this may have been arbitrarily lowered in order to present a more favorable picture. The sugar sales figures from the above source are not used because they are consistently lower than those from other sources and hence probably had a somewhat less extensive coverage. There is no reason to believe these figures were falsified, however, because the percentage increases are not markedly different from those in other sources. The 1950 and 1952 sales figures for coal and bicycles and the 1950 cigarette sales statistics are taken from this source because they do not appear in the other sources mentioned above.

g The 1957 sales figures are derived from percentage increases over 1952 given in SSB, "Communique on the Fulfillment of the First Five Year Plan," *CB*, no. 556, p. 7, except for pork, which is derived from a statement by Po I-po, "Draft Plan for the Development of the National Economy in 1958," *CB*, no. 494, p. 9, that the pork supply in 1958 was 620 million catties above 1957. The figure for rubber shoes that can be derived from the percentage increase given for 1958 over 1957 (a reported increase of 52 per cent, according to SSB, "Report on the 1958 National Economic Development Situation," *HHPYK*, April 25, 1959, p. 53) is not the same as the one derived from the percentage increase given for 1957 over 1952, but it is not radically different (the other is about 117 million pairs). One can be somewhat more certain of the base used in comparing 1957 with 1952, so this figure was the one chosen.

h The 1959 sales figures (except for total retail sales) are derived from percentage increases for 1959 over 1958 given in *Chi-hua yu t'ung-chi*, no. 2 (1960), p. 44. It is not known definitely whether or not these figures caught up with the general trend toward falsification, but the comparatively conservative increases reported would tend to make one doubt it.

i There are a number of problems in the reconstruction of cotton-cloth sales statistics. At times data are given in meters and at times in rolls (approximately 32 meters per roll), but there does not appear to be a consistently used conversion ratio. In addition, a substantial amount of cloth is used for industrial purposes. The data used here for 1950 to 1956 are from *WKKT*, p. 185, and are stated to be total consumption by urban and rural residents. These figures are consistent with the figures for cloth years (September to August) given in Ministry of Commerce, "To Cut Consumption of Cloth in Summer Use," *URS*, vol. VII, no. 17, p. 223, and the percentage increase in retail sales for 1955 to 1956 in SSB, "Report on the Results of the 1956 National Economic Plan," *HHPYK*, September 10, 1957, p. 204. For 1957, 1958, and 1959 the sources used were percentage increases of retail sales in those years (for sources see notes g and h).

j SSB, *Ten Great Years*, p. 167, gives a figure of 2170 million meters for cotton-cloth retail sales in 1950. The difference is probably explained by the fact that cotton cloth for nonconsumption purposes was sold on the retail market at this time. This difference probably only existed during the first few years.

k The 1955 statistics for salt and sugar sales are derived from percentage increases over 1950 in Chu Ching and Chu Chung-chien, "Variations in Our Rural Market Commodity Turnover," *CCYC*, June 10, 1957, p. 118.

l The figures are derived from the percentage increase given in Keng Tsun-san, "A Brief Discussion on the Existing Price of Coal," *ECMM*, no. 171, p. 38.

[251]

possibility, of course, that the central government has not called them to account for obvious discrepancies.

The high degree of internal consistency between the various data in Table 31 is further evidence of probable lack of serious falsification. These data are also consistent with other relevant types of data, such as directives dealing with grain purchases and supplies and changes in urban grain rations.

There are a number of problems in the use of statistics of retail sales of individual commodities (see Table 32). The easiest one to deal with is the tendency of Chinese journals and newspapers to use statistics of sales by state firms of a particular commodity in place of total retail sales. Before the almost complete socialization of commerce these were quite different concepts. One has to be careful, therefore, that the data one uses are those for total retail trade. In constructing a table there is also a need to rely fairly heavily on percentage increases. This, however, appears to be less serious here than, for instance, in the case of purchasing-power statistics, where there is more of a problem of definition of concepts. Where percentage increases and absolute data on retail sales coincide, there are usually only minor differences.

For some retail-sales statistics there is a serious problem of how to estimate sales on free and other decentralized markets. This last problem, however, does not arise for the commodities listed in Table 32. A number of these commodities were rationed (cotton cloth, edible oils, pork, bicycles, and coal), so that the state had both the means and necessity of keeping close track of their sales, at least for the period following institution of rationing. The remaining commodities were all important ones whose distribution was mainly effected through the central government's commercial network. Some of the data for 1950–1952 and possibly later may not be too reliable because of difficulty in obtaining adequate data from the then large and relatively uncontrolled private commercial sector.

The reason for believing that the data have not been deliberately falsified is based first of all on the fact that they present a far from universally favorable picture. The sharp drop in pork sales in 1957 is the most dramatic case in point. Statistics such as these are not, of course, presented in this way in the original Communist sources. The years reported (in any single article) are usually picked so that they show a substantial increase in sales. Second, there is a high degree of consistency between production and sales data, at least for years prior to 1959. It is worth noting that in 1959 the increase in production was generally much more rapid than the rise in sales in the four cases for which information was available. It is possible, therefore, that 1959 sales data were not falsified. Finally, the data are consistent with various nonquantitative materials such as the timing of the introduction of rationing for key commodities (see Chapter IX).

APPENDIX E

Purchasing-Power Data

Statistics on money purchasing power are crude because they are based in part on rough estimates of free-market agricultural-product sales and wage payments to the rural population (see Table 33). However, wage payments to other than rural labor are strictly controlled, and the total wage bill of each firm is one of four major plan targets. State and cooperative purchases of farm products are also carefully supervised with compulsory plan targets and, in addition, form the basis of over three-quarters of China's exports and the bulk of rationed goods. As a result, it is probable that the central authorities both demand and get fairly good estimates of these quantities. Wage payments to rural nonagricultural labor apparently were not included in agricultural plans until during or after 1958.[1] The principal exception to this may be 1959. The over-all state purchase statistics of that year may have been caught up in the more general tendency toward falsification.

Several of these statistics are derived from percentage increases. The principal difficulty with such statistics is that some writers use somewhat different concepts to represent the same thing, and, when only percentage increases are given, it is not always easy to tell precisely which concept has been used. There are, for example, two different figures given for rural purchasing power in 1950 and 1956. One set is given in Table 33 and the other is 8.1 billion yuan for 1950 and 19.1 billion yuan for 1956 (see Table 33, note b). The latter figure was rejected on the grounds that it probably represents only sales of agricultural and rural handicraft produce plus some relatively small items

[1] Chang Chi-sheng, "Some Views on the Method of Calculating Purchasing Power," *Chung-yang ho-tso t'ung-hsun,* February 11, 1959, translated in *ECMM,* no. 192, pp. 38–43.

TABLE 33. Total purchasing power and its principal components (million yuan)

Year	Purchasing power Total (1)	Index (2)	Total urban wage bill (3)	Rural[a] (4)	Agriculture and subsidiary products Total sales[b] (5)	State and cooperative purchases[c] (6)	Purchasing power of collective units (7)
1950	17,660[d]	100	—	9,500[e]	8,000[f]	780	—
1951	22,080[d]	125	—	—	10,500[f]	2,500	—
1952	27,600[d]	156	6,700[g]	16,500[h]	12,970[f]	5,630	—
1953	33,120[d]	188	8,800[g]	—	15,320[f]	8,170[i]	—
1954	37,670[d]	213	9,610[g]	—	17,360[f]	12,070[i]	—
1955	40,240[j]	228	10,000[g]	—	17,800[f]	—	—
1956	46,500[k]	263	13,600[g]	24,500[e]	18,400[f]	13,330[l]	7,440[m]
1957	47,000[n]	266	15,250[g]	25,000[o]	20,280[f]	15,620[l]	6,400
1958	54,800[p]	310	—	30,000[o]	22,760[f]	19,680[q]	—
1959	—	—	—	—	29,180[r]	—	—

[a] Column 5 plus other rural income.
[b] Column 6 plus free market purchases.
[c] Excludes purchases made on the free market.
[d] I Shih-chieh, "Discussion of the Problem of Balancing Production and Consumption," *HHPYK*, March 10, 1957, p. 88. Data derived from percentage increases.
[e] *JMJP*, May 5, 1957. There are also figures of 8.1 and 19.1 billion yuan for rural purchasing power in 1950 and 1956 respectively (*Ts'ai-ching yen-chiu*, no. 1, 1958, p. 5).
[f] SSB, *Ten Great Years*, p. 168.
[g] Schran, "The Structure of Income in Communist China," p. 277. The statistics are taken directly from Chinese Communist and Soviet sources without the addition of any arbitrary assumptions by the author. Wages and salaries of the nonagricultural labor force are not identical to urban purchasing power, but the difference is not great (urban purchasing power of individuals in 1956 is given as 14,560 million yuan by Wu Ting-ch'eng, "Explanation of Certain Problems Related to the Proposal for Computing the Social Purchasing Power," *CHCC*, September 1957, pp. 27–29. One of the amounts not included, for example, is the income paid on the capital still owned by "private capitalists" based on 5 per cent of the value of their capital. Before socialization this income was derived directly from enterprise profits. The figures for 1958 and 1959 probably show very substantial increases in the wage bill due primarily to the large increase in the nonfarm work force in 1958. The average wage given for 1958, however, is only the average for old workers (SSB, *Ten Great Years*, p. 216), whereas new workers were apparently hired at a much lower wage.
[h] This figure is derived from the reported increase in rural purchasing power between 1952 and 1958 (80 per cent; Chung Chao-hsiu, "Our People Live Better and Better Lives," Peking *TKP*, October 18, 1959, translated in *CB*, no. 606, p. 13) and the reported increases between 1950 to 1952 and 1952 to 1957 (70 and 80 per cent respectively; *Hung-ch'i*, no. 13, July 1, 1960, translated in *URS*, vol. XX, no. 7), and rounding off to the nearest half billion. There are other percentage increases given for rural purchasing power not consistent with this statistic. Percentage increases given in Chu Ching and Chu Chung-chien, "Variations in Our Rural Market Commodity Turnover," *CCYC*, June 10, 1957, p. 112, were rejected on grounds that they were exactly the same rates as those given in the same article for increases in commodities retailed in the rural areas, a figure likely to be similar but not identical with purchasing power.
[i] Wang Ping, "The Free Market in China," *ECMM*, no. 92, p. 27, gives the amount and percentage of increase between 1953 and 1954, from which absolute figures can be derived.
[j] *CHCC*, 1957, p. 7.
[k] *JMJP*, July 2, 1957, in C. M. Li, *Economic Development of Communist China*, p. 158.
[l] *TCYC* data office, "The Domestic Market Commodity Circulation Situation in 1957," *TCYC*, April 23, 1958, p. 24. Data derived from percentage increases.
[m] Wu Ting-ch'eng, "Explanation of Certain Problems," pp. 27–29.
[n] Po I-po, "Draft Plan for the Development of the National Economy in 1958," *CB*, no. 494, pp. 1–27.
[o] Chai Mou, "The Superiority of the People's Commune," *CCYC*, November 17, 1959, p. 37.
[p] Ou Ming, "Strive for Realization of the 1959 National Economic Plan," *Chung-kuo kung-jen*, April 27, 1959, translated in *ECMM*, no. 171, p. 29.
[q] SSB, "Report on the 1958 National Economic Development Situation," *HHPYK*, April 25, 1959, p. 54. Data derived from percentage increases (see text below, second paragraph).
[r] "Communes Greatly Demonstrated Their Prowess," *SCMP*, no. 2189, p. 18. Data derived from percentage increases.

such as agricultural credit. When only percentage increases are given, it is not possible to make such a check unless some of the years for which percentage increases were given coincide with years for which absolute figures are available. If not, there are occasionally other grounds for deciding between alternative estimates (see Table 33, notes b and e). It is not often, however, that such grounds are strong enough to justify a great deal of confidence in the final estimates.

Beyond these reasons, the principal basis for believing that the statistics in the table roughly represent the true picture is their high degree of internal consistency. The widening discrepancy between rural purchasing power and purchases of farm products is probably accounted for mainly by increases in the use of farm labor on nonfarm projects following the advent of cooperatives and communes.[2]

[2] For example, "How to Conduct Surveys on Commodity Supply and on the Purchasing Power of Social Commodities," *Chi-hua yu t'ung-chi,* August 23, 1959, translated in *JPRS,* no. 1023D, pp. 1–7, states that 15 per cent of the base income of pleasants and communes was derived from services to transportation, capital construction, projects of the state, remittances from the cities, and state subsidies.

Selected Bibliography

The Bibliography is organized as follows:

I. BOOKS AND DISSERTATIONS

A. IN ENGLISH

Bergson, Abram, *The Structure of Soviet Wages.* Cambridge, Mass.: Harvard University Press, 1944.

—— *The Economics of Soviet Planning.* New Haven: Yale University Press, 1964.

Berliner, J. S. *Factory and Manager in the USSR.* Cambridge, Mass.: Harvard University Press, 1957.

Buck, J. L. *Chinese Farm Economy.* Shanghai: Institute of Pacific Relations, Commercial Press, 1930.

—— *Land Utilization in China.* Nanking: University of Nanking, 1937.

Carin, Robert. *China Land Problem Series.* Research Backgrounder. 4 vols. Hong Kong: 1960.

Chandra-Sekhar, Sripati. *Red China: An Asian View.* New York: Praeger, 1961.

Chao, K. C. *Agrarian Policy of the Chinese Communist Party.* New Delhi: Asia Publishing House, 1960.

—— *Economic Planning and Organization in Mainland China.* 2 vols. Cambridge, Mass.: Center for East Asian Studies, Harvard University, 1959, 1960.

Chao Shu-li. *Sanliwan Village.* Peking: Foreign Languages Press, 1957.

Chen, Jack. *New Earth.* Peking: New World Press, 1957.

Chen Po-ta. *A Study of Land Rent in Pre-Liberation China.* Peking: Foreign Languages Press, 1958.

Cheng Chu-yuan. *Monetary Affairs of Communist China.* Communist China Problem Research Series. Hong Kong: Union Research Institute, 1954.

Chong Twanmo. *Production of Food Crops in Mainland China: Prewar and Postwar.* The RAND Corporation, Research Memorandum RM-1659, March 22, 1956.

Chou En-lai. *Report on Adjusting the Major Targets of the 1959 National Economic Plan and Further Developing the Campaign for Increasing Production and Practicing Economy.* Peking: Foreign Languages Press, 1959.

Chou Li-po. *The Hurricane.* Peking: Foreign Languages Press, 1955.

—— *Great Changes in a Mountain Village,* vol. I. Peking: Foreign Languages Press, 1961.

Crook, David and Isabel. *Revolution in a Chinese Village.* London: Routledge and Kegan Paul, 1959.

Development of the Economies of the People's Democracies, 1961. Bulletin of Foreign Commercial Information Supplement, U.S. Department of Commerce, no. 4, 1962.

Directory of Chinese Communist Leadership. Hong Kong: American Consulate General, November 1960; revised version, May 9, 1962.

Ecklund, George. *Taxation in Communist China, 1950–1959.* Washington, 1961.

Eckstein, Alexander. *The National Income of Communist China.* Glencoe, Ill.: Free Press, 1961.

Eighth National Congress of the Communist Party of China. 2 vols. Peking: Foreign Languages Press, 1956.

Far Eastern Economic Review, Yearbook, 1962. Hong Kong: 1962.

Far Eastern Economic Review, Yearbook, 1964. Hong Kong: 1964.

Fei Hsiao-tung and Chang Chih-i. *Earthbound China.* London: Routledge and Kegan Paul, 1948.

First Five Year Plan for Development of the National Economy of the People's Republic of China in 1953–1957. Peking: Foreign Languages Press, 1956.

Granick, David. *Management of the Industrial Firm in the USSR.* New York: Columbia University Press, 1954.

Greene, Felix. *Awakened China.* New York: Doubleday, 1961.

Grossman, Gregory, ed. *Value and Plan.* Berkeley and Los Angeles: University of California Press, 1960.

Guillain, Robert. *The Blue Ants.* London: Martin Secker and Warburg, 1957.

Hollister, W. W. *China's Gross National Product and Social Accounts, 1950–1957.* Glencoe, Ill.: The Free Press, 1958.

Holzman, F. D. *Soviet Taxation.* Cambridge, Mass.: Harvard University Press, 1955.

Hsia, Ronald. *Government Acquisition of Agricultural Output in Mainland China, 1953–1956.* The RAND Corporation, Research Memorandum RM-2207, September 3, 1958.

Hsiao Chi-jung. *Revenue and Disbursement of Communist China.* Communist China Problem Research Series. Hong Kong: Union Research Institute, 1955.

Hsieh, S. C., and T. H. Lee. *The Role of Demand Projection in Agricultural Planning in Taiwan.* Taiwan, n.d.

Hsueh Mu-chiao, Su Hsing, and Lin Tse-li. *The Socialist Transformation of the National Economy in China.* Peking: Foreign Languages Press, 1960.

Hughes, Richard. *The Chinese Communes.* London: The Bodley Head, 1960.

Hughes, T. J., and D. E. T. Luard. *The Economic Development of Communist China, 1949–1958.* London: Oxford University Press, 1959.

Kirby, E. S., ed. *Contemporary China.* 5 vols. Hong Kong: Hong Kong University Press, 1956–1963.

Kuan Ta-tung. *The Socialist Transformation of Capitalist Industry and Commerce in China.* Peking: Foreign Languages Press, 1960.

Labin, Suzanne. *The Anthill.* London: Stevens, 1960.

Lerner, Abba P. *The Economics of Control.* New York: Macmillan, 1944.

Lethbridge, H. J. *China's Urban Communes.* Hong Kong: Dragonfly Books, 1961.

Lewis, J. W. *Leadership in Communist China.* Ithaca: Cornell University Press, 1963.

Li, C. M. *The Economic Development of Communist China.* Berkeley and Los Angeles: University of California Press, 1959.

———— *The Statistical System of Communist China.* Berkeley and Los Angeles: University of California Press, 1962.

Liu Shao-ch'i. *Address at the Meeting in Celebration of the 40th Anniversary of the Founding of the Communist Party of China* (June 30, 1961). Peking: Foreign Languages Press, 1961.

Liu, T. C., and K. C. Yeh. *The Economy of the Chinese Mainland: National Income and Economic Development, 1933–1959.* 2 vols. The RAND Corporation, Research Memorandum RM-3519, April 1963.

Lockwood, W. W. *The Economic Development of Japan.* Princeton: Princeton University Press, 1954.

Ma Feng-hwa. "The Financing of Public Investment in Communist China," unpub. diss. University of Michigan, 1959.

MacFarquhar, Roderick. *The Hundred Flowers Campaign and the Chinese Intellectuals.* New York: Praeger, 1960.

Mao Tse-tung. *The Question of Agricultural Cooperation.* Peking: Foreign Languages Press, 1955.

Ohkawa, Kazushi. *The Growth Rate of the Japanese Economy since 1878.* Tokyo: Kinokuniya Bookstore, 1957.

Orleans, L. A. *Professional Manpower and Education in Communist China.* Washington: National Science Foundation, 1961.

Reports and Abstracts of the Chinese Maritime Customs, 1863–1948.

Rostow, W. W. *The Prospects for Communist China.* Cambridge, Mass., and New York: Technology Press and Wiley, 1954.

Schran, Peter. "The Structure of Income in Communist China," unpub. diss. University of California, 1961.

Schwartz, Harry. *Russia's Soviet Economy.* New York: Prentice-Hall, 1954.

Shen, T. H. *Agricultural Resources of China.* Ithaca: Cornell University Press, 1951.

Snow, Edgar. *The Other Side of the River: Red China Today.* New York: Random House, 1962.

Starlight, L. L. "Monetary and Fiscal Policies in Communist China, 1949–1954," unpub. diss. Harvard University, 1957.

State Statistical Bureau. *Ten Great Years.* Peking: Foreign Languages Press, 1960.

Tawney, R. H. *Land and Labor in China.* New York: Harcourt Brace, 1932.

Third Five Year Plan (1961). Government of India, Planning Commission.

Tung Ta-lin. *Agricultural Cooperation in China.* Peking: Foreign Languages Press, 1959.

Vogel, Ezra. Unpublished manuscript (in process).

Wiles, P. J. D. *The Political Economy of Communism.* Cambridge, Mass.: Harvard University Press, 1962.

Wu Ai. *Steel and Tempered.* Peking: Foreign Languages Press, 1961.

Wu Yuan-li. *An Economic Survey of Communist China.* New York: Bookman Associates, 1956.

Yang, C. K. *A Chinese Village in Early Communist Transition.* Cambridge, Mass.: Technology Press, 1959.

Yang, M. C. *A Chinese Village — Taitou, Shantung Province.* New York: Columbia University Press, 1945.

Yin, Helen and Y. C. *Economic Statistics of Mainland China (1949–1957).* Cambridge, Mass.: Center for East Asian Studies, Harvard University, 1960.

B. IN JAPANESE

Ishikawa, Shigeru. *Chugoku ni okeru shihon chikuseki kiko* (Capital formation in China). Tokyo: Iwanami Bookstore, 1960.

C. IN CHINESE

Chao I-wen. *Hsin Chung-kuo-te kung-yeh* (New China's industry). Peking: Statistical Press, 1957.

Chien-kuo shih-nien, 1949–1959 (Ten years of national construction, 1949–1959). 2 vols. Hong Kong: Chi-wen Press, 1959.

Chung-hua jen-min Kung-ho-kuo fa-kuei hui-pien (Collection of laws of the Chinese People's Republic). 12 vols. Peking: Law Press, 1956–1962.

Chung-kung shih-nien (Ten years of Chinese Communism). Hong Kong: Union Press, 1960.

Chung-kuo Kung-ch'an-tang Ti-pa-tz'u Ch'uan-kuo Tai-piao Ta-hui Wen-hsien (Eighth National Congress of the Communist Party of China). Peking: People's Press, 1957.

Handicraft Industry Team of the Economic Research Office of the Chinese Scientific Institute. *Yi-chiu-wu-szu-nien ch'uan-kuo kuo-t'i shou-kung-yeh t'iao-ch'a tzu-liao* (Research materials on the individual handicraft industry in the entire country in 1954). Peking: San-lien Bookstore, 1957.

Hsia Yen. *K'ao-yen* (The test). Peking: People's Literature Press, 1959.

Hsin Chung-kuo kung-shang-yeh-chia-te tao-lu (New China's road to industrialization and the development of commerce). Hong Kong: Overseas Chinese Economic Press, 1950.

I-chiu-wu-szu-nien kuo-chia yu-suan (The national budget of 1954). Peking: Financial and Economic Press, 1954.

Kung-yeh ch'i-yeh-te sheng-ch'an chi-hua (Industrial enterprise production planning). Statistical Office of the Northeast Planning Committee, 1950.

Liu Hung-chu. *Wo kuo-te ma* (Our country's fibers). Peking: Financial and Economic Press, 1956.

Ministry of Communications. *Shui-yun yun-chia hui-pien* (Compendium of water transport prices). Peking: People's Communications Press, 1956.

Ministry of Fuel Industries. *Chu-yau she-pei chi ts'ai-liao ku-chia piao-chun mu-lu* (Standard catalogue for estimating prices of important equipment and materials). Peking, 1951.

Nankai University Economic Research Office. *Nankai chih-shu tzu-liao hui-pien, 1913–1952* (Compilation of Nankai index data, 1913–1952). Peking: Statistical Press, 1958.

Shanghai chieh-fang ch'ien-hou wu-chia tzu-liao hui-pien (A collection of

Shanghai pre- and postliberation price materials). Shanghai Economics Institute, Academica Sinica, and the Institute of Economics of the Shanghai Academy of Social Sciences. Shanghai: Shanghai People's Press, 1958.

Shanghai kung-shang tzu-liao (Shanghai industrial and commercial materials). 1952.

State Planning Commission. *Fa-chan kuo-min ching-chi-te ti-i-ko wu-nien chi-hua-te ming-tz'u chien-shih* (A simple selection of terms used in the first five year plan for the development of the national economy). Peking: People's Press, 1955.

Wo-kuo kang-t'ieh, tien-li, mei-tan, chi-chieh, fang-chih, tsao-chih kung-yeh-te chin-hsi (Our country's iron and steel, electric power, coal, machinery, textile, and paper industries, past and present). Peking: Statistical Publishing Office, 1958.

Yang Chien-pai. *Chieh-fang i-lai wo-kuo kuo-min ching-chi-chung chi-chung chu-yau pi-li kuan-hsi-te pien-hua* (Changes in several important ratios in our national economy since the liberation). Shanghai: New Knowledge Press, 1957.

Yang Po. *Kuo-chia kuo-tu shih-ch'i-te shang-yeh* (State commerce during the transition period). Peking: Workers' Press, 1956.

II. ARTICLES, REPORTS, AND SPEECHES

A. IN ENGLISH

"Agricultural Study Forecasts Another Hungry Spring for Communist China," *Current Scene* (Hong Kong), vol. I, no. 23 (January 22, 1962), pp. 1–21.

"Agriculture in China, 1963," *Current Scene* (Hong Kong), vol. II, no. 27 (January 15, 1964), pp. 1–11.

"Back to Normal," *Far Eastern Economic Review,* XLI (August 15, 1963), 370–371.

Bergson, Abram. "Reliability and Usability of Soviet Statistics: A Summary Appraisal," *The American Statistician,* vol. VII (June–July 1953), pp. 13–16.

Bornstein, Morris. "The Soviet Price System," *American Economic Review,* LII (March 1962), 64–103.

"Changes and Muddle," *China News Analysis* (Hong Kong), no. 299 (October 30, 1959), pp. 1–7.

Chao Kang. "Testing the Reliability of Industrial Output Data of Communist China," unpublished paper presented to the First Research Conference of the Social Science Research Council on the Economy of China, Berkeley, January 31-February 1, 1963.

Chao, K. C. "The Organization and Functions of the People's Communes," in E. S. Kirby, ed., *Contemporary China,* III, 131–145. Hong Kong: Hong Kong University Press, 1960.

Chapman, Janet. "Real Wages in the Soviet Union, 1928–1952," *Review of Economics and Statistics*, XXXVI (May 1954), 134–156.

Chi Ping. "The Effects of the Commercialization of Agriculture in Southern Hopei," in *Agrarian China: Selected Source Materials from Chinese Authors*. London: Allen and Unwin, 1939.

"Coal Mines," *China News Analysis* (Hong Kong), no. 266 (February 27, 1959), pp. 1–7.

"Composition of Membership of the Chinese Communist Party," in E. S. Kirby, ed., *Contemporary China*, II, 141. Hong Kong: Hong Kong University Press, 1958.

Donnithorne, Audrey. "Background to the People's Communes: Changes in China's Economic Organization in 1958," *Pacific Affairs*, XXXII (December 1959), 339–353.

———— "The Organization of Rural Trade in China since 1958," *The China Quarterly*, no. 8 (October–December 1961), pp. 77–91.

Eason, Warren. "Population and Labor Force," in Abram Bergson, ed., *Soviet Economic Growth*, chap. iii. Evanston: Row, Peterson, 1953.

Eckstein, Alexander. "Moscow-Peking Axis: The Economic Pattern," in H. L. Boorman and others, *Moscow–Peking Axis: Strengths and Strains*, pp. 54–111. New York: Harper, 1957.

Emerson, J. P. "Chinese Communist Party Views on Labor Utilization before and after 1958," *Current Scene* (Hong Kong), vol. I, no. 30 (April 20, 1962), pp. 1–10.

Falcon, W. P. "Farmer Response to Price in a Subsistence Economy: The Case of West Pakistan," *American Economic Review*, LIV (May 1964), 580-591.

"Food Supply Improved," *Far Eastern Economic Review*, XL (April 11, 1963), 55–56.

Gerschenkron, Alexander. "Reliability of Soviet Industrial and National Income Statistics," *The American Statistician*, vol. VII, no. 2 (April–May 1953), p. 19.

Hodgman, D. R. "Soviet Monetary Controls through the Banking System," in Gregory Grossman, ed. *Value and Plan*, pp. 105–124. Berkeley and Los Angeles: University of California Press, 1960.

Hoffman, Charles. "Work Incentive Policy in Communist China," *The China Quarterly*, no. 17 (January–March 1964), pp. 92–110.

Holzman, F. D. "Comment," in Gregory Grossman, ed. *Value and Plan,* pp. 125–131. Berkeley and Los Angeles: University of California Press, 1960.

Kirby, E. S. "Bad Weather or Bad System? The Agricultural Crisis in Mainland China," *Current Scene* (Hong Kong), vol. I, no. 5 (June 29, 1961), pp. 1–8.

Kojima, Reiitsu. "Grain Acquisition and Supply," in E. S. Kirby, ed., *Contemporary China*, V, 65–88. Hong Kong: Hong Kong University Press, 1963.

Lange, Oscar. "On the Economic Theory of Socialism," in Oscar Lange and Fred Taylor, *On the Economic Theory of Socialism,* pp. 55–142. Minneapolis: University of Minnesota Press, 1938.

Li, C. M. "Statistics and Planning at the *Hsien* Level in Communist China," *Current Scene* (Hong Kong), vol. I, no. 28 (March 27, 1962), pp. 1–11.

Liu, T. C. "Structural Changes in the Economy of the Chinese Mainland, 1933 to 1952-1957," *American Economic Review, Papers and Proceedings of the Seventy-First Annual Meeting of the American Economics Association,* vol. XLIX, no. 2 (May 1959), pp. 84–93.

Ma Feng-hwa. "The Financing of Public Investment in Communist China," *Journal of Asian Studies,* XX (November 1961), 33–48.

MacDougall, Colina. "Modernising Farms," *Far Eastern Economic Review,* XLII (November 21, 1963), 382–383.

MacFarquhar, Roderick. "Communist China's Intra-Party Dispute," *Pacific Affairs,* XXXI (December 1958), 323–335.

"Mainland Chinese Exports," *Far Eastern Economic Review,* XXXI (January 26, 1961), 178.

"Major Party Decisions," *China News Analysis* (Hong Kong), no. 258 (January 2, 1959), pp. 1–7.

Montias, J. M. "The Soviet Economic Model and the Underdeveloped Countries," in Nicholas Spulber, ed., *Study of the Soviet Economy,* pp. 57–82. Bloomington: Indiana University Press, 1961.

Nathan, Andrew. "China's Work-point System: A Study in Agricultural 'Splittism,' " *Current Scene* (Hong Kong), vol. II, no. 31 (April 15, 1964), pp. 1–13.

" 'Plain Living and Hard Struggle': An Economic Assessment," *Current Scene* (Hong Kong), vol. II, no. 28 (February 15, 1964), pp. 1–8.

"Press Communique of National People's Congress," *Peking Review,* no. 49 (December 6, 1963), pp. 6–9.

"Red China: The Mechanical Man," *Time,* October 12, 1959, pp. 28–32.

Schran, Peter. "Unity and Diversity of Russian and Chinese Industrial Wage Policies," *Journal of Asian Studies,* XXIII (February 1964), 245–251.

Schurmann, Franz. "Economic Policy and Political Power in Communist China," *The Annals of the American Academy of Political and Social Science,* CCCXLIX (September 1963), 49–62.

Skinner, G. W. "Marketing and Social Structure in Rural China, Part I," *Journal of Asian Studies,* XXIV (November 1964), 3–43.

"Transition to Communism (I) and (II)," *China News Analysis* (Hong Kong), nos. 278–279 (May 29 and June 5, 1959), pp. 1–7.

"What Do People Eat?" *China News Analysis* (Hong Kong), no. 364 (March 17, 1961), pp. 1–7.

"Who is Mao Tse-tung? Four Answers," *Current Scene* (Hong Kong), vol. I, no. 22 (January 5, 1962), pp. 1–10.

B. TRANSLATED INTO ENGLISH

"Bank Deposits Increase in China," NCNA, August 1, 1960, translated in *SCMP*, no. 2312, p. 14.

Basic-level Organization Section, Finance and Trade Department, Chinese Communist Party Tientsin Municipal Committee. "Further Implement the System of Responsibility of Directors under the Leadership of Party Committees," Peking *TKP*, November 20, 1961, translated in *SCMP*, no. 2643, pp. 8–12.

"A Brief Description of the State Distribution of Commodities during the Past Year," *TCKT*, July 14, 1957, translated in *ECMM*, no. 97, pp. 21–30.

Chang Chi-sheng. "Some Views on the Method of Calculating Purchasing Power," *Chung-yang ho-tso t'ung-hsun*, February 11, 1959, translated in *ECMM*, no. 192, pp. 38–43.

Chang Chih-hua. "Try Hard to Lower the Production of Nondirectly Productive Personnel in Enterprises," *Lao-tung*, May 18, 1962, translated in *ECMM*, no. 322, pp. 1–4.

Chang Ch'un-ch'iao. "Break Away from the Idea of the Bourgeois Right," *JMJP*, October 13, 1958, translated in *CB*, no. 537, pp. 1–5.

Chang Hsuan-wen. "Do a Good Job of the Oils Supply for 1957," *Shang-yeh kung-tso*, February 14, 1957, translated in *ECMM*, no. 79, pp. 14–16.

Ch'en Hsi-ya. "The 1958 Banking Work and the 1959 Tasks," *Chung-kuo chin-jung*, May 25, 1959, translated in *ECMM*, no. 178, pp. 28–39.

Ch'en Yun. "On Commercial Work and Industrial Commercial Relations," speech to the National People's Congress, June 30, 1956, translated in *CB*, no. 398, pp. 1–8.

——— Speech, *Eighth National Congress of the Communist Party of China*, II, 157–176. Peking: Foreign Languages Press, 1956.

Ch'eng Fang. "Balance in the Economic System and Planning," *Hsin chien-she*, August 1958, translated in *ECMM*, no. 146, pp. 40–47.

Ch'eng Yuan-yeh. "Strengthen the Concept of the Integral Whole, Manage Credit Funds Properly," Peking *TKP*, June 13, 1962, translated in *SCMP*, no. 2771, pp. 4–8.

Ch'i Liang. "Carry Out More Properly Production of Non-staple Foodstuffs in Organizations and Enterprises," Peking *TKP*, March 20, 1962, translated in *SCMP*, no. 2720, pp. 16–20.

——— "What Advantages Are There to Opening a State Led Free Market?" *Shih-shih shou-ts'e*, November 10, 1956, translated in *ECMM*, no. 64, pp. 27–42.

Chia To-fu. "Speech at Outstanding Workers' Conference," *Kung-jen jih-pao*, May 9, 1956, translated in *URS*, vol. III, no. 17, pp. 234–244.

Chinese Communist Party Committee of the Commerce Bureau, Kingtechen Municipality. "Thoroughly Enforce the Party Committee System in Enterprises and Fully Develop the Role of Collective Leadership," Peking *TKP*, March 28, 1962, translated in *SCMP*, no. 2725, pp. 1–8.

"Chinese People's Liberation Army Self-sufficient in Vegetables," NCNA, November 14, 1961, translated in *SCMP*, no. 2622, p. 18.

Chou En-lai. "Report on the Proposals for the Second Five Year Plan for Development of the National Economy," *Eighth National Congress of the Communist Party of China*, I, 261–328. Peking: Foreign Languages Press: 1956.

———— "Report on the Work of the Government" (September 29, 1954), *Documents of the First Session of the First National People's Congress*, pp. 75–130. Peking: Foreign Languages Press, 1955.

———— "Press Communique on Speech at the Third Session of the Second National People's Congress of the People's Republic of China," NCNA, April 16, 1962, translated in *CB*, no. 681, pp. 1–4.

Chou Po-p'ing. "The Policy of Unified Purchase and Sale of Grain Shall Not Be Frustrated," *Liang-shih*, July 1957, translated in *ECMM*, no. 101, pp. 26–33.

———— "This Year's Condition of Food Supply in China," *Chung-kuo hsin-wen*, October 3, 1959, translated in *URS*, vol. XVII, no. 6, pp. 79–84.

Chu Ching-chih. "A Review of Urban Food Rationing and Some Suggestions for Improvement of the System," *Liang-shih*, August 25, 1957, translated in *ECMM*, no. 110, pp. 29–37.

Chung Chao-hsiu. "Our People Live Better and Better Lives," Peking *TKP*, October 18, 1959, translated in *CB*, no. 606, pp. 12–15.

"Communes Greatly Demonstrated Their Prowess in Last Year's Massive and Rapid Purchase of Farm Products," NCNA, January 26, 1960, translated in *SCMP*, no. 2180, pp. 18–20.

"Credit Work's Role in the Promotion of Production," Peking *TKP*, May 24, 1960, translated in *JPRS*, no. 3869, pp. 1–3.

Fan Jo-yi. "More on the Price Policy for Heavy Industry Products," *CCYC*, June 17, 1957, translated in *ECMM*, no. 93, pp. 14–31.

Fang Fa. "Some Common Knowledge of the National Economic Plan," *Hsueh-hsi*, October 2, 1956, translated in *ECMM*, no. 65, pp. 38–41.

"Finance Minister Po I-po Presents the Budgetary Report at the 16th Meeting of the Central People's Government Council," August 10, 1952, translated in *CB*, no. 214, pp. 12–14.

Grain Production Bureau of the Ministry of Agriculture. "Our Country's Grain Production during the First Five Year Plan Period," *Chung-kuo nung-pao*, March 8, 1958, translated in *URS*, vol. XI, no. 4, pp. 45–58.

Ho Wei. "How and Why to Compare the Present Prices of Farm Produce with the Prewar Level," *Hsueh-hsi,* April 3, 1957, translated in *ECMM,* no. 89, pp. 20–25.

———— "New Problems in Unified Purchase and Marketing of Grain," *Cheng-chih hsueh-hsi,* October 13, 1956, translated in *ECMM,* no. 58, pp. 16–19.

Ho Yu-chung. "A New Page in the History of China's Machine Building Industry," *Ching-chi tao-pao,* June 14, 1957, translated in *ECMM,* no. 92, pp. 31–34.

Hou Chien-chung. "Some Understanding of the 'Make Up Shortage by Plenty' Policy," *Liang-shih,* September 25, 1957, translated in *ECMM,* no. 106, pp. 22–24.

"How to Conduct Surveys on Commodity Supply and on the Purchasing Power of Social Commodities," *Chi-hua yu t'ung-chi,* August 23, 1959, translated in *JPRS,* no. 1023D, pp. 1–7.

Hsiao Ku. "A Preliminary Study of the Agricultural Tax in the Next Couple of Years," *Ts'ai-cheng,* December 5, 1956, translated in *ECMM,* no. 66, pp. 27–36.

Hsiao Kung-ju. "The Principle Underlying Wage Increase," *Hsueh-hsi,* August 3, 1957, translated in *ECMM,* no. 106, pp. 12–14.

Hsing Ch'ung-chih. "Carry Out Properly the Work in Connection with Youths Returning to the Rural Areas," *Chung-kuo ch'ing-nien,* June 1, 1962, translated in *ECMM,* no. 322, pp. 16–21.

Hsing Yu-hung. "Make a Good Job of Labor Allocation for 1957," *Lao-tung,* June 3, 1957, translated in *ECMM,* no. 94, pp. 22–26.

Huang K'o. "How We May Settle the Disequilibrium between Social Purchasing Power and the Supply Volume of Goods in 1958," *CHCC,* November 9, 1957, translated in *ECMM,* no. 119, pp. 30–36.

Hung-ch'i commentator. "Simultaneous Development and Mutual Promotion of Grain Production and Hog Breeding," *Hung-ch'i,* April 16, 1961, translated in *ECMM,* no. 260, pp. 28–31.

Investigation and Study Team, Canton Municipal Bureau of the Chemical Industry. "Spend Less Money and Do More Work," *Nan-fang jih-pao,* June 2, 1962, translated in *SCMP,* no. 2780, pp. 13–16.

Jen Ching-lu. "Prices in Trading at Rural Fairs and the Role of the Law of Value," Peking *TKP,* May 12, 1961, translated in *SCMP,* no. 2508, pp. 1–5.

JMJP editorial. "Conscientiously Implement Policies of Rural People's Communes," *JMJP,* April 2, 1961, translated in *SCMP,* no. 2476, pp. 24–27.

———— "Develop Undertaking of Hog Rearing by Rearing Hogs Privately and Publicly at the Same Time," *JMJP,* December 2, 1960, translated in *SCMP,* no. 2425, pp. 12–14.

———— "The Three-Level Ownership System with the Production Brigade as the Basic Level Is the Basic System for People's Communes at the Present Stage," *JMJP*, December 21, 1960, translated in *SCMP*, no. 2408, pp. 10–14.

Jung Tzu-ho. "The Question of Equilibrium for the State Budget, for the State Credit Plan, and for Supply and Demand of Commodities," *Ts'ai-cheng*, June 5, 1957, translated in *ECMM*, no. 90, pp. 11–16.

—— "Summary of the 1950 Financial Work and Policy and Tasks for 1951," *JMJP*, March 28, 1951, translated in *CB*, no. 214, pp. 6–11.

Ke Chih-ta and Wang Cho. "On Several Interrelations in Finance and Banking," Peking *TKP*, November 17, 1961, translated in *SCMP*, no. 2650, pp. 3–11.

Keng Tsun-san. "A Brief Discussion on the Existing Price of Coal," *CCYC*, March 17, 1959, translated in *ECCM*, no. 171, pp. 36–39.

Kuan Ta-t'ung. "Firmly Enforce the Policy of Activating Rural Trade Fairs," Peking *TKP*, January 26, 1961, translated in *SCMP*, no. 2456, pp. 1–6.

Kuo Chih-chun and Ouyang Tou. "Some Questions of How to View Trade at Rural Fairs," Peking *TKP*, December 25, 1961, translated in *SCMP*, no. 2660, pp. 18–22.

Kweichow jih-pao editorial. "Adjusting the Price of Autumn Crops," *Kweichow jih-pao*, August 30, 1959, translated in *SCMP*, no. 2142, pp. 42–44.

Li Fu-chun. "Report on the Draft 1960 National Economic Plan" (March 30, 1960), *Second Session of the Second National People's Congress of the People's Republic of China (Documents)*, pp. 1–48. Peking: Foreign Languages Press, 1960.

—— Speech, *Eighth National Congress of the Communist Party of China*, II, 288–303. Peking: Foreign Languages Press, 1956.

Li Hsien-nien. "The Implementation of the State Budget for 1957 and the Draft State Budget for 1958" (February 1, 1958), NCNA, February 12, 1958, translated in *CB*, no. 493, pp. 1–22.

—— "The 1954 Final Accounts and the 1955 Budget," Hong Kong *TKP*, July 1955, translated in *CB*, no. 336, pp. 1–25.

—— "Report on the Final State Accounts for 1959 and the Draft State Budget for 1960" (March 30, 1960), *Second Session of the Second National People's Congress of the People's Republic of China (Documents)*, pp. 49–73. Peking: Foreign Languages Press, 1960.

—— Speech, *Eighth National Congress of the Communist Party of China*, II, 206–224. Peking: Foreign Languages Press, 1956.

Li Hsueh-feng. Speech, *Eighth National Congress of the Communist Party of China*, II, 304–317. Peking: Foreign Languages Press, 1956.

Liang-shih commentator. "Certain Basis and Ideas for Wheat Collection and Purchases," *Liang-shih*, May 25, 1957, translated in *ECMM*, no. 89, pp. 3–6.

Lin Chiang-yun. "Certain Problems in the Control of Labor Power," *Lao-*

tung, November 15, 1955, translated in *ECMM,* no. 27, pp. 22–26.

Liu Shao-ch'i. Speech, *Eighth National Congress of the Communist Party of China,* I, 13–111. Peking: Foreign Languages Press, 1956.

Liu Yuan. "Food Grain Prices Fixed by the State Are Reasonable," *Liaoning jih-pao,* September 20, 1957, translated in *SCMP,* no. 1658, pp. 13–18.

Ma Yin-ch'u. "A New Principle of Population," *JMJP,* July 5, 1957, translated in *URS,* vol. VIII, no. 6, p. 93.

"Many Enterprises in Peking Do Away with the Piece Wage System," NCNA, October 21, 1958, translated in *CB,* no. 537, pp. 22–24.

Men Cho-min. "Heed the Lessons from Work of Supply of Material Resources in 1956," *CHCC, February* 9, 1957, translated in *ECMM,* no. 80, pp. 28–33.

Ministry of Commerce. "Report on the 1957 Supply of Cotton Cloth," *JMJP,* April 20, 1957, translated in *URS,* vol. VII, no. 17, pp. 220–224.

―――― "To Cut Consumption of Cloth in Summer Use: To Ensure Supply in Winter," *JMJP,* April 20, 1957, translated in *URS,* vol. VII, no. 17, pp. 220–224.

"More Savings Deposits Being Made by People in City and Town throughout the Country," NCNA, November 20, 1959, translated in *SCMP,* no. 2144, p. 2.

Nan-fang jih-pao editorial. "Work on All Projects Not in the Plan Must Stop at Once," *Nan-fang jih-pao,* May 15, 1962, translated in *SCMP,* no. 2757, pp. 1–3.

"The Nature of Private Plots of Land and Family Subsidiary Production of Commune Members," Peking *TKP,* March 15, 1961, translated in *SCMP,* no. 2478, pp. 17–19.

Niu Chung-huang. "Computation of Labor Productivity and the Fixing of the Wage Scale," *Hsueh-hsi,* May 3, 1957, translated in *ECMM,* no. 91, pp. 8–11.

"No Work Should Be Begun without Planning," *JMJP,* June 16, 1951, translated in *CB,* no. 119, p. 3.

Noirot, P. "Facts on the Evolution of the Standard of Living," *Economie et politique,* special issue, nos. 66–67 (January–February 1960), pp. 121–145, translated in *JPRS,* no. 3639, pp. 44–78.

"On Raising Hogs and Accumulating Manure," Peking *TKP,* August 31, 1961, translated in *SCMP,* no. 2595, pp. 21–24.

Ou Ming. "Strive for Realization of the 1959 National Economic Plan," *Chung-kuo kung-jen,* April 27, 1959, translated in *ECMM,* no. 171, pp. 28–31.

Pan Ching-yuan. "The Struggle between the Road of Socialism and the Road of Capitalism on the Free Market," *Hsin chien-she,* March 13, 1958, translated in *ECMM,* no. 136, pp. 27–33.

―――― "Why Is It Necessary to Have a Free Market?" *Cheng-chih hsueh-hsi,* November 13, 1956, translated in *ECMM,* no. 61, pp. 31–34.

"Party Bulletin of Pao-an hsien, Kwangtung," September 22, 27, 30, October 6, 8, 1961, translated in *URS,* vol. XXVII, nos. 7–8 (April 24, 1962).

"People Enthusiastic in Making Savings," *JMJP,* January 12, 1960, translated in *SCMP,* no. 2180, pp. 3–4.

Pilmin, A. M. "The Role of Public Finance in the Enforcement of the Economy and Austerity Program," *CCYC,* October 17, 1955, translated in *ECMM,* no. 21, pp. 33–42.

Po I-po. "Draft Plan for the Development of the National Economy in 1958" (February 3, 1958), NCNA, February 13, 1958, translated in *CB,* no. 494, pp. 1–27.

———— "For New Victories in Industrial Production and Construction in Our Country," *Hung-ch'i,* February 1, 1961, translated in *ECMM,* no. 250, pp. 9–17.

———— "Report on the 1953 State Budget of the People's Republic of China," supplement to *People's China,* March 16, 1953.

———— Speech, *Eighth National Congress of the Communist Party of China,* II, 45–62. Peking: Foreign Languages Press, 1956.

———— Speech to National People's Congress, *Nan-fang jih-pao,* July 31, 1955, translated in *CB,* no. 353, pp. 1–7.

"Political Work Is the Lifeline of All Work," *Hung-ch'i,* March 31, 1964, translated in Current Scene (Hong Kong), supplement, vol. I, no. 1, pp. 1–10.

"A Production Brigade in Kwangtung Province Is Successful in Developing Hog Breeding," *Nan-fang jih-pao,* February 23, 1962, translated in *SCMP,* no. 2711, pp. 7–10.

SC. "Report on the Organization of the Coal Market for 1957" (March 18, 1957), in K. C. Chao, *Economic Planning and Organization in Mainland China,* II, 41–43. Cambridge, Mass.: Center for East Asian Studies, Harvard University, 1960.

Secretariat of the National Conference for Small Scale Ore Dressing Plants. "A Small Copper Ore Dressing Plant Built and Put into Operation in Only 21 Days," *Yu-se chin-shu,* February 18, 1959, translated in *JPRS,* no. 1080D, pp. 1–9.

Shih Ching. "Don't Let Money Assume Command," *JMJP,* October 16, 1958, translated in *CB,* no. 537, pp. 5–8.

Shih Hsiu-lin. "Some Views on the Nature of Land Retained for Private Use," Peking *TKP,* June 21, 1961, translated in *SCMP,* no. 2547, pp. 13–17.

SSB. "Communique on the Fulfillment of the First Five Year Plan," NCNA, April 13, 1959, translated in *CB,* no. 556, pp. 1–9.

Statistics Unit, Department of Planning, Ministry of Heavy Industry. "Analysis of Results of State Plans Administered by the Ministry of Heavy Industry during the First Quarter of 1956," *Chung-kung-yeh t'ung-hsun*, May 1, 1956, translated in *ECMM*, no. 42, pp. 19–26.

———— "The Execution of Production Plans in 1955," *Chung-kung-yeh t'ung-hsun*, January 1, 1956, translated in *ECMM*, no. 35, pp. 19–25.

Sun Chien and Tung Chia-chen. "On Prices of Vegetables in 1958," *CCYC*, March 17, 1959, translated in *ECMM*, no. 171, pp. 34–35.

Sun Shang-ch'ing. "On the Nature and Destiny of Our Current Piece Rate Wage System," *CCYC*, April 17, 1959, translated in *ECMM*, no. 180, pp. 35–40.

Sun Yi-min. "Strengthen Leadership over the Free Market," *CHCC*, December 23, 1956, translated in *ECMM*, no. 77, pp. 14–20.

Sung Jen-chiung. Speech, *Eighth National Congress of the Communist Party of China*, II, 147–156. Peking: Foreign Languages Press, 1956.

"Surplus Labor in Canton Should Return to the Countryside to Participate in Rural Production," *Nan-fang jih-pao*, December 30, 1955, translated in *SCMP*, supplement, no. 1261, p. 5.

"A Survey of the Work of Savings during the First Five Year Plan Period," *Chung-kuo chin-yun*, March 7, 1958, translated in *URS*, vol. XI, no. 3.

TCKT data office. "Price Gaps between Industrial Products and Farm Products: Their Changes in Post-Liberation Years," *TCKT*, September 14, 1957, translated in *ECMM*, no. 104, pp. 20–29.

TCKTTH data office. "Questions Concerning Socialist Industrialization," *TCKTTH*, November 14, 1956, translated in *ECMM*, no. 69, pp. 29–35.

Teng Tse-hui. Speech, *Eighth National Congress of the Communist Party of China*, II, 177–198. Peking: Foreign Languages Press, 1956.

TKP editorial. "Satisfactorily Control and Use the Circulating Funds of Industry," Peking *TKP*, June 20, 1961, translated in *SCMP*, no. 2543, pp. 5–6.

———— "Work According to Plan," Peking *TKP*, May 25, 1962, translated in *SCMP*, no. 2763, pp. 8–10.

Ts'ai-cheng editorial. "Implement Agricultural Tax Regulations and Endeavor to Complete Agricultural Reform," *Ts'ai-cheng*, July 5, 1958, translated in *ECMM*, no. 139, pp. 40–44.

Tsao Jui-hsiang. "Questions of Raising the Procurement Prices for Rapeseed," *Liang-shih kung-tso*, October 14, 1956, translated in *ECMM*, no. 58, pp. 25–27.

Tseng Chih. "To Handle Well Some Interrelated Matters of Fiscal Work," *Ts'ai-cheng*, May 24, 1959, translated in *ECMM*, no. 176, pp. 26–34.

Tu Shao-po and Wang I-cheng. "Why the Changeover from the Supply System to the Wage System," *Shih-shih shou-ts'e*, September 25, 1955, translated in *ECMM*, no. 19, pp. 27–29.

"Unified Purchase Prices for Autumn Crops in Kweichow Province

Raised," *Kweichow jih-pao*, August 30, 1959, translated in *SCMP*, no. 2142, p. 42.

Wage Office, Labor Wage Bureau, Ministry of Commerce. "Draw up the 1957 Labor Plan for Commercial Organizations on 'Increasing Production without Increasing Men' Principle," *Lao-tung*, April 3, 1957, translated in *ECMM*, no. 86, pp. 29–31.

Wang Kuei-ch'en. "Carrying out Seriously the Principle Underlying Exchange of Equal Values," *Chung-kuo ch'ing-nien pao*, August 30, 1961, translated in *SCMP*, no. 2586, pp. 11–15.

Wang Ping. "The Free Market in China: Its Scope and Changes," *TCKT*, June 14, 1957, translated in *ECMM*, no. 92, pp. 24–27.

Wang Tieh-sheng. "To Understand Better the Relationship between Light Industry and Capital Accumulation," *Hsueh-hsi*, March 18, 1957, translated in *ECMM*, no. 86, pp. 20–22.

Wang Tzu-ying. "Improve the Fiscal System and Strengthen Fiscal Discipline," *Ts'ai-cheng*, April 5, 1957, translated in *ECMM*, no. 87, pp. 15–22.

Wei Yi. "The Problem of Speeding Up the Development of Light Industry," *Hsueh-hsi*, September 2, 1956, translated in *ECMM*, no. 60, pp. 27–34.

Wen Shih-yun. "Concentrate Our Efforts, Solve Problems One by One," *Hung-ch'i*, December 16, 1960, translated in *ECMM*, no. 249, pp. 10–20.

"Why are Supply Plans for Certain Commodities under Unified Distribution and Ministry Control To Be Placed in the Hands of Provincial and Municipal Governments?" *Shang-yeh kung-tso*, September 12, 1957, translated in *ECMM*, no. 118, pp. 44–46.

Wu Sheng-kuang and Ts'ai Jung-shu. "A Cursory Discussion of the Previous Year's Surplus," Peking *TKP*, April 9, 1962, translated in *SCMP*, no. 2756, pp. 1–4.

Wu Shuo. "An Inquiry into the Grain Situation during the Transition Period," *Liang-shih*, January 25, 1957, translated in *ECMM*, no. 85, pp. 5–15.

Yao Yi-lin. "Development of Domestic Commerce during the Past Three Years," *JMJP*, October 3, 1952, translated in *CB*, no. 219, pp. 33–38.

Yeh Chun. "An Inquiry into a Change for the Agricultural Planning System in China," *CHCC*, February 9, 1957, translated in *ECMM*, no. 80, pp. 15–19.

Yi Ch'ien. "Seriously Implement the Principle of Exchange of Equal Values," *Kung-jen jih-pao*, January 28, 1961, translated in *SCMP*, no. 2460, pp. 14–16.

Yonezawa, Hideo. "Japanese Analysis on Purchase and Sales Prices in Communist China," *Ajia keizai jumpo*, July 1, 1960, translated in *JPRS*, no. 4042, pp. 1–11.

Yuan Feng. "The Ratio of Increases between Labor Productivity and Wages," *Hsin chien-she*, December 3, 1956, translated in *ECMM*, no. 71, pp. 10–18.

C. IN JAPANESE

Mizoguchi Toshiyuki. "Examination of Price Index Materials in China," in Ishikawa Shigeru, ed., *Chugoku keizai hatten no tokeiteki kenkyu* (Research on statistics of Chinese economic development), vol. I, chap. ii. Tokyo: Asia Economics Research Institute, 1960.

D. IN CHINESE

Chai Mou. "The Superiority of the People's Commune as Seen from Our Work in Finance and Trade," *CCYC*, November 17, 1959, pp. 34–37.

Chang Ch'uan-shu. "The Anshan Financial Office on How to Strengthen Enterprise Financial Overseeing Work," *Ts'ai-cheng*, January 5, 1958, pp. 25–27.

Chang Liu. "The Differential between the Prices of Industrial and Agricultural Products," *HHYP*, November 25, 1950, pp. 112–113.

Chang Meng-tseng. "The Problem of Product Prices in the State Coal Industry," *Ts'ai-cheng*, March 5, 1958, pp. 14–15.

"Changes in the Standard of Living of Shanghai Workers during the Past 27 Years," *TCKT*, July 14, 1957, p. 6.

Ch'en Ch'i-hsiang. "Understand Clearly the New Cotton–Grain Price Ratio," *HHYP*, May 25, 1953, pp. 182–183.

Chin Liu-fan. "A Preliminary Analysis of Cotton Yarn Prices in Our Country," *CCYC*, December 17, 1959, pp. 44–50.

Ching-chi chou-pao editorial. "Clearly Understand the New Cotton–Grain Price Ratio in Order to Complete Agricultural Production Duties," *Ching-chi chou-pao*, no. 14 (1953), pp. 2–3.

Chu Ching and Chu Chung-chien. "Variations in Our Rural Market Commodity Turnover," *CCYC*, June 10, 1957, pp. 100–126.

"Discussion of Ending of the Advance Purchases of Cotton," *HHYP*, May 25, 1953, p. 183.

"Effectiveness of the First Half Year of the 1958 National Economic Plan," *HHPYK*, August 25, 1958, pp. 68–70.

Fan Jo-i. "A Brief Discussion of the Profit Rate on Capital," *CHCC*, August 23, 1958, pp. 21–23.

Fu I-kang. "Raise the Financial Work of State Enterprises One Step," *HHYP*, September 20, 1950, pp. 1376–1377.

"Government Affairs Council Issues Directive on the Advance Purchase of Tea, Silk, Hemp, Tobacco, and Wool," *HHPYK*, March 6, 1956, pp. 129–130.

"The Great Success of Agricultural Production Leadership in 1950," *HHYP*, March 25, 1951, pp. 1068–1070.

Ho Cheng and Wei Wen. "Discussion of Rural Market Trade," *CCYC*, April 17, 1962, pp. 11–15.

"How to Analyze Worker and Employee Wage Problems," *TCKT*, April 14, 1957, pp. 8–11.

Hsing Yu-hung. "In Order to Continue to See Clearly the New Objectives and Struggles of Labor Employment," *HHYP*, July 25, 1954, p. 141.

Hsueh Mu-ch'iao. "Preliminary Views on the Present Plan Management System," *CHCC*, September 9, 1957, p. 27.

I Shih-chieh. "Discussion of the Problem of Balancing Production and Consumption," *HHPYK*, March 10, 1957, pp. 86–88.

JMJP columnist. "The Correct Way of Settling Industrial Circulating Capital Problems," *HHPYK*, September 10, 1958, pp. 122–123.

JMJP editorial. "Directive on the 1954 Advance Purchase Work," *HHYP*, April 25, 1954, pp. 164–165.

——— "Do We Still Want to Plan?" *HHPYK*, October 6, 1956, p. 62.

——— "Properly Adjust the Relative Price of Cotton and Grain and the Grain–Cloth Seasonal Price Differential," *HHYP*, May 25, 1953, pp. 181–182.

——— "Reform the New Joint Public–Private Enterprises' Wage System," *HHPYK*, November 21, 1956, pp. 106–107.

——— "Reform of the Railroad Price System," *HHYP*, June 28, 1955, pp. 128–129.

——— "Settling Vegetable Supply Problems from the Bottom Up," *HHPYK*, July 10, 1957, p. 150.

——— "Supply and Marketing Cooperatives Should Adjust Retail Prices," *HHYP*, March 28, 1955, p. 148.

——— "Why Do We Want to Issue Local Economic Construction Bonds?" *HHPYK*, June 25, 1958, pp. 91–92.

Joint Cooperative Board. "Temporary Methods of Handling 1951 Advance Cotton Purchases," *HHYP*, April 25, 1951, pp. 1338–1339.

Li Hsien-nien. "Report on the Final State Accounts for 1954 and the Draft State Budget for 1955" (July 6, 1955), *FKHP*, II, 489–522.

——— "Report on the Final State Accounts for 1955 and the Draft State Budget for 1956," in *Chung-hua Jen-min Kung-ho-kuo Ti-i-chieh Ch'uan-kuo Jen-min Tai-piao Ta-hui ti-szu-tz'u hui-i hui-kan* (The fourth meeting of the First National People's Congress of the People's Republic of China), pp. 57–92. Peking: People's Press, 1957.

——— "Report on the Final State Accounts for 1957 and the Draft State Budget for 1958" (February 1, 1958), *FKHP*, VII, 116–142.

——— "Report on the Final State Accounts for 1958 and the Draft State Budget for 1959" (April 21, 1959), *FKHP*, IX, 63–74.

Lo Keng-mo. "The Question of the Turnover Tax on Heavy Industrial Products," *CCYC*, June 17, 1956, pp. 26–32.

Local Party Committee Investigation Team. "Management of Subsidiary Production Is Not a Small Thing; Why Is So Little Attention Paid It?" *HHPYK*, October 10, 1956, pp. 63–64.

Ma An. "The Relationship between the State, the Cooperative, and Cooperative Members as Seen from the Situation in Chao-szu Cooperative," *TCYC*, May 23, 1958, pp. 36–41.

Ma Wen-jui. Speech in *Chung-hua Jen-min Kung-ho-kuo Ti-i-chieh Ch'uan-kuo Jen-min Tai-piao Ta-hui ti-san-tz'u hui-i hui-k'an* (The third meeting of the First National People's Congress of the People's Republic of China), pp. 733–743. Peking: People's Press, 1956.

Ministries of Agriculture, Foreign Trade, Textile Industries, Forestry, and Second Commerce. "Report on the Nationwide Silkworm Production Conference" (April 30, 1958), *FKHP*, VIII, 225–232.

Ministry of Finance. "Report on Questions Pertaining to Present Enterprise Finance Work" (February 25, 1959), *FKHP*, IX, 132–134.

Nan Ping and So Chen. "The Value of the Means of Production and the Function of the Law of Value under the Socialist System," *CCYC*, February 17, 1957, pp. 38–51.

"Nationwide Lowering of the Retail Prices of 13 Types of Important New Model Agricultural Tools," *JMJP*, September 10, 1955.

"New Situation, New Problems," *CHCC*, August 23, 1956.

"The 1960 Agricultural Battle Line." *Hung-ch'i*, no. 2 (1960), reprinted in *Jen-min shou-ts'e, 1960*, p. 423. Peking: *TKP*, 1960.

"Northeast Ministry of Industry's Investigation of the Financial Situation in State Factories and Mines," *HHYP*, September 20, 1950, pp. 1376–1377.

"On the Question of Industrial and Agricultural Standards of Living," *TCKT*, July 14, 1957, p. 4.

"Our Cooperative Wants to Raise 20,000 Hogs," *Jen-min shou-ts'e, 1957*, p. 487.

"Our Country's Development of Tea Leaf Production," *TCKT*, February 14, 1957, p. 33.

People's Bank of China. "Report on the Clearing Up of Agricultural Credit Problems" (September 5, 1957), *FKHP*, VI, 341–344.

———— "Report on Eliminating the Use of Commercial Credit between State Industries and between State Industries and Other State Enterprises as a Substitute for Bank Balances" (March 30, 1955), *FKHP*, I, 270–273.

SC. "Report on the Lowering of the Prices of Farm Pumping Power Machinery" (April 8, 1958), *FKHP*, VII, 310–315.

———— "Report on Several Questions Regarding Present Enterprise Financial Affairs Work" (February 25, 1959), *FKHP*, IX, 131–134.

SC spokesman. "Discussion of the Market Price Problem with an NCNA Reporter," *HHPYK*, May 25, 1957, pp. 109–110.

"Second Nationwide Large and Medium Cities Subsidiary Food Production Conference" (December 11, 1959), *Jen-min shou-ts'e, 1960,* pp. 430–431. Peking: *TKP,* 1960.

"Several Points of View on Setting Up and Reforming Agricultural Producers' Cooperatives Plan Work," *CHCC,* October 23, 1956, pp. 16–19.

"Some Problems Concerning the Increase in Employees and Workers in Shanghai Industrial Enterprises in 1956," *TCKT,* August 14, 1957, pp. 29–31.

SSB. "Report on the First Five Year Plan to Develop the National Economy (1953–1957)" (April 13, 1959), *HHPYK,* April 25, 1959, pp. 48–51.

—— "Report on the 1958 National Economic Development Situation" (April 14, 1959), *HHPYK,* April 25, 1959, pp. 51–54.

—— "Report on the Results of 1954 Economic Development and State Planning," *HHYP,* October 28, 1955, pp. 166–170.

—— "Report on the Results of the 1956 National Economic Plan," *HHPYK,* September 10, 1957, pp. 201–205.

"State Grain Purchase and Supply Work Situation in the Past 4 Years," *HHYP,* April 28, 1954, pp. 161–162.

"State Unified Purchase and Sale Situation of Edible Oils and Oil Materials," *HHYP,* October 25, 1954, p. 247.

Sun Yeh-fang. "A Discussion of 'Gross Value of Output,' " *TCKT,* July 14, 1957, pp. 8–14.

Sung Hai-wen. "A Discussion of the Problem of Retained Plots of Land in Agricultural Producers' Cooperatives," *CCYC,* August 17, 1957, pp. 7–17.

Sung Pao-szu. "Our Cooperative Wants to Raise 20,000 Hogs," *Jen-min shou-ts'e, 1957,* pp. 487–489. Peking: *TKP,* 1957.

Survey Team, cosponsored by the Shanghai Economics Institute, Academica Sinica, and the Institute of Economics of the Shanghai Academy of Social Sciences. "Report on the Examination of the Commodity Economics of the Li-shan and the Ling-ch'iao People's Commune of Fu-yang Hsien in Chekiang," *CCYC,* June 17, 1959, pp. 47–55.

T'an Chen-lin. "A First Step in Research on Farm Income and Standard of Living," *HHPYK,* June 10, 1957, pp. 105–111.

TCKT data office. "The Basic Situation with Respect to Our Country's Unified Purchase and Sale of Grain," *HHPYK,* November 25, 1957, pp. 171–172.

TCKTTH data office. "The Breakdown and Organization of the Number of Workers and Employees in Our Country in 1955," *HHPYK,* January 25, 1957, pp. 87–89.

—— "The 1956 Domestic Market Price Situation," *HHPYK,* May 25, 1957, pp. 114–115.

—— "The 1956 Labor Wage Situation," *HHPYK,* May 25, 1957, pp. 115–116.

―――― "The Situation with Respect to Our Socialist Industrialization," *HHPYK*, January 25, 1957, pp. 54–62.

TCYC data office. "Changes in 1957 Market Prices and Their Influence on the People's Livelihood," *TCYC*, April 23, 1958, pp. 25–26.

―――― "The Domestic Market Commodity Circulation Situation in 1957," *TCYC*, April 23, 1958, pp. 24–25.

―――― "The Flying Leap in Our Industrial Construction," *TCYC*, September 23, 1958, pp. 4–5.

―――― "The Great Leap Forward in Basic Construction Work," *TCYC*, September 23, 1958, pp. 10–12.

―――― "Research Materials on Income Distribution in 228 Agricultural Producers' Cooperatives in 1957," *TCYC*, August 23, 1958, pp. 8–12.

"This Year's Spring Rural Market Situation in . . . ," *CHCC*, May 23, 1956, pp. 15–16.

T'ien Huo-nung. "How to Determine and Put into Effect Agricultural Production Planning," *HHYP*, December 25, 1950, pp. 377–378.

Tseng Ling. "Does Inflation Exist in China Today?" *CCYC*, October 17, 1957, pp. 36–49.

―――― "The Effects of Agricultural Cooperation on Rural Monetary Circulation," *CCYC*, December 17, 1956, pp. 39–58.

―――― "The Rural Market in the Surging Tide of Agricultural Collectivization," *CCYC*, March 1, 1956, pp. 1–29.

"Understanding the Compiling of Ex-Factory Prices of Important Products by Local State Run Industry," *CHCC*, January 23, 1957, pp. 22–24.

"Views on Compiling the 1957 Agricultural Production Plan," *CHCC*, November 23, 1956, p. 11.

"Views on Setting Up Agricultural Producers' Cooperatives Plan Work," *CHCC*, June 23, 1956, pp. 11–13.

Wang Tzu-ying. "Some Lessons from Compiling and Putting into Effect the 1956 State Budget," *HHPYK*, March 19, 1957, pp. 91–93.

Wang Wei-ts'ai. "Progress in Developing the People's Deposit Business," *HHYP*, March 28, 1955, pp. 147–148.

"Why Is There a Stopping of Production and an Obstruction of Sales of Double-wheeled Double-bladed Plows?" *CHCC*, September 23, 1956, pp. 1–4.

"Why Were the Prices of These Commodities Raised?" *HHPYK*, May 25, 1957, pp. 110–111.

Wu Ting-ch'eng. "Explanation of Certain Problems Related to the Proposal for Computing the Social Purchasing Power," *CHCC*, September 1957, pp. 27–29.

Young Pei-hsin. "The Road to Raising the Agricultural Development Fund," *CCYC*, January 17, 1958, pp. 22–37.

―――― "A Study on the Problem of Balance among the Financial Revenue and Expenditure, Cash Income and Outgo, and the Supply

and Demand of Commodities," *CCYC*, October 17, 1957, pp. 50–63.
Young Po. "Planned Purchase and Planned Supply and the National Construction of Socialism," *CCYC*, February 17, 1956, pp. 33–42.
Yu Tai-ch'ien. "Can We Use 'Profit' in Place of 'Production Value?'" *TCKT*, March 14, 1957, p. 16.

III. REGULATIONS AND DIRECTIVES

A. TRANSLATED INTO ENGLISH

Agricultural Bank of China. "Provisional Regulation on Loans Extended to the Agricultural Producers' Cooperatives," translated in K. C. Chao, *Economic Planning and Organization in Mainland China*, I, 242–244. Cambridge, Mass.: Center for East Asian Studies, Harvard University, 1959.
CCPCC. "Resolution on Some Questions Concerning the People's Communes" (December 10, 1958), translated in E. S. Kirby, ed., *Contemporary China*, III, 213–234. Hong Kong: Hong Kong University Press, 1960.
"The Constitution of the Communist Party of China" (September 26, 1956), translated in *Eighth National Congress of the Chinese Communist Party*, pp. 135–228. Peking: Foreign Languages Press, 1956.
"Draft Regulations of the Weihsing People's Commune" (August 7, 1958), translated in E. S. Kirby, ed., *Contemporary China*, III, 235–252. Hong Kong: Hong Kong University Press, 1960.
"Model Regulations for an Advanced Agricultural Producers' Cooperative" (June 30, 1956), translated in Tung Ta-lin, *Agricultural Cooperation in China*, pp. 145–179. Peking: Foreign Languages Press, 1959.
"Model Regulations for an Agricultural Producers' Cooperative" (March 17, 1956), translated in Tung Ta-lin, *Agricultural Cooperation in China*, pp. 93–143. Peking: Foreign Languages Press, 1959.
SC. "Provisional Measures for the Unified Purchase and Supply of Grain in Rural Districts" (August 25, 1955), translated in K. C. Chao, *Economic Planning and Organization in Mainland China*, II, 24–31. Cambridge, Mass.: Center for East Asian Studies, Harvard University, 1960.
——— "Provisional Regulations on the Examination and Approval of Plans and Budgetary Estimates for Capital Construction" (July 12, 1955), translated in K. C. Chao, *Economic Planning and Organization in Mainland China*, I, 77–81. Cambridge, Mass.: Center for East Asian Studies, Harvard University, 1959.
——— "Provisional Regulations Governing the Wages for Ordinary and Miscellaneous Workers in Enterprises, Business Units, and Government Agencies," NCNA, February 10, 1958, translated in *CB*, no. 497, pp. 2–3.

—————— "Regulations on the Restrictions on Certain Agricultural Products and Other Commodities Which Are Subject to Planned Purchase or Unified Purchase by the State" (August 9, 1957), translated in K. C. Chao. *Economic Planning and Organization in Mainland China*, II, 43–47. Cambridge, Mass.: Center for East Asian Studies, Harvard University, 1960.

B. IN CHINESE

All China Cooperative Organization. "Temporary Methods of Handling 1951 Advance Cotton Purchases" (March 20, 1951), *HHYP*, April 25, 1951, pp. 1338–1339.

CCPCC. "Directive on Doing Agricultural Producers' Cooperative Production Management Work Well" (September 14, 1957), *HHPYK*, October 10, 1957, pp. 136–137.

—————— "On the Question of the Establishment of People's Communes in Rural Areas" (August 29, 1958), *FKHP*, VIII, 1–5.

CCPCC and SC. "Decision on the Development of Live Hog Production" (February 28, 1957), *FKHP*, V, 231–235.

—————— "Directive on Doing Vegetable Sowing Work Well so as to Strengthen Vegetable Production and Supply Work" (July 17, 1958), *FKHP*, VIII, 238–239.

—————— "Directive on Handling Well Summer Distribution Work" (June 14, 1957), *FKHP*, V, 258–263.

—————— "Directive on Organizing Rural Market Trade" (September 25, 1959), *Jen-min shou-ts'e, 1960*, pp. 380–381. Peking: *TKP*, 1960.

—————— "Directive on Prohibiting the Blind Outflow of the Rural Population" (December 18, 1957), *HHPYK*, January 25, 1958, pp. 119–120.

—————— "Directive on Strengthening Leadership over Vegetable Production and Supply Work so as to Have a Timely and Well Handled Fall Vegetable Sowing Season" (July 17, 1958), *FKHP*, VIII, 238–239.

—————— "Directive on Strengthening Production Leadership and the Organization of Construction in Agricultural Producers' Cooperatives" (September 12, 1956), *HHPYK*, October 6, 1956, pp. 53–59.

—————— "Directive on This Year's Cotton Unified Purchase Work" (September 7, 1957), *FKHP*, VI, 370–373.

—————— "Regulation Changing the Method of Examining and Approving the Plans for Above Limit Basic Construction Items" (September 24, 1958), *FKHP*, VIII, 102–105.

—————— "Regulation on Spheres of Price Control and the Commercial Management System" (April 11, 1958), *FKHP*, VII, 315–318.

—————— "Several Regulations on Advancing the Commodity Distribution System" (September 24, 1958), *FKHP*, VIII, 100–101.

"Draft Regulations of the Ch'i-li Ying People's Commune," *HHPYK*, September 25, 1958, pp. 76–80.

Financial and Economic Committee. "Directive on the Relative Price of Cotton and Grain in 1953" (April 1, 1953), *HHYP*, May 25, 1953, pp. 180–181.

——— "Directive on the Relative Price of Cotton and Grain in 1954," *HHYP*, April 25, 1954, p. 166.

——— "Methods of Enforcing Currency Management and Compiling Currency Income and Outgo Plans" (December 25, 1950), *HHYP*, January 25, 1951, pp. 610–615.

——— "Regulations Concerning the Relative Price of Fibers and Grain and the Settling of Purchase and Grain Fertilizer Supply Problems" (March 17, 1951), *HHYP*, April 25, 1951, p. 1341.

Government Affairs Council. "Decision on the Labor Employment Problem" (July 25, 1952), *HHYP*, August 25, 1952, pp. 28–30.

——— "Directive on Increasing Production of Oil Materials Crops" (December 25, 1953), *HHYP*, January 25, 1954, pp. 157–158.

——— "Directive on 1953 Agricultural Tax Work" (August 28, 1953), *HHYP*, September 25, 1953, pp. 161–162.

——— "Directive on 1954 Advance Purchase Work," *HHYP*, April 25, 1954, pp. 164–165.

——— "Directive Ordering the Putting into Effect of the Planned Purchase of Cotton" (September 14, 1954), *HHYP*, October 25, 1954, pp. 241–242.

——— "Order Putting into Effect the Planned Purchase and Supply of Grain," *HHYP*, April 25, 1954, pp. 158–159.

——— "Regarding Settlement of the Unification of the Nation's Financial and Economic Work" (March 3, 1950), *HHYP*, April 15, 1950, pp. 1393–1395.

Labor Employment Committee of the Government Affairs Council. "Methods for the Unified Registration of Unemployed Personnel" (August 27, 1952), *HHYP*, September 25, 1952, pp. 42–43.

Ministries of Agriculture and Commerce. "Directive on the Relative Price of Cotton and Grain in 1955" (April 22, 1955), *FKHP*, I, 322.

Ministries of Agriculture and Foreign Trade. "Directive on Strengthening the Development of Tea Leaf Production" (May 19, 1955), *FKHP*, I, 391–394.

Ministries of Trade and Agriculture. "Directive on Clearly Understanding Cotton Price Policy" (October 19, 1950), *HHYP*, November 25, 1950, p. 115.

Ministry of Agriculture of the Northeast People's Government. "Trial Regulations for Agricultural Producers' Cooperatives in the Northeast" (January 5, 1953), *HHYP*, March 25, 1953, pp. 149–151.

Ministry of Commerce and People's Bank of China. "Regulation Eliminating Commercial Credit within the State Commercial Network and between Various Departments" (May 28, 1955), *FKHP*, I, 278–286.

Ministry of Finance. "Methods of Dividing and Using Profits of State Enterprises in Excess of the Plan in 1954" (October 18, 1955), *FKHP*, II, 523–524.

—— "Regulation on the Agricultural Tax Land Area and the Fixed Standard for an Ordinary Year's Production" (September 16, 1950), *HHYP*, September 20, 1950, pp. 1360–1361.

—— "Regulation on the Distribution and Use of 1956 State Enterprise Profits in Excess of the Plan" (October 11, 1956), *FKHP*, IV, 267–268.

Ministry of Finance and People's Bank, "Several Regulations Reforming Methods of Supplying State Enterprises' Circulating Capital" (May 17, 1961), *FKHP*, XII, 74–78.

Ministry of Grain. "Directive on Conscientiously Handling the Fall Unified Purchase of Oil Materials in 1957" (September 14, 1957), *FKHP*, VI, 349–351.

—— "Directive on Summer's Unified Purchase of Rapeseed" (April 30, 1959, *FKHP*, IX, 150–153.

—— "Notification on Rewards for Exceeding the Planned Unified Purchase Duties for Oil Products and Oil Materials" (June 5, 1959), *FKHP*, IX, 147–148.

Northeast People's Government. "Temporary Regulations on the State Enterprise Financial System" (August 27, 1950), *HHYP*, September 20, 1950, pp. 1378–1379.

SC. "Directive on Adjusting Several Types of Commodity Prices" (October 16, 1959), *Jen-min shou-ts'e, 1960*, p. 388. Peking: *TKP*, 1960.

—— "Directive on the Advance Purchase of Cotton in 1955," *HHYP*, April 28, 1955, p. 141.

—— "Directive on Raising the Purchase Price of Rapeseed" (September 29, 1956), Shanghai Price Book, pp. 594–595.

—— "Directive on Raising the Sales Prices of Vegetable Oil, Sesame Oil, Tea Oil, Tung Oil, Wood Oil, Tallow Oil, and Northeast and Inner Mongolian Bean Oil" (March 22, 1957), *FKHP*, V, 185–186.

—— "Directive on Strengthening Leadership over Bank Deposit Work and Positively Developing People's Deposit Work" (June 5, 1959), *FKHP*, IX, 137–140.

—— "Directive Ordering Various Areas Not to Raise on Their Own Authority Purchase Prices of Agricultural Subsidiary Products Which the State Unifiedly Purchases" (November 14, 1956), *FKHP*, IV, 333.

—— "Handling Rewards for Exceeding Oil Products and Oil Materials Unified Purchase Duties" (February 19, 1959), *FKHP*, IX, 146–147.

—— "Industrial and Commercial Unified Tax Regulations and Tax Rate Schedule (Draft)" (September 13, 1958), *FKHP*, VIII, 126–137.

—— "Notification of an Adjustment in the Purchase Price of Live Hogs" (February 15, 1957), *FKHP*, V, 181–182.

—— "Notification of the People's Bank of China's Report on Progress in Developing the People's Deposits" (November 5, 1955), *FKHP*, II, 547–548.

—— "Notification on the Unification of the Management of Village Subsidiary Production" (October 22, 1957), *FKHP*, VI, 447–449.

—— "Regulation on the Adjustment of the Agricultural Tax on Economic Crops the Income from Which Is Relatively Large" (December 20, 1957), *FKHP*, VI, 338–339.

—— "Regulation on State Planned and Unified Purchase of Agricultural Products and Other Commodities Not Allowed to Enter the Free Market" (August 17, 1957), *FKHP*, VI, 366–369.

—— "Regulation Putting into Effect the Enterprise Retained Profits System" (May 22, 1958), *FKHP*, VII, 239–242.

—— "Regulations on Reforming the Basic Construction Financial Management System" (July 5, 1958), *FKHP*, VIII, 123–124.

—— "Regulations on the Work of the People's Commune Credit Department and State Enterprise Circulating Capital" (December 20, 1958), *FKHP*, VIII, 156–158.

—— "Revised Regulations on Changing the Basic Construction Management System" (May 20, 1959), *FKHP*, IX, 135–137.

—— "Revised Regulations Putting State Enterprise Circulating Capital under the Unified Management of the People's Bank" (February 3, 1959), *FKHP*, IX, 121–125.

—— "Supplementary Regulation on Grain Unified Purchases and Sales" (October 11, 1957), *FKHP*, VI, 351–354.

—— "Temporary Methods of Handling Urban Fixed Grain Supply," *HHYP*, September 28, 1955, pp. 163–164.

—— "Temporary Regulation on Bonuses for the Working Personnel of State Administrative Organs" (October 26, 1957), *HHPYK*, November 25, 1957, pp. 88–90.

Standing Committee of the National People's Congress. "Decision on the Increase of the Retained Plots of Members of Agricultural Producers' Cooperatives" (June 25, 1957), *FKHP*, V, 263.

—— "Draft Regulations of an Agricultural Producers' Cooperative" (November 9, 1955), *FKHP*, II, 624–657.

IV. NEWSPAPERS

Ch'ang-chiang jih-pao.
Chekiang jih-pao.
Chieh-fang jih-pao. Shanghai.
Chungking jih-pao.
Hong Kong Tiger Standard.
Jen-min jih-pao. Peking.
Nan-fang jih-pao. Canton.

Ta kung pao. To 1955, Tientsin; from 1956 on, Peking.
Tientsin jih-pao.
Tsingtao jih-pao.
Wen hui pao. Hong Kong.
Yunnan jih-pao.

Index